Old Testament
Turning
Points

Old Testament
Turning
Points

The Narratives That Shaped a Nation

Victor H. Matthews

Baker Academic
Grand Rapids, Michigan

©2005 by Victor H. Matthews

Published by Baker Academic
a division of Baker Publishing Group
P.O. Box 6287, Grand Rapids, MI 49516-6287
www.bakeracademic.com

Printed in the United States of America

Library of Congress Cataloging-in-Publication Data
Matthews, Victor Harold.
    Old Testament turning points : the narratives that shaped a nation / Victor H. Matthews.
        p.   cm.
    Includes bibliographical references and indexes.
    ISBN 0-8010-2774-8 (pbk.)
    1. Bible O.T.—History of biblical events. 2. Bible. O.T.—Criticism, Narrative.
I. Title.
BS1197.M33 2005
221.9′5—dc22   2005015272

Contents

Preface

Tell me a story!
Tell me a story that everyone knows!
Tell me a story that echoes throughout time!

The biblical story was never intended to be told only once. Its lively nature and its rich social texture demand constant retelling and reexamination. Recognizing this, many people make a serious commitment to read and reread their Bible. I applaud that commitment, and I hope that it becomes a lifelong pursuit. Nothing gives me greater personal pleasure than reading a familiar biblical story and discovering a new insight or a better understanding of what is going on in the narrative. However, I also realize as I read that there is an undercurrent of meaning that was originally aimed at the ancient audience. These ancient people experienced a world unlike our own, but the questions that they asked about their world, their God, and themselves are not unfamiliar to us. Of course, the very human emotions, desires, and ambitions of the characters in the biblical narrative are shaped by their cultural environment, but they can be read with some measure of understanding by modern audiences.

What may be more difficult for modern readers is identifying the insider information implicit in the words of the story and the key plot highlights that make the whole tale comprehensible. For example, when reading an epic novel like Tolkien's *Lord of the Rings*, a reader may enjoy individual episodes but have a more difficult time knowing when a key event has transpired that affects the overall plot. After multiple readings, however, some of these subtle aspects of the author's purpose may become clearer. Alternatively, a Tolkien scholar can provide an orientation to the text that makes even an initial reading more fruitful (and invites the reader to savor those critical moments in the narrative). It therefore is often helpful to have a guide who can explain the references to everyday life that are mentioned in the biblical story. These social signposts are there but must be pointed out to those not used to looking for them. In addition, the guide can sketch out the bigger picture that includes major themes, rhetorical techniques, and references to events that form the basic structure of Israelite identity.

With that in mind, it is my hope that readers will benefit from the following discussion of a series of major turning points in biblical tradition. Each chapter contains a synopsis of the narrative, an examination of the social and literary background of the text, and then provides an explanation and graphic depictions of what I am calling "echoes" of these traditions in the writings of biblical historians, poets, and prophets. I will also try to take into account that ancient audiences did not read the stories—they heard them told. A written form of the biblical text will not begin to appear until late in their history, and even then its contents will be passed on orally either by professional storytellers or by parents telling their children what is most important about their world. It will be these "tellings" that will preserve the stories in the popular mind. Thus the "echoes" that I will point out are designed to show how the storytellers and prophetic figures attempted to touch their audience by repeatedly referring to well-known stories from their past while casting them in a new light that was relevant to their own time.

In my selection of turning points, I looked for instances that go beyond just the recorded events in the history of the people. My aim is to emphasize those moments in time and space that are retold, recalled, and reckoned as essential to the identity of ancient Israel as a nation. Each of the narratives I have chosen reaches to the very heart of the Israelites' identity as a people of the covenant. Since no other ancient people was granted covenant status, it was essential that each generation of Israelites pass on to their children the essence of their cultural portfolio. This included the terms of the covenant promise; the ethical character of Yahweh in comparison to the amoral, capricious gods of their neighbors; and the justification for God's punishment of those who violate the covenant (an aspect of theodicy).

Each chapter therefore focuses on a significant event or story that in turn provides the primary hooks upon which to hang important biblical themes and traditions as they are employed in subsequent writings. The intent is to help readers identify such basic story elements as a creation story, a wilderness theme, a contest between gods, a reference to the founding of the monarchy and David's special relationship with God, or another example of the evil brought on the nation by "Jeroboam's sin" in their various narrative and prophetic guises. This should open up the text to richer understanding and lively discussion. It should also demonstrate how the biblical writers over the centuries between the establishment of the monarchy (ca. 1000 BCE) and the postexilic era (ca. 500 BCE) made use of their own traditions and stories.

Each chapter contains numerous insets pointing out how particular themes and traditions are retold in the light of later history. For example, we can see how the prophets many times began their message with a variation on the phrase "I brought you up out of the land of Egypt" (Amos 2:10; Hosea 11:1; Mic. 6:4), echoing the exodus event and reminding the people just what they owe to God. Similarly, it is interesting to see the way in which the editor of the books of Kings provides summary judgments of the reigns of the kings of Israel and Judah based on whether each "did what was right in the sight of the LORD just as his ancestor David had done" (2 Kings 18:3), or "did what was evil in the sight of the LORD, walking in the way of Jeroboam and in the sin that he caused Israel to commit" (1 Kings 15:34). This transcends politics, wars, and the petty concerns of everyday administration and centers instead on what the biblical editors felt was the most important criterion for an Israelite ruler.

In becoming attuned to the way in which the biblical writers drew on their own traditions, we can more successfully appreciate the implications of their message. Thus I have often chosen to examine the structure of particular narratives, including their recurring motifs and themes, and I have analyzed the emphasis placed by the biblical writers on aspects of law, ritual purity, and religious practice. In addition, where possible I have discussed the insider viewpoint of the biblical storytellers and their original audience. To do this, I have employed literary and social scientific methods. I hope that this will allow modern readers to make more effective use of these materials as they strive to understand how the stories can be applied to our own day. In the process we will continue the tradition set forth by the biblical writers to tell and retell the old familiar stories.

What follows is a capsule summary of each of the chapters in this volume. Each section of the book represents a self-contained study, although they all share the common theme of identifying later echoes of biblical tradition. Thus readers can turn immediately to the topic that interests them the most without feeling that they need to read them in sequence. Readers will also be aided by a glossary of technical terms used in the text, as well as by subject and Scripture indexes. A bibliography of works cited is included for those who would like to read in more depth on these subjects.

1. Adam and Eve Are Expelled from Eden

On the surface, Eden represents God's first gift to humankind, an idyllic place for the first humans to explore and glory in to their hearts' content. However, it also allows the author and the audience to explore a host of explanations or etiologies of what we consider the basic aspects of our lives: marriage, reproduction, why we must work, our relationship to the rest of creation, and the inevitability of death. Also integral to the story is the issue of obedience and the consequences of disobedience. Throughout the Bible humans are continually making decisions that either allow them to obtain a richer relationship with God or drive a wedge between them. This account therefore provides the first example of many in which humans make the decision to seek wisdom or power at the expense of their allegiance to their Creator.

2. Yahweh Establishes a Covenant with Abraham

The covenant promise of land and children made to Abraham and Sarah forms the basis for the relationship between the Israelites and their God throughout their history. The various episodes in Genesis in which the covenant promise is made progressively demonstrate how Yahweh successfully challenges the power of all other gods and thereby provides the theological alternative to the fertility cults of the ancient Near East. This chapter examines the implications of God's covenant with Abraham and Sarah and then traces the echoes of how that covenant relationship becomes the basis for Israelite identity, their claims to the promised land, and the central theme of the prophets, who repeatedly call the people back to obedience and right conduct under the terms of the covenant with God.

3. Moses Leads the Israelites out of Egypt

Next to the establishment of the covenant with Abraham, the story of the exodus from Egypt is the most important event in Israelite salvation history. The subsequent story of the history of the nation and much of the prophetic material use the escape from Egypt as the premise for obedience to God's commands and the covenant. The exodus narrative also features the first national Israelite figure, one who is the model for all future leaders (until David becomes king) and who becomes the model for the later prophetic figures. It should be understood that the exodus narrative not only serves as a chronicle of events that tell the story of the origin of Israel as a people but also sets out a series of precedents that form the basis for legal, religious, and social activities. Each event in the narrative and each legal or religious precedent will have a ripple effect on later Israelite tradition and history and will be cited repeatedly as the foundation of authority for practice or belief.

4. King David Makes Jerusalem His Capital

What begins as a political move on David's part to provide a capital city for his newly formed nation becomes in the end an origin story for the presence of Yahweh in Jerusalem. Both David and Jerusalem will eventually become idealized social icons within Israelite tradition. David's rise to power marks the shift away from tribal society to central government, and the "everlasting covenant" made with his dynasty creates a divine-right principle of leadership and provides an idealized model of kingship that endures even when the monarchy comes to an end. Jerusalem serves as the physical capital city as well as the metaphorical perfect city, the place (i.e., the temple) where God caused his name to dwell, the place tied to the hope of return after the exile.

5. Jeroboam Leads the Secession of the Northern Tribes

The history of every nation, including ancient Israel, includes examples of political strife and rebellion. These stories contain both exemplary and evil individuals. Jeroboam, who is initially chosen by the prophet Ahijah to rule the nation of Israel when the northern tribes break away from the Davidic dynasty, ultimately becomes the arch-apostate in the account of the Deuteronomistic Historian (see the glossary). His record of covenant violations will serve as a measure for all future kings. The king's shrines in the northern kingdom at Dan and Bethel—as well as the local high places, the non-Levitical priesthood, and the revision of the festival-year celebrations—are condemned by the biblical writers and the prophets, and Jerusalem as the place where God's name dwells is given even more prestige. Ultimately, the destruction of Israel will be laid at the feet of those who continued "to walk in the sin of Jeroboam."

6. Samaria Falls to the Assyrians

This is the story of the death of a nation. One might envision a bold headline in the Jerusalem newspaper heralding the terrible message: "Samaria falls to the Assyrians!" Some would see this event as a potential threat to Judah and Jerusalem, since the Assyrians had already put a heavy burden of tribute payments on them and the rampaging nature of the Assyrian army was well known to the people of the ancient Near East. The Judeans could easily be next on the Assyrians' list of conquests. At the same time there are also voices, prophets among them, who explain Samaria's fall as a direct result of the "sin of Jeroboam." According to their interpretation, that king's policies had allowed Israel to engage in idolatrous practices and ignore their covenantal obligations. Despite the fact that Judah and Jerusalem continue to survive past 721 BCE, the destruction of Samaria and the deportation of the Israelites of the northern kingdom mark a critical point for the people as a whole.

7. Nebuchadnezzar Destroys Jerusalem and Deports the People of Judah

Despite all that had happened to Judah and Israel during the eighth and seventh centuries, the one abiding belief of the people and their leaders was that Jerusalem would remain sacrosanct because it contained the temple where God had "caused his name to dwell." While towns and villages throughout the kingdoms were ravaged by the armies of Assyria, Jerusalem continued to stand as a beacon of hope that God would relent and allow the people to survive. This was made particularly clear when Sennacherib did not capture the city. However, in the century after 701 BCE, as Judah became increasingly subservient to Assyria, the likelihood of its continued survival amid the storm of international conflict became less clear. Then, as the Assyrian Empire faded and a new Mesopotamian superpower emerged, centered once again in Babylon, Judah faced an even more uncertain future.

After the Babylonian king Nebuchadnezzar drove the Egyptians out of most of Syria-Palestine in 603, the rulers of Jerusalem did not reconcile themselves to their new political masters. What followed was a political and social tragedy that would end with the capture of Jerusalem in 598 and the transport of an initial group of hostages to Babylon. A decade later, again as a result of Egyptian plotting and a failure to judge the political situation correctly, Jerusalem fell again, and this time it was substantially destroyed and a large proportion of its people were taken into exile. Yet the history of the people of the covenant did not end here. Despite the dislocation of the exile, the story of ancient Israel continued. The emotions expressed in Psalm 137 of depression, resolution, and a desire for retribution speak to the complexity of what had just happened and point to new solutions like that expressed by Jeremiah in his letter to the exiles offering them the opportunity to worship Yahweh outside Judah. This chapter will explore the events that led to this devastating loss and the ways in which the story of Jerusalem's fall continued to be told for generations.

8. Cyrus Captures Babylon, and the Exiles Return Home

When the Persian king Cyrus captured Babylon, he issued a decree that among other things gave the exiled communities the opportunity to return to their homelands, and he provided funds for them to rebuild the temples of their gods. However, only a small minority of the exiles from Judah chose to return to Jerusalem. This divided the covenant community into two segments, those of the Diaspora (the lands of exile) and those who took up residence in Judah (Persian Yehud). A Jewish identity movement had preserved their cultural and religious heritage, but the Jerusalem temple, rebuilt with the blessing of the Persian government, with its restored priestly community and its claim to be the center of Yahweh worship, would not serve the needs of the Diaspora. Even though a coherent community in Yehud (formerly Judah) was created, conflict with the status quo is found among the people who did not wish to restrict membership in the covenant community (see Isa. 58 and the books of Ruth and Jonah). In addition, Isaiah's triumphant call to "prepare the way of the LORD, make straight in the desert a highway for our God," would have to come to terms with a succession of political changes that helped to shape postexilic Judaism.

Abbreviations

Old Testament

Genesis	Gen.	Ecclesiastes	Eccles.
Exodus	Exod.	Song of Solomon	Song of Sol.
Leviticus	Lev.	Isaiah	Isa.
Numbers	Num.	Jeremiah	Jer.
Deuteronomy	Deut.	Lamentations	Lam.
Joshua	Josh.	Ezekiel	Ezek.
Judges	Judg.	Daniel	Dan.
Ruth	Ruth	Hosea	Hosea
1 Samuel	1 Sam.	Joel	Joel
2 Samuel	2 Sam.	Amos	Amos
1 Kings	1 Kings	Obadiah	Obad.
2 Kings	2 Kings	Jonah	Jon.
1 Chronicles	1 Chron.	Micah	Mic.
2 Chronicles	2 Chron.	Nahum	Nah.
Ezra	Ezra	Habakkuk	Hab.
Nehemiah	Neh.	Zephaniah	Zeph.
Esther	Esther	Haggai	Hag.
Job	Job	Zechariah	Zech.
Psalms	Ps. (Pss.)	Malachi	Mal.
Proverbs	Prov.		

New Testament

Matthew	Matt.		1 Timothy	1 Tim.
Mark	Mark		2 Timothy	2 Tim.
Luke	Luke		Titus	Titus
John	John		Philemon	Philem.
Acts	Acts		Hebrews	Heb.
Romans	Rom.		James	James
1 Corinthians	1 Cor.		1 Peter	1 Pet.
2 Corinthians	2 Cor.		2 Peter	2 Pet.
Galatians	Gal.		1 John	1 John
Ephesians	Eph.		2 John	2 John
Philippians	Phil.		3 John	3 John
Colossians	Col.		Jude	Jude
1 Thessalonians	1 Thess.		Revelation	Rev.
2 Thessalonians	2 Thess.			

Adam and Eve Are
Expelled from Eden

Eden and Afterward

The account of Adam's and Eve's experience in the Garden of Eden has fascinated students and scholars of the Bible for centuries. In its basic simplicity, their tale provides us with a host of literary, religious, and cultural themes that weave their way through many other passages in the Bible. On the surface, Eden represents God's first gift to humankind, an idyllic place for the first humans to explore and glory in to their hearts' content. However, it also allows the author and the audience to explore a host of explanations or etiologies of what we consider the basic aspects of our lives: marriage, reproduction, why we must work, our relationship to the rest of creation, and the inevitability of death. Also integral to the story is the issue of obedience and the consequences of disobedience. Throughout the Bible, humans are continually making decisions that either allow them to obtain a richer relationship with God or drive a wedge between them. This account therefore provides the first example of many in which humans make the decision to seek wisdom or power at the expense of their allegiance to their Creator.

The story of the Garden of Eden and the expulsion of Adam and Eve from the garden (Gen. 2:4b–3:24) is part of a larger creation account

---

Issues to Consider in This Chapter

- What was God's purpose in placing the humans in Eden?
- Why were restrictions placed on what the humans could consume in the garden?
- Why is the serpent allowed to raise a question that leads the humans to disobey?
- Why must the humans be expelled from Eden?
- What is the result of the expulsion from Eden?

---

that is designed to provide the foundation for ancient Israel's understanding of their relationship to nature and to God. The portrayal of an unchanging, totally harmonious, primeval paradise creates an ideal model against which all other places can be measured. It also provides a set of origin stories that explain (1) who the Creator is, (2) the obligation of humans to care for all of God's creation, (3) the ability of humans to function as creators through reproduction, and (4) the limitations placed on humans as mortal beings. Ultimately, the story revolves around the wisdom dialogue between Eve and the serpent that explores humanity's role and their relationship to God. The crisis of belief then comes when Eve and Adam take it upon themselves to disobey the divine command. This step proves to be fatal, at least to the extent of their ability to remain in Eden. Once they are expelled, they develop an even stronger desire to return to Eden. It is this path from creation to emerging inquisitiveness to nostalgia that we will explore in this chapter.

Outline of the Story

Since the purpose of each of these chapters is to note the ripples that emanate from each of these seminal stories, I begin with a basic outline of the account of the Garden of Eden. Elements of this tale will then be examined below, but the reader can always return to this outline as a check on the details.

A. **God creates the earth and the heavens** (2:4b–14)
   - Initially, without rain, the land is sterile with no plant or animal life (2:5).
   - The only source of water is a "stream" or spring welling up (2:6).
   - God creates a human from the dust, giving him life by infusing him with the breath of life (2:7).

- God plants a garden in Eden (in the east) and places the human there (2:8).
- God creates plants, including the Tree of Life and the Tree of the Knowledge of Good and Evil (2:9).
- The river flowing out of Eden, with its four branches (Pishon, Gihon, Tigris, Euphrates), is described, providing a simple geography of the world (2:10–14).

B. **God interacts with the human(s)** (2:15–23)

- It is repeated that God places the human in Eden, adding the task to till and maintain it (2:15).
- God voices the first command to the human—eat of every tree except the Tree of the Knowledge of Good and Evil—warning that death is the consequence of disobedience (2:16–17).
- Judging the lack of companionship for the human "not good," God makes a "helper" by creating out of the earth all animal life (2:18–19a).
- God allows the human to name each beast—a sign of dominion (2:19b–20a).
- Since the animals are not found to be "a helper" or "partner" to the human, God places the human in a deep sleep and forms a woman out of one of the human's ribs (2:20b–22).
- The human recognizes this new creation as his true companion and calls her "Woman" (2:23).

C. **Editor's comment** (2:24–25)

- Later marriage arrangements are explained (2:24).
- A clue is given to the audience about the first couple's lack of clothing and lack of shame (2:25).

D. **Dialogue between the serpent and the woman** (3:1–7)

- The "crafty" serpent asks the first question voiced in Genesis: Did God restrict you from eating from any of the garden's trees? (3:1).
- The woman's answer is not a verbatim repetition of God's command, noting that they must not eat from the tree "in the middle of the garden" or touch it lest they die (3:2–3).
- The serpent assures her they will not die and that this restriction is just God's way of preventing their "knowing good and evil" and becoming gods (3:4–5).
- Attracted by the sensual aspects of the tree and its fruit, the woman eats and gives some to her husband, who also eats (3:6).

- The humans are transformed intellectually, recognize their nakedness, and clothe themselves with skirts made of fig leaves (3:7).

E. **Expulsion from the garden** (3:8–24)

- The humans hide when they hear God approaching, and God calls to them: "Where are you?"—a rhetorical question (3:8–9).
- The man responds, voicing fear and saying he is naked, to which God responds with two questions: "Who told you that you were naked?" and "Have you eaten from the [forbidden] tree?" (3:10–11).
- The man blames his action on the woman whom God gave to him, and the woman, when questioned, blames her action on the tricky serpent (3:12–13).
- God curses the serpent (3:14–15), pronounces the woman's fate of painful childbirth and reliance on her husband (3:16), and requires the man to work the soil to support and feed them (3:17–19a).
- God recounts the circle of life, telling them, "You are dust, and to dust you shall return" (3:19b).
- The man names his wife Eve—"mother of all living" (3:20).
- God clothes the humans in garments of skins (3:21).
- To prevent the humans from eating from the Tree of Life, God expels them from Eden, barring the east entrance with armed cherubim (3:22–24).

Ultimately, this story provides an explanation of the origin of human-divine relations and sets the stage for all of human history. The gift of life given to the human couple, which might have extended through the ages, is shortened to a brief lifetime by the decisions made by the humans to disobey the divine command in order to seek knowledge. In order to better understand the various aspects and implications of this story for later Israelite traditions, we will examine five principal themes.

Utopia Theme

By definition, a **utopia** is a "totally other" place, completely removed from society and the world as we know it, and free of competition and suffering, since it provides all needs without work or request. Although the technical term *utopia* cannot be applied to ideal societies prior to Thomas More's coining of the word in 1516, the concept of creating ideal societies is as old as civilization itself. More took the term from the Greek word *outopos*, meaning literally "no place." In the England

> ## Themes and Influences
> ## Attached to the Eden Story
>
> 1. **Utopia theme**—an idyllic place, unassociated with the regular world, that contains absolute peace and harmony.
> 2. **Etiology theme**—precedents are set and explanations given for human origins and our present condition as mortal beings capable of reproduction and forced to work with and manipulate nature to survive.
> 3. **Wisdom theme**—since humans were created without divine omniscience, they strive to obtain knowledge and its attendant power.
> 4. **Gift-giving theme**—life, purpose, and place are gifts to humanity. The principle of reciprocity then comes into play to balance the obligation that accompanies these gifts.
> 5. **Return theme**—the desire to return to Eden is expressed in both the covenant with God, which is designed to draw humans back into a closer relationship with the divine presence, as well as the wilderness theme of both the exodus event and the exile. These periods of purification are to lead a righteous remnant into a "promised land" that could be seen as the new Eden.

of More's time social institutions that had held society together during the Middle Ages were starting to collapse, and new economic initiatives were laying the groundwork for the introduction of capitalism. In the process of economic and social change, thousands of English people were driven from their villages as farmland was enclosed for sheep rearing. In the face of this landmark shift in village and rural culture, More wrote *Utopia* as a protest statement against the wanton destruction of the Old World order and as a call to seek out what "Reason would construct as a good society" (Fortier and Fortier 1992: ii). His book shares a number of the primary characteristics found in previously developed utopian literature, such as Plato's *Republic* (Carey 1999: xi–xii).

Eden and Utopia

In the semi-arid conditions found in both the ancient and the modern Near East, perfection is found in well-watered gardens filled with fragrant and lush vegetation. By this definition the Garden of Eden is the exact model of such a perfect place. A close examination of the Genesis account of the Garden of Eden (Gen. 2:4b–3:24) demonstrates the obvious contrast between the abundance of the garden and the stark emptiness prior to its creation. The land is virtually sterile, watered

---

Characteristics of Utopian Literature

1. A utopia is the expression of human desire for a place of perfect harmony.
2. Ordinary people cannot exist in a utopia since they occupy the world that we know and the world that we wish to change.
3. The author of a utopian work criticizes the present as a time of great unhappiness.
4. The utopia is thus an alternative society, inhabited by beings who are without selfish desires and who can therefore live free of suffering, injustice, and heartbreak.

---

only by springs welling up from the earth. It is in this unattractive environment that God creates a human from the dust. At that point, light is suddenly shone upon a nearly dead world by the "planting" of the Garden of Eden "in the east" and the physical transport of the newly created human into this paradise. The author then provides a detailed description of the benefits to be found in Eden, all of which serve as a further contrast with the outside world (2:9–14). Every plant and tree needed to support human life and to bring joy to the eye are planted here along with the two trees (of Life and of Knowledge) that will form the basis for the subsequent drama that explains the expulsion of humans from the garden. Providing life-giving water to the garden is a river that then branches into four streams that radiate out from Eden, carrying with them a measure of the blessings of Eden to the outside world (Stordalen 1992: 17).

Of particular importance here is that Adam is created not in Eden but elsewhere, and then he, and later the animals, are brought into Eden by God. Adam alone serves as caretaker of Eden's delights (2:15) until Eve is created (2:21–22). One could argue that Eve is the only creature formed by God within the confines of Eden. However, her substance is taken from Adam's body, and he had been formed from the dust of the earth outside the garden. Thus the presence of humans and animals in the Garden of Eden is simply part of the divine design to create an idyllic place. They live there at the sufferance of God, not because they are entitled to space there. True ownership and sovereignty in Eden belongs to God alone. It is that initial sense of perfect harmony as the proper condition of Eden's existence that is matched by what occurs within this divine paradise. Therefore, even though Adam receives a measure of sovereignty over the animals, being given the power to name them (2:19–20), there is no sense that he in any way abuses or mistreats them. Humans and animals complement each other without the need to harm

Comparisons with Eden in the Prophets

Ezekiel 31:8—In his oracle against Egypt, the prophet Ezekiel metaphorically compares that nation to Assyria, which had been created by God as a beneficial tree, a "cedar of Lebanon," a sort of "cosmic tree" standing at the foundation or center point of creation (Cook 1999: 124–25). Assyria is said to have been so beautiful that "the cedars in the garden of God could not rival it." Having thus created an image of idyllic splendor, Ezekiel then goes on, using the loss of Eden's glory to humans as a backdrop, to describe how Assyria, this mighty "tree," has been cast down to the underworld (Sheol) "as its wickedness deserves" because of its excessive pride (Ezek. 31:10–18). In this way Assyria's fall provides an object lesson to other nations like Egypt that human institutions are temporary and subject to God's will (Galambush 1999: 153).

Isaiah 51:3—The postexilic voice of Isaiah provides another example of the way in which the prophets use Eden as a measure of comparison when he describes the restoration of Zion's "wilderness" (a euphemism for Judah after the Babylonian destruction of Jerusalem) and its transformation by God into a new Eden.

Joel 2:3—The postexilic prophet Joel provides a stark contrast in the fortunes of the land of Judah prior to its devastation by invading armies. He says that the land was once "like the garden of Eden," but in the face of God's wrath in the form of these invaders it had become a "desolate wilderness."

or feed off each other. Furthermore, all those things that might create strife, such as precious stones (2:11–12) and sexual tension (2:25), are absent from Eden (Amit 1990: 15).

A basic incongruity surfaces, however, as it becomes clear that the humans are apparently unable to be content in Eden. Given the impetus of the serpent's question (3:1) to consider their role in creation and the desire to test the rules, these first representatives of the human race quickly find themselves outside Eden and in the real world. Then, perhaps regretting their decision, they discover that their existence has been transformed forever. It is also at this point that Eden becomes an actual utopia by our definition. While it was God's creation originally, it has now become a true expression of human desire, a place so perfect that humans cannot remain there and to which they eternally hope to return.

Echoes of Eden as Utopia

Eden is to be distinguished from all other space and by definition is a perfect and perfectly isolated locale in which God plants a botanical garden and harbors animals and humans in an atmosphere in which they never have to struggle to survive. In this utopia called Eden or the "garden of God," there is no need to strive to achieve. There are no ambitions and there is no need for change. However, such an idyllic place also functions as a model against which other places can be contrasted in the prophetic literature.

Perhaps the best examples of these echoes of Eden's glory are in Ezekiel's oracles against Tyre in chapter 28. In this judgmental prophetic statement, Ezekiel draws on the image of Eden as a utopian locale while he condemns the proud king of Tyre (Block 1998: 106). The prophet reminds this foolish monarch that "you were in Eden, the garden of God," full of wisdom and enthroned amid vast riches, including gold and silver, wondrous jewels, which he had amassed as a result of a wide-ranging trading network. A further tie to the Genesis account is found in the equation of the king's position with the "primal human" of Genesis 2–3, who had been set in Eden's primordial garden and who was eventually driven from his place because of disobedience (see also Job 15:7–8). Thus the prophet uses clear references to the Eden story to make his point that excessive pride and the desire to be "a god" (Ezek. 28:2) leads to the king's being cast out of "the mountain of God" by a guardian cherub (28:16; compare the cherubim in Gen. 3:24; Callender 2000: 178–79).

Etiology Theme

The primary purpose of an etiology is to answer the basic question, How did this come about? Among the elements that the storyteller employs in composing an etiological tale are direct revelation from a deity, a compilation of received traditions that are considered both authoritative and inspired in their transmission through time, and personal commentary on conditions that are current in the time of the storyteller (Lohfink 1994: 18–19). This last element in the storytelling process would be a form of social reflection based on the examination of society as it exists in the time of the writer and the formulation of a primordial story to explain such things as the origin of the universe, the place of humanity within creation, and the basis for the existence of evil in the world.

In many cases, an etiology is designed to relate tradition to history at a later point. For instance, there are a number of stories in 1 Samuel about the origins of the monarchy in ancient Israel (1 Sam. 8–12).

The storyteller is working from the historical reality that a monarchy existed in his own time. The etiology then provides the answer to our question about origins and blends oral tradition, political annals, and other data into a cogent narrative. The Eden story is more difficult to relate to historical circumstances since it involves events in a place separate from normal human existence. However, the story's concern with the realities of the human condition—mortality, pain and suffering, the need to work, the relationship between God and humanity—makes it one that relates to many periods of human history. These conditions exist throughout time and can be tied to many of the accounts associated with specific historical events. As von Rad (1961: 91–92) has suggested, however, the etiology of Eden also may be described as a theodicy, that is, a theological explanation with the intent of absolving God of responsibility for all the suffering that now exists in the world.

An Etiology of Death

At its heart, however, the story of Adam's and Eve's experience in the Garden of Eden is an explanation of why humans are mortal (Barr 1992: 4). A careful reading of the story demonstrates that the pair have access to the Tree of Life, since God does not forbid them from eating from the fruit of that tree. Immortality is therefore within their grasp, but it is lost when they choose to eat from the Tree of Knowledge (Propp 1990: 192–93). Therefore, the story of the Garden of Eden becomes an etiology of death, explaining why humans are mortal. The elements in the story that bring about death are (1) the specially endowed trees in the garden, (2) the serpent's questions, and (3) the exercise of moral autonomy by Eve. When the climax of the story is reached, it is immediately evident that there is no possibility of going back.

The element of choice that is so crucial to the Eden story is also found in the Mesopotamian story of Adapa. When this epic hero angers the gods by breaking the wing of the north wind and bringing drought on the earth, he is called into the divine council and offered the food and drink of immortality. However, Adapa had been warned by his patron god, Ea, not to eat or drink anything that the gods offer him. Following these instructions, the hero is tricked out of becoming immortal and therefore all humanity is similarly doomed to die. Unlike Adam and Eve, whose loss is the result of disobedience to divine command, his loss is based on obedience. However, the result is the same. Both stories explain why humans are mortal and why they are

---

The Story of Adapa

Ea created Adapa to be wise,
   He had not created him to be immortal.
When the wise Ea began to create Eridu,
   He made Adapa to be a just man. . . .

"When Anu offers you bread to eat,
   Do not eat it.
When Anu offers you water to drink,
   Do not drink it.
When Anu offers you a garment and oil for your body,
   Clothe and anoint yourself." (Matthews and Benjamin 1997:
      42–43)

---

subject to divine direction and cannot perceive the intricate designs of the deity.

Reflection on what the humans lose as a result of their disobedience simply reinforces the idyllic image of Eden as a place where humans may wish to live but from which they have been expelled. In Eden there is no competition between humans and animals, no need to work to obtain their daily bread; but it is also a place in which Adam grows lonely until Eve is created, and paradise apparently is not enough to keep the couple from disobeying God's command. As a result, the story then revolves around how Adam and Eve are provided with the initial spark to question their surroundings and their place within creation (see the "Wisdom Theme" section below). The serpent, rather than being the source of evil in the world, serves as a catalyst for change, a necessary ingredient in any story. In this way, the Eden story can explain the physical reality that humanity no longer inhabits Eden.

This spatial shift from within the garden to the outside world is accomplished through the serpent's intermediary role. Life as we know it could then begin, and the fallow soil outside the garden could begin to bloom as a result of human toil (Stordalen 1992: 22–23). In this way, Adam and Eve bring some of the benefits of Eden with them even as they are exiled from that unearthly paradise. This also may explain why God does not remove Noah from the earth following the flood, in contrast to the Mesopotamian gods, who transport the flood hero of the Gilgamesh Epic, Utnapishtim, to an unearthly realm "between the rivers." Instead, Noah and his family are charged to "be fruitful and multiply, and fill the earth" (Gen. 9:1), because in that way humans fulfill their role as stewards of the earth and achieve their immortality through procreation, even if they are denied access to the Tree of Life (3:22). Humans live on the earth while they dream of Eden.

Thus the ultimate etiology in this narrative filled with etiologies may be the explanation for why human existence is earthbound. The ideal nature of Eden coupled with the rebelliousness that cast Adam and Eve out of Eden then led later storytellers to speculate on why we were created, why life is never perfect, and why we must work to live. As the psalmist says, "What are human beings that you are mindful of them, mortals that you care for them?" (Ps. 8:4). In addition, every generation has wrestled with questions such as why new life comes into being as a result of intimacy that involves loss of personal control of the emotions and some physical functions, why birthing is such a painful process, and why relationships are built and often founder on issues of self-identity and personal worth. Just as Eve is told "your desire shall be for your husband" (Gen. 3:16), the woman in the Song of Solomon states, "I am my beloved's, and his desire is for me" (7:10).

Finally, in the end, we question the necessity for the death that claims us all. Why should we spend a lifetime acquiring knowledge and skills only to have them disappear with our last breath? Is the writer of Ecclesiastes correct to say that all is vanity and that we have no real legacy of enduring accomplishment upon which to justify our existence on earth (Eccles. 1:2–11)? The answer may be that in our struggle to make a life for ourselves and establish an identity as a member of a people or nation, we act on the knowledge gained through disobedience in Eden. In that context, while we cannot return to Eden, we can strive to make this world a better, more Eden-like place. Thus it is best to take the advice to "not let your hands be idle" (Eccles. 11:6) and to "rejoice in" all the years we are given (11:8).

Wisdom Theme

Since one of the main purposes behind the story of the Garden of Eden is to describe how humans first began their search for knowledge, it is appropriate to look at how this story relates to the larger genre of Wisdom literature in the Bible and the ancient Near East. By its very nature, Wisdom literature recognizes and celebrates differences. Its task is therefore to question, through discourse and analysis, the substance of reality and truth. Thus the serpent provides an opportunity for Eve to test the truth by suggesting to her that she "will not die" if she eats from the Tree of Knowledge (Gen. 3:4). This is precisely what "the Satan," functioning as a sort of prosecuting attorney figure, does when he questions God's assertion that Job is a truly righteous man (Job 1:8–12). By accepting that we live in a complex world with many different and often opposing viewpoints on how a society should be constructed and administered, Wisdom literature exhorts us to consider carefully our own depths of knowledge and understanding. As Stratton (1995: 224) says, biblical Wisdom literature also "reminds us that, while we should think and plan, God is also involved in our lives and will work with how life turns out."

Although Genesis 2–3 is generally not identified as Wisdom literature, it does contain a number of distinctive wisdom themes. These include the search/desire for knowledge, the serpent's role and apparent cleverness, the polar opposites—good and evil—and Adam's classifying of nature by giving names to the animals (Alonso-Schökel 1976: 472–73). Perhaps the most important of these wisdom features, however, is the presence, in addition to aboriginal humans, of at least one other sentient being in this story, a talking serpent. The serpent is not a magical being or a creature whose intent and purpose is to strive against God (compare the Leviathan in Isa. 27:1 or the beastly serpent [nahash] at the bottom of the sea in Amos 9:3). Instead, the serpent of Eden is just another of the animals that populate the garden (Sawyer 1992: 66). However, its narrative purpose is found in the serpent's formulating the first question in the Genesis account, "Did God say, 'You shall not eat from any tree in the garden?'" (Gen. 3:1; Sawyer 1992: 69). To this point in the story, all that has been said are words of command by God or Adam's naming of the animals and his poetic explanation for Eve's name (2:23). By injecting a question where none had existed before, the possibilities for self-examination are created and a wisdom dialogue can begin. Indeed, a major step has been taken with what seems like a very simple query toward actually exercising the capability of discerning the difference between good and evil.

Perhaps the real question here is whether Eve possessed the capacity for critical thinking before consuming the fruit of the Tree of Knowledge (see Sasson 2000: 207–8). If she did not, then it would have been impossible for the serpent to reason with her. Instead, however, she responds to his query by repeating God's command and elaborating on it, adding a prohibition against touching the tree (compare Gen. 2:17 with 3:3). After the serpent's second prompt, which supplies a motive for why God might wish to prevent the humans from eating this special "brain food," it would have required reasoning skills to analyze, as Eve does, the various merits of the tree: she "saw" that (1) "the tree was good for food," (2) "it was a delight to the eyes," and (3) "the tree was to be desired to make one wise" (3:6). Such a close inspection is reminiscent of God's repeated certification that each aspect of creation was "good" (1:10, 12, 18, 21, 25, 31). Eve's ability "to see" here is the first time that attribute is ascribed to a human, and yet it seems to come quite naturally and does not particularly surprise her. The conclusion would then be that Adam and Eve already possessed the tools of rational and analytical thought prior to the serpent's question. However, they either had not chosen to exercise this ability, trusting in the need to obey God's command, or they had not thought to do so. Of course, this is an etiological moment, and the personalities of the characters have not been explored or even described to this point in the story. In other words, what we find here is the creation, or the awakening, of Eve's intellectual curiosity, rather than a newly bestowed gift of reasoning.

Once the couple choose to consume this fruit, they have, through their assertion of moral autonomy, obtained a new form or aspect of wisdom. Their "eyes [are] opened" to the extent of being about to recognize and be ashamed of their nakedness. In a world in which everyone is naked, there is no need or even reason to be ashamed. But Adam and Eve are no longer the same persons that they were, and they have actually taken an etiological step that prepares them for life outside Eden, where clothing is a mark of status, gender, and economic condition (Simkins 1994: 188). Having emerged from a childlike state of innocence and been transformed into adults, they now discover the same truth as the naïve, elemental creature Enkidu, who eventually becomes the companion of the legendary king Gilgamesh in a Mesopotamian epic. Originally, he had run with the animals until he was "civilized" by a prostitute sent to him by the gods. Afterward, because he now smelled like a human, Enkidu was shunned by his former beastly pack and was forced to seek out other humans. In the same way, Adam and Eve discover that once personal identity, role, and a sense of worth have been established, there is no going back to a primeval, "innocent" condition. The rite of passage from childhood to adulthood has been completed (see 1 Cor. 13:11).

Why then do Adam and Eve take this step if they know the difference between obedience and disobedience? The question raised by the serpent may simply have been a nagging thought that had troubled Eve's unconscious mind. Her elaboration of God's command, adding the prohibition against even touching the tree and its fruit, may be a defense mechanism designed to add further weight to the problem. Of course, the result of their consuming the fruit is not a vast store of wisdom or an omniscient mind like God's. What they receive is the knowledge that humans do not belong in Eden, especially if they are to fully exercise their knowledge of each other and populate the earth. For them, as noted in Proverbs 3:18, the desire to embrace knowledge and to thereby obtain wisdom "is a tree of life," substituting for that tree found only in Eden. Of course, the fact that eating from the Tree of Knowledge does not supply Adam and Eve with all knowledge, much less ultimate wisdom, is simply a way to explain the human condition (Murphy 1996: ix–xi). As Job discovered (42:3), it is not possible to plumb the depths of God's store of knowledge; and as the

Hellenistic Jewish sage Jesus ben Sirach notes, "The first man did not know wisdom fully, nor will the last one fathom her" (Sirach 24:28).

The wisdom that does derive from the events in Eden is to be found in the prospects set forth for humans, who have now become creators but find that they must operate within a finite lifetime. They may seek out knowledge and strive to achieve great things, reveling in "the fountain of life" that wisdom brings them (Prov. 16:22; 1 Cor. 13:2). However, their limitations are clearly defined by the God whose wisdom created all things (Prov. 3:19) and then allowed them to make the choice that sent them out of Eden. If, however, Adam and Eve had never been expelled from Eden, then the effort that is the basis for most human achievement, as well as both good and bad actions, would not exist. Without expulsion there also would be no drive to restore the severed relationship with the Divine, no attempt to join ourselves once again with the God who created us. Considering the reflections of the author of Ecclesiastes once more, it does ring true that "God made human beings straightforward, but they have devised many schemes" (Eccles. 7:29).

Gift-Giving Theme

Given that Eden eventually proves itself to be an unsuitable place for humans, how could it then be considered a gift of God to the newly created humans? While it is an ideal setting, it seems to be more of a trophy case for the display of all of God's creations rather than a proper habitat of humans. Furthermore, if the Garden of Eden is a gift, the question arises whether this gift requires reciprocation. Very few gifts are given simply for the joy of giving to others. Traditional societies, such as those that existed in the ancient Near East, gauge themselves and their basic identities on the need to achieve personal and group honor and avoid shame. This is often achieved through the ritualized exchange of presents. Within these ancient Near Eastern cultures, the concept of reciprocity was a common mechanism of social interaction designed to protect one's household and to bring honor to both the one who gives a gift and to the recipient of the gift (Prov. 19:6). This exchange, based on a social protocol, could take the form of offering hospitality to strangers or simply sharing one's wealth with others, both in terms of material goods as well as wisdom (Matthews 1999: 95).

A social system that includes obligatory exchange as part of everyday behavior is open to abuses as well as strategically orchestrated advances on the part of the donor. Some gift givers may simply wish to bribe the powerful (Sirach 20:29) or curry favor with the leadership (Prov. 18:16). In some cases, the donor may try to test the intent of the recipient and thereby determine whether a balanced exchange can or will occur

> ## The Protocol of Gift Giving
>
> 1. Gifts must be given by a patron for every service rendered by a client.
> 2. All gifts must be equally measured so that there is no advantage to be gained by either side of the exchange.
> 3. Failure to give an appropriate gift dishonors the donor and insults the recipient.
> 4. The recipient may not contest the gift offered, but a demur, based on the honor of the household, may be employed either to refuse the gift or to negotiate a change in the gift.

(Sherry 1983: 159). Any attempt to coax or coerce another person into an exchange, however, may be damaging to either the gift giver or the recipient or both. The choice to refuse a gift may result in a moral dilemma, and that may in turn result in a loss of honor or status.

In the Wisdom literature of the ancient Near East, it is made quite clear that the head of a household may obtain honor through his generosity. For instance, in the Egyptian "Teachings of Ptah-hotep" (ca. 2500 BCE), the sage states that if you obtain a position of authority, you should "be generous with the wealth that the divine assembly gives you, and take care of your hometown now that you can" (Matthews and Benjamin 1997: 269). Similarly, the Egyptian wisdom sayings of Amenemope (eleventh century BCE) caution that it is "better to be praised for loving your neighbor than loving your wealth" (Matthews and Benjamin 1997: 280). This model of generosity is also heralded in the Hellenistic writings of ben Sirach, who states that "with every gift show a cheerful face" since the Lord "will repay you sevenfold" (Sirach 35:11–13). These examples, however, are forms of nonobligatory giving. They simply represent a form of moral behavior. It may be expected of the rich and powerful, but their gifts do not carry the burden of obligatory response by the recipient.

Based on this definition of social exchange, it is clear that Adam and Eve cannot repay God for giving them the gift of life. Such a gift can only be seen as a nonobligatory bequest, not requiring reciprocation. Where the principle of reciprocation does enter the story, however, is in their being hosted in Eden. In fact, this story of gift giving, uncertainty, and logic that turns to action becomes the prototypical hospitality tale (compare Abraham's hosting of three guests in Gen. 18:1–15). While Adam and Eve enjoy the hospitality of Eden granted to them by God, they are only guests, not permanent residents. When they abuse the privileges accorded to a guest by their host, they cease to be protected by the protocol of hospitality and may be expelled without further delay (see Matthews 1991a). A reuse of this tradition can be found in the oracle against Tyre in Ezekiel 28:11–19. In this prophetic passage, the wise and "blameless" king of Tyre is given all manner of costly, jewel-encrusted raiment and installed within the Garden of Eden as its steward with a cherub as his guardian. However, because of the king's arrogance and excessive pride (hubris) in his success as a master of international trade, he is banished from the garden and shamed before other nations. Like Adam and Eve, his personal desires outweigh his gratitude to his bene-factor, and he then faces the consequences of his own actions (Block 1998: 117–19).

In both of these passages, the audience is taught to recognize that (1) the roles of guest and host are strictly regulated as a means of insur-ing continuity and the meeting of social expectations in their culture, and (2) the pursuit of knowledge has its price. Adam and Eve choose to serve their own needs rather than honoring the sanctity of their host's domain. The shocking result is therefore part of the educational process for them and for their audience. It is understood that no proposition can be left unquestioned once that first step is taken in the educational process—defined as the exercise of critical-thinking skills that demand examination, experimentation, and realization that there is no turning back. This turning point in the human story is an inevitable consequence of creation. If humanity is truly created in the image of God, then there is an inherent element of free thinking that is an integral part of our mental makeup. Adam and Eve could not have remained as they were forever. If they were truly human, then the curiosity that stirred the ancients to discover uses for fire, stone, and animals demanded that they be awakened to their destiny, which was not in Eden.

Return Theme

The one recurring theme attached to the story of the expulsion from Eden is the desire to return to that place or a similar place character-ized by perfect peace and harmony. Such a desire is common to many cultures, for human storytelling is filled with nostalgia for a primordial paradise and the hope or expectation of a return to the paradisiacal condition that had been lost at the dawn of time (Eliade 1975: 59–60). Some central elements in the paradise story, both in its original incar-nation and in the restoration motif, include "abundant fertility, cosmic harmony, life, bliss, and peaceful tranquility, forming a contrast with chaos, infertility and death" (Cornelius 1988: 43).

For example, it will be the desire to return to Eden that is then trans-formed during the account of the wilderness wanderings into the desire to reach the "promised land" (i.e., "Yahweh's Land"; Ottosson 1988: 187). And, as in the case of the Eden story, it will be the lack of obedience and faith in God's word that will prevent the majority of the people from reaching that desired place (see the account of the failed invasion of Canaan in Num. 14:26–45). Once they do enter Canaan, the Israelites will find that like Adam they are tenants of a land that belongs to God. They can expect that the "land will yield its fruit," but only if they obey God's statutes (Lev. 25:18–23). The comparative echoes with the Eden story are then applicable to their later history as the superpowers of Egypt and Mesopotamia ravage their towns and villages, and the prophets explain to the Israelites that these disasters are the direct result of the people's disobedience and their inability to consistently fulfill the requirements of the covenant (Isa. 10:1–6). Like Adam and Eve, they will ultimately be expelled from the land that is associated with their close proximity to God (Hosea 9:3). That expulsion, in turn, will become in the prophetic materials the basis for a deep longing to return to Jerusalem/Zion, which is equated with the benefits of Eden. This is seen in Ezekiel's description of life-giving water flowing eastward from beneath the temple, providing sustenance to "every living creature" (Ezek. 47:1–12). This echo of Eden's character is also expressed in Zechariah's apocalyptic vision of the future "day of Yahweh" when restoration of the nation takes the form of "living waters" that "flow out of Jerusalem" (Zech. 14:8; Tuell 2000: 174–76).

This is particularly evident in the writings of the Hebrew prophets of the late monarchy period (750–586 BCE), who face the Assyrian and Babylonian menace to Judah's survival. In order to create as stark a contrast as possible, the "return to paradise" theme is couched in exaggerated language that highlights the manifest differences between the real world and the abundance to be found in divinely endowed space. In the prophets this language takes the form of predictions of Israel's restored fortunes, when its ruined cities are rebuilt and the true harmony of life is reestablished for all time (Amos 9:14–15).

This dualistic state of affairs, with its concern over current social ills and its expectation of future hope and divinely inspired transformation (cf. Dan. 7:26–27), also is typical of the apocalyptic and eschatological themes in the postexilic prophets (Cook 1995: 23–24). The stresses caused by the exile and the physical and social dislocation that required the faithful to shape their identity through reference to their history and traditions led these visionaries to describe a future time when Yahweh's sovereignty would transform the wilderness that Israel and Judah had become into an Eden-like world free of the problems that surrounded them (Isa. 51:3; Hanson 1975: 11). It should be made clear, however, that when they envisioned a world in which the "wolf and the lamb

Eden-Like Prophetic Visions of Restoration

The prophets often use aspects of Eden's idyllic character to describe the restoration of the nation and their land after they have been devastated by invading armies. This provides the opportunity to highlight both how the people have brought these disasters upon themselves and how God is still willing to restore them and their land to fertility and to covenantal relationship if they return to proper behavior and faith.

Amos 9:13—The early-eighth-century prophet Amos predicts a time when the fertility of the land is so great that the workers cannot keep up with the productive power of their fields and vineyards.

Hosea 2:21–22—The late-eighth-century prophet Hosea describes the "day of the LORD" as a time when the earth will answer God's call to bring forth grain, wine, and oil in abundance.

Joel 3:18—The postexilic prophet Joel speaks of mountains dripping with sweet wine, hills flowing with milk, and every wadi (streambed) in Judah flowing with life-giving water.

shall feed together" (Isa. 65:25) and in which the lion shall no longer stalk travelers (Isa. 35:9), the prophets were speaking of a return (if not physically, then spiritually) to a place that has no crime, no war, and in which all creatures can live in harmony together (Ezek. 36:33–35; Zech. 8:12).

A situation such as this provides a direct contrast with the expulsion from Eden and the curse of pain and hard labor imposed on Adam and Eve in Genesis 3:17–19 (Cornelius 1988: 49, 53). In this way the prophets can speak of an energized, superfertile world in Eden-like terms as they envision an end to exile and the destructiveness of invading armies, without actually calling on a physical return to the garden. Thus the conditions at the end of history can be "paradise but not the same Paradise from which knowledge of good and evil was excluded" (McClung 1983: 18). While understanding that the lessons of history cannot be forgotten or swept away, the prophets can still say that the lost Tree of Life is to be replaced with an arboreal image of Yahweh as "an evergreen cypress" or "the olive tree" bringing life to the people of faith (Hosea 14:5–8).

Given a common theme in the Genesis account, the Hebrew prophets, and the apocryphal literature of the Second Temple period, it seems that one of the primary purposes of the story can be found in the writer's

desire to explain to his audience that while we cannot physically return to Eden, we can strive to restore a measure of the relationship
between God and these first humans while they were in Eden (Amit
1990: 16). Even when the hope of return was transferred to a return to
the "promised land" after the exile, the apocalyptic vision is one that
retains aspects of Eden's paradisiacal qualities. Peace and contentment
can be found in obedience to God's command and a personal effort to
rise above the need for dominance over others, either politically, economically, or sexually.

2

Yahweh Establishes a Covenant with Abraham

The covenant promise of land and children made to Abram and Sarai forms the basis for the relationship between the Israelites and their God throughout their history. The various episodes in Genesis in which the covenant promise is made progressively demonstrate how Yahweh successfully challenges the power of all other gods and thereby provides the theological alternative to the fertility cults of the ancient Near East. Thus Abram is persuaded to leave his Mesopotamian homeland and his gods behind. The ancestors of the Israelite people are repeatedly promised not only numerous offspring but both nations and kings from their lineage. What is demanded of them is obedience to God's word and faith in Yahweh's ability to provide what has been promised to them. The narrative is held together by a series of theophanies that assure Abram of God's protection and blessing. God will instruct him to traverse the promised land, and he will experience visions illustrating the covenant promise. Abram and his wife will have their names changed, and the newly named Abraham will be commanded to institute the tradition of circumcision as a sign of membership in the covenant community. A long-awaited heir will finally be born and then inexplicably be demanded as a sacrifice by God. Throughout this complex and entertaining narrative, the ancestors are repeatedly tested. In this way, they prove themselves worthy of the title of father and mother of nations. It is therefore the

Abraham's Covenantal Legacy

The legacy of Abraham's covenant, promising land and children to his descendants, becomes a hallmark for Israelite identity and a justification for their claim to Canaan. Only the reference to God's saving act in the exodus event is mentioned more often in the Old Testament than the establishment of the covenant. It legitimizes the Israelites' claim to the promised land, functions as the reason for God to continually act on behalf of the people, and serves as a reminder to the people of their obligation to God.

Exodus 33:1—After receiving the law at Mount Sinai, Moses is charged by God to lead the people out of the wilderness into the "land . . . I swore to Abraham, Isaac, and Jacob."

Joshua 24:3—Following the conquest of Canaan, Joshua recounts to the assembled Israelites how God "took your father Abraham from beyond the River and led him through all the land of Canaan and made his offspring many."

2 Kings 13:23—The editor of the royal annals assures the people that despite the long-standing oppression of Israel by Hazael of Aram (Syria), God had no intention of abandoning the nation. Instead, God would have compassion on Israel, remembering "his covenant with Abraham, Isaac, and Jacob," and would not allow them to be destroyed.

Nehemiah 9:7–8—In the postexilic period (ca. 400 BCE) Ezra recounts the salvation history of the people beginning with God's choice of Abram, and he notes that God "found his [Abraham's] heart faithful before you, and made with him a covenant" that included a land for his descendants.

Isaiah 51:2—The postexilic voice of the prophet gives the people hope by saying: "Look to Abraham your father and to Sarah who bore you; for he was but one when I called him, but I blessed him and made him many."

Sirach 44:19–21—The second-century BCE wisdom writer extols Abraham as one who "kept the law . . . entered into a covenant with him [God] . . . and when he was tested he proved faithful" and thus gained blessings for the nations and offspring "as numerous as the dust of the earth."

task of this chapter to examine the implications of God's covenant with Abraham and Sarah and then to trace the echoes of how that covenant relationship becomes the basis for Israelite identity, their claims to the promised land, and the central theme of the prophets, who repeatedly call the people back to obedience and right conduct under the terms of the covenant with God.

A Covenant Is Established

God's decision to establish a covenant relationship with Abram and Sarai is the first seminal event in Israelite history. It creates a "founding parents" story, similar in some ways to the story of Adam and Eve, since both involve the origins of the nations of the earth; but for the ancestors of Israel it becomes the origin of their special tie to Yahweh as the "chosen people." What is particularly important about it, of course, is that God selected Abram and by extension his descendants for this special distinction. There is no specific reason given for this decision in the initial references to the covenant in Genesis 12, 13, and 15, in contrast to the flood narrative, in which Noah is chosen to survive because he is "righteous" (6:9). However, the apparently capricious decision on God's part is quickly justified by Abram's model behavior, and God explains the purpose for choosing the patriarch in 18:19 as a means of teaching the paths of righteousness and justice to those who will inherit the covenant promise.

Initial Call to Obedience (Gen. 12:1–3)

The story of Abram and Sarai begins in Genesis 11:27–32. We are told about Abram's father, Terah, Abram's marriage to Sarai, Sarai's infertility problem, and the trip from Ur of the Chaldees to Haran. This biographical sketch provides several clues to upcoming events and sets the stage for much of the rest of the book of Genesis. To begin with, it firmly establishes that the ancestors of the nation of Israel had their origins in Mesopotamia. If "Ur of the Chaldees" refers to the old Sumerian city near the Persian Gulf on the Euphrates River, then Terah and his family would have been very familiar with the urban-based, cosmopolitan culture of southern Mesopotamia. This would have included its warring city-states, its sense of kingship "sent down" from the gods, its huge temple and palace complexes, its economic contacts throughout the region, and its polytheistic religious system. A move to Haran, several hundred miles to the north in what is today northeastern Syria, would have involved a prolonged journey up the Euphrates, probably in the company of caravans or other travelers. It would also have involved a cultural shift away from a large urban setting to a much smaller town in the hinterland, away from the major political events of the day and sleepily engaged in a mixed economy of farming and herding (Matthews 1981). The text gives no indication why Terah chose to take his family to Haran other than its possible ties to his brother's family, but it will be in this place that God's call to Abram will come, and it serves as a good jumping-off point for Canaan.

One could ask whether a call by a god to serve would have been an extraordinary experience for Abram. Certainly, there are stories from the

Call to Obey God's Voice

The precedent of obedience to God's voice that is set by Abram in the ancestral narratives is echoed throughout the biblical text as later writers regularly include a strident call to be obedient. They also repeatedly remind the people that the consequences of disobedience are various forms of divine punishment.

Exodus 19:5—On reaching Mount Sinai after the exodus from Egypt, the Israelites are exhorted to "obey my voice and keep my covenant" in order to become "my treasured possession out of all the peoples."

Deuteronomy 11:26–28—As the people enter the promised land, they are warned that blessing comes from obeying "the commandments of the LORD," and curses come if they disobey God's commands.

Joshua 24:19–28—Joshua calls on the people, who had gathered at Shechem following the conquest, to renew the covenant and pledge to serve and obey God.

1 Kings 6:12—After building the Jerusalem temple, God tells Solomon that he will be blessed like his father David if he "will walk in my statutes, obey my ordinances, and keep all my commandments."

Jeremiah 26:13—The prophet Jeremiah offers hope that God will spare Jerusalem if the people amend their ways and "obey the voice of the LORD."

Zechariah 6:15—The prophet Zechariah predicts the return of the exiles to rebuild the temple in Jerusalem if they "obey the voice of the LORD."

ancient Near East that speak of heroes and kings who are confronted by a god or goddess (Gilgamesh, Adapa, Utnapishtim, Aqhat), and this could serve as preparation for a theophany. What Abram may not have been prepared for was a demand by this god that he break his ties to all that was familiar and take his family into the unknown (Gen. 12:1). The incentive for taking this risky step is the promise of children to an elderly man (age seventy-five) whose wife is barren (12:2) and a compact assuring divine protection for his household and blessings for those who ally themselves with Abram's family (12:3).

The offer is apparently one that Abram cannot refuse, and the story continues without any personal reflection or concerns being raised. This seems unusual in the light of Abram's polytheistic background. The people of the ancient Near East worshiped many gods. This allowed them to focus their attention on particular problems like the need for rain, a plague, or devastating earthquakes by praying and sacrificing to the god associated with that specific aspect of nature. Furthermore, there was a hierarchy among the gods, so that, if one god did not respond, the worshiper could go to another deity higher up and ask for relief or favor. Having only one god meant that there would be no opportunity to seek help elsewhere. This would have been a frightening prospect, and that is what makes Yahweh's command to Abram such an important and life-changing event.

Given this cultural background, the storyteller chooses to report only that Abram and his household, including his nephew Lot and a body of servants, left Haran for Canaan (hundreds of miles to the southwest). The narrative is extremely short on details, simply saying in one verse that they departed and in the next that they arrived near the city of Shechem in the central hill country of Canaan (Gen. 12:5–6). Telling a story with such an obvious narrative gap is an indication that the storyteller wishes to emphasize just one of Abram's attributes. The events during their journey may have been exciting and interesting, but what matters to this compiler of traditions is the bottom line: Abram obeyed God's command. In this way it can be said that the founding figure of the nation set a precedent from the very beginning of obeying God's voice, a quality that is echoed in later narratives and in prophetic speech.

Upon reaching Canaan, a second theophany occurs when God appears at the oak of Moreh near Shechem and once again promises "to give this land" to Abram's descendants (Gen. 12:6–7). This is expressed in the narrative in what could be called an action-reaction sequence: God commands, and Abram obeys; and when Abram obeys, then God renews the promise of land and children. Yet another precedent is set for later ritual practice when Abram constructs crude stone altars at Shechem and then at Bethel (12:8) and sacrifices to Yahweh. Each time this occurs, the presence of Yahweh is invoked in this place, marking the cultic beginnings for Israel. In addition, in a political and legal sense, the building of the altars functions as a staking out of the land, indicating Abram's claim to settle here. The construction of the altars also sets these places aside as significant, and they will reappear repeatedly as the sites of important events in later Israelite history (Matthews 2002: 6–11). There will be a series of narrative echoes (see the sidebar on the next page) that emanate from the initial action taken there by Abram. Each echo plays on the authority attached to the initial event at that place and reemphasizes its importance within Israelite tradition.

Sites of Abram's Altars

Place Name	Initial Event	Echo Event #1	Echo Event #2	Echo Event #3
Shechem	Abram first arrives in Canaan, builds altar to God (Gen. 12:6–7)	Rape of Dinah, massacre of men of Shechem by Jacob's sons (Gen. 34:2–26)	Joshua stages covenant-renewal ceremony after conquest (Josh. 24:1–32)	Rehoboam meets with tribal elders—kingdom divides (1 Kings 12:1–17)
Bethel	Abram builds altar to God (Gen. 12:8)	Jacob has theophany and names the place Bethel (Gen. 28:11–22)	Jeroboam builds northern kingdom shrines at Bethel and Dan (1 Kings 12:29)	Amos prophesies against Israel at Bethel (Amos 7:10–13)
Hebron	Abram builds altar to God (Gen. 13:14–18)	Abraham buys burial cave of Machpelah (Gen. 23:2–19)	David becomes king in Hebron (2 Sam. 2:11; 1 Kings 2:11)	Absalom begins his revolt from Hebron (2 Sam. 15:7–10)

Call to Survey the Promised Land (Gen. 13:14–18)

Two episodes intervene in the narrative at this point (Gen. 12:10–13:13) that contain (1) a contest-between-gods story (discussed in more detail in chap. 3 below) and (2) a disqualification story involving Abram's nephew Lot. Each of these episodes falls into a subtheme involving the endangerment of the covenant promise. Abram and Sarai had been promised that they would become the ancestors of "a great nation" (12:2), but they are an aged and childless couple. For this reason they had brought their nephew Lot with them, and the implication is that Abram planned to adopt Lot as his heir. Compounding this problem is a famine (12:10) that forces the new immigrants to flee from Canaan to Egypt, where they can purchase food and perhaps work for a time as itinerant laborers. The wife-sister deception that Abram concocts prior to their entrance into Egypt (12:11–13) is designed to protect his life from a covetous pharaoh, but it places both Sarai and the covenant promise in jeopardy since any child she might bear from that point on would be Pharaoh's and not Abram's. God intervenes to protect Sarai and forces the god-king pharaoh to return her to Abram (along with the riches that had been paid as a bride price), and the covenant promise is preserved (Gen. 12:14–20).

The return to Canaan then involves yet another decision. Lot and Abram cannot pasture their sheep together without exhausting the grazing too quickly. They choose to separate, but Lot disqualifies himself as Abram's heir by deciding to leave the promised land and settle near

Sodom east of the Jordan River (Helyer 1983). This leaves Abram without an heir, and it is at this point that he experiences a third theophany in which God instructs this ancestral character first to view the land in every direction and then to "walk through the length and the breadth of the land" (13:14–15, 17). All that he sees and traverses shall be an inheritance for his countless offspring (Gen. 13:16). The geographic dimensions of the promised land are intentionally inclusive. For example, the reference to every point of the compass in Genesis 13:14 fits into the ancient Near Eastern concept of universality. In this way Abram's sovereignty, and that of his descendants, over the promised land is established. Furthermore, as the divine donor of this land, Yahweh's position as Lord of all the earth is demonstrated.

Points of the Compass and Universalism

A common expression found in both ancient Near Eastern royal inscriptions and in the Bible referring to a king's or a god's sovereignty over the whole earth is the phrase "from sunrise to sunset." Their days were computed by the passage of the sun across the horizon, and it was therefore logical to refer to the length and breadth of the land (as in Gen. 13:14–17 = the dimensions of the promised land) as stretching from one horizon to the other.

Karatepe Inscription—An eighth-century ruler of southern Turkey proclaims: "I have become both father and mother of the Danunians . . . extending their land from sunrise to sunset" (Matthews and Benjamin 1997: 162).

Psalm 75:6–7—The psalmist proclaims that justice does not come from the east or west or from the wilderness, "but it is God who executes judgment." In this way God's sovereignty over all creation is certified.

Psalm 107:2–3—The psalmist describes how God has gathered the exiles from every land, "from the east and from the west, and from the north and from the south." Thus there is no place in all the world that is free from God's sovereign command (see also Isa. 41:8–9 and 49:8–12).

Isaiah 45:6—Speaking of God's use of Cyrus of Persia to free the exiles in Babylon, the prophet says God has done this "so that they may know, from the rising of the sun and from the west, that there is no one besides me." In this way all nations will be expected to recognize the power of Yahweh.

Malachi 1:11—God proclaims through the prophet that "from the rising of the sun to its setting my name is great among the nations."

Once again Abram does not question God's promise. He travels another
stage south into the land, settling near Hebron by the oaks of Mamre,
and yet again builds an altar to worship God in this place (Gen. 13:18).
Each of the places where Abram constructs his altars (Shechem, Bethel,
Hebron) will function as a major religious and political center in later
Israelite history (see the sidebar on page 42). Repeatedly tying a site
to significant events allows later characters to play on the authority
attached to this sacred space and associate themselves with Abram's
act of faith.

To this point very little of Abram's character has been revealed. He
has been forced into situations that he cannot control, and in each case
he must depend upon Yahweh to rescue or direct him. That, of course,
is the theological paradigm that the biblical storyteller is trying to con-
vey to the audience. Like Abram, they should be willing to take a leap
of faith into the unknown, being assured that God would be there to
protect them and reward their obedience.

A Twofold Covenant Promise (Gen. 15)

A more complete expression of the covenant promise to Abram is
found in Genesis 15. Only here are the covenant elements of land and
children coupled by God with an elaborate ritual (Moberly 1990: 119).
A quick examination of the chapter indicates that it has a two-part
structure that can be divided into verses 1–6 and verses 7–21. While each
portion includes a covenant promise, the chapter may contain originally
separate covenant stories that have been molded together by the editor
of these traditions. Since there is a clear relationship between the two
sections, however, it is possible to argue for narrative unity based on
the connection between the assessment of Abram's righteousness and
the promise of progeny and land (Wenham 1987: 326; Van Seters 1992:
251). Regardless of its original provenance, this chapter provides yet
another reiteration of the terms of the covenant while adding some new
features and predictions of coming events.

In the first section (15:1–6) the mute and unprotestingly obedient
Abram finally finds his voice during his fourth theophany, this time in
the form of a vision or dream. God exhorts Abram to "fear not" and
proclaims that he is Abram's "shield" and that his rewards will be great
(15:1). This is an appropriate poetic image for the divine protector after
Abram's battle with the Mesopotamian kings described in 14:14–16, and
it is repeated often as either a quality of God (Deut. 33:29; Pss. 3:3; 7:10;
18:2) or as one of God's names: "Give thanks to the shield of Abraham"
(Sirach 51:12). Furthermore, since the Hebrew word for shield (*magen*)

can also be translated as "giver/donor," this phrase can be tied to a sense of benefaction as well as to protection (Rendsburg 1992: 267–68).

An apparently astonished and frustrated Abram speaks out here about the unbelievable aspects of God's promise and asks what is to be done. He had seen his nephew Lot eliminated from the heirship, and Abram now is told that his adopted servant Eliezer of Damascus may not serve as his heir either (Gen. 15:2–4). Disregarding Abram's concern and his failed attempts to obtain an heir through legal means, God once again repeats the covenant promise that Abram will have a son of his own, and then God elaborates on this with the metaphor of the starry sky to express how numerous Abram's offspring will be (compare the metaphor of the "dust of the earth" in 13:16).

Most important in this dialogue between Abram and God is the statement expressed in the third person in 15:6 that because Abram believed what God had said, "the LORD reckoned it to him as righteousness." This is the only place in the Bible where the two Hebrew words for "believe" and "righteousness" are used together in a single sentence. Given the brevity of the passage, the implication is that Abram is reckoned to be righteous because of his faith in God's word rather than in an action or set of actions he has performed (Alexander 1994: 14). Furthermore, the form of the word for "righteousness" implies continuous or long-standing practice (Moberly 1990: 103–5). Yahweh's assessment of Abram therefore is that he has continuously shown himself to be righteous based on his expressed faith in God's word, and once again the audience for this story is confronted with a role model and a criterion for divine blessing. Indeed, the religious idiom of "reckoned righteousness" indicates "a convergence between human and divine action," which both enhances a person's relationship with God and leads "to a kind of overflow such that enduring blessing" is bestowed on Israel as well (Moberly 1990: 126).

An echo of this form of divine reckoning of righteousness is also found in the psalmist's retelling of the story of Phinehas in Psalm 106:28–31 (based on his actions in Num. 25:1–13). Like Abram, God makes a covenant with Phinehas because of his "zeal for God" (Num. 25:13), and like Abram's covenant, it has an effect on future generations. Yet another expression of righteousness is found in a passage in which God muses over Abraham's purpose (Gen. 18:19). God states that he has chosen Abraham so that the patriarch can teach his children "to keep the way of the LORD by doing righteousness and justice," and they in turn will benefit from "what he [God] has promised" their ancestor.

It is a concern for these later generations that is of greatest importance for the biblical editor, who is compiling these materials in the

The Rewards of Righteousness

The value of righteousness, as exemplified by Abraham's obedience to God's command, is often extolled in the biblical text. This quality that centers on obedience to the covenant is found in the annals of the kings, in Wisdom literature, and in the words of the prophets. Furthermore, it is described as the basis upon which God rewards those who continuously pursue this path of proper behavior.

1 Samuel 26:23—After sparing the king's life, David expresses the maxim to Saul: "The LORD rewards everyone for his righteousness and his faithfulness."

2 Samuel 22:21—In a song of thanksgiving, David states, "The LORD rewarded me according to my righteousness."

Proverbs 11:19—The wisdom writer proclaims: "Whoever is steadfast in righteousness will live, but whoever pursues evil will die" (compare Rom. 6:23).

Isaiah 32:17—In the face of the looming Assyrian threat to Judah at the end of the eighth century, Isaiah posits how the political and social order can be transformed: "The effect of righteousness will be peace, and the result of righteousness, quietness and trust forever."

Ezekiel 33:24–29—After Jerusalem's fall, Ezekiel warns the survivors in Judah that they cannot claim the land as theirs by saying, "Abraham was only one man, yet he got possession of the land; but we are many; the land is surely given us to possess." Their lack of righteousness will only lead to further destruction of the people and the land.

Hosea 10:12—The prophet urges the people: "Sow for yourselves righteousness; reap steadfast love."

late-monarchic or postexilic period. The assumption is that Israel has benefited from these early traditions, and they hope that the blessings of the covenant will continue. Their concern also extends, after the return from exile, to the question of who are the true descendants of Abraham and are thus entitled to claim the land promised to him in the covenant (Noort 1995: 143).

There is a definite thematic logic that connects the second segment of Genesis 15, verses 7–21, to the first segment. This is based on the tie between the promise of land and children in both of these sections and the "reckoning" of Abram's righteousness that activates God to fulfill that promise (Van Seters 1992: 248–49). Both segments, excluding verses 12–16, which are probably a later addition, contain similar elements, suggesting a basic unity (see the sidebar on the next page).

Literary Links in Genesis 15

Divine introduction—"your shield" (v. 1) and "the LORD who brought you from Ur" (v. 7)

Abram's question—"What will you give me?" (v. 2) and "How am I to know that I shall possess it?" (v. 8)

Divine promise—"your very own issue shall be your heir" (v. 4) and "give you this land to possess" (v. 7)

Divine command—"count the stars" (v. 5) and cut animals in two (vv. 9–11)

One unusual elaboration that separates the two promise theme statements in verses 4–5 and 18–21 is a ceremonial act that finds a biblical parallel only in the curse text in Jeremiah 34:18–20, which describes the fate of covenant breakers. In the Genesis 15 account, God commands Abram to cut the bodies of several different species of animals in half (15:9–11). This is followed by God's passing, in the form of a smoking fire pot and a flaming torch, between the pieces (v. 17). Such an unusual set of actions lends itself to numerous interpretations, and many commentators have tried to draw parallels from ancient Near Eastern cultic performance (see Hasel 1981 and his discussion of Hittite and Mari texts). The difficulties of establishing clear parallels with second-millennium Mesopotamian texts (such as Alalakh text 456) make a definitive statement on either cultural borrowing or even dating of the ritual impossible at this point (Hess 1994: 64–65). Even defining the ritual has proven difficult, with some scholars suggesting that it may be a form of elaborate sacrificial rite, a self-cursing performance, or an aspect of a treaty-making ceremony (see Zevit 2001: 534; Harran 1997: 218–19). What it does seem to foreshadow is the exodus experience in which God leads the people in the form of a pillar of cloud and a pillar of fire (Exod. 13:21–22). This narrative tie is strengthened by the mention in verse 11 of Abram driving away birds of prey from the bodies of the divided animals, which may represent his defense of his covenantal descendants and God's rescue of the people from Egyptian slavery (Wenham 1987: 332–33).

Renaming and Circumcision as Signs of the Covenant (Gen. 17)

While the twofold covenant statement in Genesis 15 centers on an apparently unconditional promise of land for Abram's descendants (vv. 5 and 18–21), there is no explicit mention of an ongoing relationship between God and these descendants (Alexander 1994: 21). That omission is rectified in Genesis 17, and an additional element, circumcision, is added to the condition of membership within the covenant community.

Furthermore, there is a new emphasis in this chapter, in comparison to Genesis 15, on an "everlasting covenant" with Abraham's offspring. A connection is made repeatedly between "exceedingly numerous" offspring (17:2) and an "exceedingly fruitful" ancestor (17:6, 20) as a sign of how God's blessing will be demonstrated under the terms of the covenant (see a similar statement in 12:2; P. Williamson 2000: 153). This in turn brings new focus to the search for the proper heir that had begun in Genesis 12 with Lot and will now be completed with the disqualification of Ishmael and the certification of Isaac as Abraham's God-given heir.

In this fifth theophany experienced by Abram, the patriarch is addressed by a God calling himself El Shaddai, "God Almighty." This new name for God, most often used in the Jacob cycle of stories (Gen. 28:3; 34:14; 35:11; 48:3; 49:25), foreshadows the revelation of new elements in the covenant promise. Its sudden appearance is explained by the editors of Exodus 6:3, who indicate that El Shaddai was the name for God known to the ancestors before the name Yahweh was revealed to the people in Moses' time. That the name Yahweh does appear several times in the Genesis accounts can thus be explained as narrative aids for the later audience so they can make the connection between Yahweh and the various El-based names used in these ancestral stories (Brett 2000: 62). There is also an example of the name Shaddai appearing in Canaanite culture in the ninth-century BCE Deir Alla inscription. This text indicates that Canaanite religion used *shaddayin* to refer to a group of protective deities (Hackett 1984: 85–89).

Once again the importance of obedience to God's command prefaces all else, even though Abram has previously shown his willingness to comply (leaving Haran—Gen. 12:1–4; accepting the disqualification of Lot and Eliezer—15:2–6). In this chapter, however, Abram's loyalty must be shown. He must no longer rely on his own devices to survive (journey to Egypt—12:10–20) or to obtain an heir (Fleishman 2001: 20). He is exhorted to be "blameless" (see 6:9, where Noah is certified as having this quality), and this will take the form of obedience to God's command to circumcise all males in Abram's household (Brett 2000: 62–63).

To signify the maturing relationship between God and the ancestors, God changes Abram's name to Abraham and Sarai's to Sarah. In doing this the Deity transforms the very character of these individuals, marking both of them as his covenantal partners and implying the destiny that has been set aside for them (Sarna 1989: 124). The universal character of this couple's role again evokes images of Adam and Eve. Like that first couple, God charges Abraham and Sarah with the task of becoming "parents" to many nations (Hamilton 1990: 464; P. Williamson 2000:

155). The name changes, along with the command to circumcise the males in Abraham's household, are thus part of the final cultural transition from Mesopotamian traditions to a newly formed social group in Canaan (Fleishman 2001: 23).

Structural Features

One way to better understand Genesis 17 is to examine its basic structure (see P. Williamson 2000: 149). Its literary framework consists of (1) a series of divine commands requiring obedience to God's word, (2) several repetitions of the basic covenant promise followed by both elaborations on the theme and an extension to later generations, and (3) the command to circumcise all males in his household, followed by both a legal expansion and the physical act of circumcising Abraham's encampment (compare Lev. 12:3 and Josh. 5:2–7). One additional element embedded in the narrative is the annunciation (divine birth announcement) and certification of Isaac as Abraham's heir. This is done explicitly at the expense of Ishmael's claim to that title, although that son of Abraham by the Egyptian slave woman Hagar is provided a separate legacy of his own (Gen. 21:17–21). Dividing the principal segments of the chapter are the two occasions when Abraham acknowledges God's sovereignty and bows to the ground (v. 3 and v. 17).

While there are several familiar features in these covenant promises, the chief difference between Genesis 17 and previous episodes in Genesis is found in its elaborations on the theme and the prominent role played by Sarah. She is no longer a pawn who can be used by her husband when he feels endangered by local rulers (see the wife-sister motif in Gen. 12:10–20 and Gen. 20). Instead, Sarah is essential to the covenant promise as the mother of Abraham's true heir (Turner 1990: 78). Another elaboration on previous themes can be seen by comparing the narrative elements found in Genesis 17 with those in 12:1–3, 7. In the Genesis 12 account, God commands Abram to leave Haran and promises that Abram will be the ancestor of "a great nation," a blessing to them and their allies, and they will be given their own land. These same promises are repeated in 15:5, 18–21, with some variation and elaboration on the theme. However, the degree to which this covenant language is expounded upon is far greater in 17:2, 4, 6–16. In addition to extreme fertility, there are also promises of kings as his and Sarah's descendants and the fivefold repetition of extending the covenant and its blessings of land and children to their "offspring." The key phrases that recur in this version and thus tie the various elements of the chapter together are "offspring" (vv. 7, 8, 9, 10, 19) and "everlasting covenant" (vv. 7, 13, 19).

Structural Scheme of Genesis 17

1. **Divine commands—**
   "Walk before me and be blameless" (v. 1)
   "Your name shall be Abraham" (v. 5)
   "You shall keep my covenant, you and your offspring" (v. 9)
   "Every male among you shall be circumcised" (v. 10)
   "Sarah shall be her name" (v. 15)
   "Your wife Sarah shall bear you a son, and you shall name him
   Isaac" (v. 19)
2. **Divine covenant promises—**
   a. Promise to Abraham:
      "I will make you exceedingly numerous" (v. 2)
      "You shall be the ancestor of a multitude of nations" (v. 4)
      —Elaboration (1) "I will make you exceedingly fruitful" (v. 6)
      —Elaboration (2) "I will make nations of you, and kings shall
      come from you" (v. 6)
   b. Promise to Abraham's offspring:
      "I will establish my covenant between me and you, and your
      offspring . . . for an everlasting covenant, to be God to you
      and to your offspring after you" (v. 7)
      "I will give to you, and to your offspring after you, the land . . .
      all the land of Canaan, for a perpetual holding" (v. 8)
   c. Promise to Sarah:
      "I will bless her . . . give you a son by her . . . and she shall
      give rise to nations; kings of peoples shall come from her"
      (v. 16)
   d. Promise to Isaac:
      "I will establish my covenant with him [Isaac] as an everlasting
      covenant for his offspring after him" (v. 19)
3. **Responses to God's statements—**
   Abraham "falls on his face" before God (vv. 3 and 17)
   Abraham pleads unsuccessfully for Ishmael (v. 18)
   Abraham circumcises all the males in his household (v. 23)

Also unique to this example of the covenant promise in Genesis 17 is the institution of circumcision as a ritual act and a sign of membership in the covenant community (Fleishman 2001: 25; Fox 1974). Although the practice of male circumcision is not unique to the ancient Israelites (see Hamilton 1990: 469) and may have been borrowed from the Egyptians or another Northwest Semitic group (Sasson 1966), its chief function is to provide an unmistakable, physical proof of membership. There is also a sacrificial aspect since it involves the shedding of blood, and it can thus be tied to the apotropaic use of blood to ward off the angel of death in the tenth plague in Exodus 12:3–13.

As described in Genesis 17:12, the prescribed practice involves cutting off the foreskin of every male who is at least eight days old. Obviously, Abraham was an adult at the time of this command, as were most of the males in his household. It is possible that performing circumcision at the time of puberty or later was an acceptable option (compare the mass circumcision in Josh. 5:2–7) that was eventually normalized by the time of the postexilic period (per Lev. 12:3; Fox 1974: 593). Given the strong emphasis expressed in Genesis and Leviticus, however, it seems more likely that "late" circumcisions were done in extraordinary rather than ordinary circumstances.

The significance of waiting until the eighth day is unclear, although it may be related in a cultic sense to the dedication on the eighth day of firstborn animals that will be offered as sacrifices (Exod. 22:29; Lev. 22:27;

Echoes of Abraham's Offspring

Such a clear emphasis on the transmission of the covenant promise to all future generations would have been extremely important to the people of Israel in later historical periods. Their basic sense of identity, especially after the destruction of Jerusalem in 586 BCE, would have been fortified by the "everlasting" covenant promise made to their ancestor Abraham. Thus to be called the "offspring of Abraham" was a comforting phrase used by a psalmist and several of the prophets.

Psalm 105:5–8—The psalmist reminds the people of the "wonderful works" performed by God on their behalf and calls on them to be thankful. He then refers to them as the "offspring of his [God's] servant Abraham," who have benefited from the actions of their just God, who "is mindful of his covenant forever."

Isaiah 41:8—The prophet reassures the people during their Babylonian exile of God's willingness to help them as the "offspring of Abraham, my friend."

Jeremiah 33:15, 26—In the face of Judah's imminent defeat and destruction by the Babylonians, the prophet foretells a day when God will restore the nation and raise up a "righteous Branch" of David's line to rule over them. This promise is based on the people's status as "the offspring of Abraham, Isaac, and Jacob."

4 Maccabees 18:1—This Roman-era (50 BCE–70 CE) writer exhorts the "offspring of the seed of Abraham" to be obedient to the law in order to enjoy God's blessings.

Sarna 1989: 125). On a practical level, waiting until the eighth day may be a way of establishing the viability of the child in a world in which infant mortality was quite high. It also provides an "x + 1 formula" for a ritual that takes place one day after the traditional seven-day creation period.

Because it involves the male sex organ, the ritual of circumcision is also tied to fertility, a principal component of the covenant promise (Eilberg-Schwartz 1990: 146–48). By performing this act in each successive generation, the Hebrews tied themselves to Abraham's original compliance with God's word and created a link to God's promise to bless them with fertility and ownership of the land "throughout their

---

Circumcision as Covenant Marker and Sign of Obedience

On a physical level, the law of circumcision functions as a tie to Israel's origins as a people of the covenant, and its occurrence at moments of crisis provides a renewal of the obligation by the people to be in compliance with God's command.

Exodus 4:24–26—Moses is threatened by God until Zipporah circumcises their son and brings them into compliance with the law.

Joshua 5:2–7—After the Israelites miraculously cross the Jordan River and enter the promised land, God orders Joshua to circumcise all males, since this practice had not been continued during the wilderness wanderings. They are then prepared, being in compliance with the law, to conduct the conquest.

In prophetic texts, however, circumcision becomes a metaphor for obedience to the covenant, going beyond the physical ritual of removing the foreskin. In this way, the common theme of obedience over ritual (see 1 Sam. 15:22) is given another guise.

Jeremiah 4:1–4—Citing a similar statement in Deuteronomy 10:16, the prophet calls on the people to return to truth, justice, and uprightness and to "circumcise yourselves to the Lord, remove the foreskin of your hearts," or God's wrath will break out against them.

Jeremiah 9:25–26—In his frustration over hollow worship that goes through the motions but has no substance in faith, the prophet condemns those "who are circumcised only in the foreskin" and cries out that "all the house of Israel is uncircumcised in heart."

generations" (Gen. 17:7). Since failure to perform this required act cut an individual or a group off from the covenant (v. 14), circumcision was added to the laws regarding Passover. No male (including resident aliens) could celebrate the Passover if he had not been circumcised (Exod. 12:48–49).

To reinforce this legal requirement and as a means of teaching the community about the covenant and its obligations, it is quite likely that a traditional lesson was recited or a drama performed during the circumcision of each newly born male infant (see Eilberg-Schwartz 1990: 144–45 for this practice in other cultures). Although the biblical text does not contain an elaborate liturgy based on the circumcision ceremony (compare that for Passover in Exod. 12:1–28), this certainly would have been an appropriate occasion for telling the story of Abraham's first mass circumcision of his household (see Goldberg 1996: 26–31).

Hospitality as a Framework for Covenant Promise (Gen. 18:1–15)

There is a logical progression in the narrative from Abraham's circumcision of his household in Genesis 17:23–27 to the prediction of Isaac's birth in 18:1–15. In these two chapters the patriarch proves himself to be obedient once again in the matter of circumcision and with regard to the hospitality protocol common to the Near East. It is therefore appropriate that he and his wife will receive, at long last, the fulfillment of the promise, made so often, that they will have a son of their own. Completing the cycle of these events, Isaac will be the first male in the household to be circumcised on the mandated eighth day after birth (21:4). Adding to the interest attached to these stories, the sixth and final theophany in the sequence of episodes outlining the covenant promise introduces yet another narrative innovation—one that will have an immediate impact on the audience (see the animal ritual in Gen. 15; renaming and circumcision in Gen. 17). In chapter 18 the covenant theme of command and right behavior is tied to the strict adherence to the steps of the hospitality protocol, one of the central survival-based traditions of the ancient Near East.

As a social institution, hospitality in the Near East, in both ancient and more modern times, adheres to a model of behavior based on the fulfillment of obligation and social expectations. The concept of hosting as a form of political strategy and social obligation originated in the need for aid when away from home (Janzen 1994: 43). Travel was often difficult and dangerous, and a strategy must have quickly emerged that allowed both the traveler and the host to achieve a sense of security. Thus hospitality is offered to the traveler who is neither part of one's extended family nor a resident of the general area (Hobbs 2001: 16). Reciprocal actions and expectations grow out of this need for security and allow the stranger to be invited into an encampment, village, or town. The liminal stranger, unknown and therefore a potential threat, is given temporary status as a guest, thereby removing the hostile overtones associated with the different and the unfamiliar (Malina 1986: 181). In this way, the host obtains honor within his household and his community as well as a certain degree of moral superiority by extending the offer of hospitality (Douglas 1992: 156–57). However, if at any point the pattern of behavior that governed the relationship between the host and guest is violated, by either party, then overt hostility can occur. The protection and comfort to which the guest is entitled and which the host is obligated to give are no longer required. In order to prevent violence by either the stranger or the host, strict adherence to the social code of hospitality is required.

It is therefore interesting to note that Abraham is involved in the only two examples in the Old Testament (the other is in Gen. 24) in which strict adherence to the protocol of hospitality occurs. In all other instances in which hospitality is a key factor in the narrative, it is the violations of the protocol that drive the story rather than obedience to social custom (see Gen. 19; Judg. 4 and 19; Matthews 1991a; 1992). As always, Abraham is the model for proper behavior against which all other characters can be measured. His handling of the hospitality opportunity in Genesis 18:1–15 can be outlined as follows:

1. Sphere of hospitality: As one living in an encampment, Abraham's sphere of hospitality obligation likely stretches either by line of sight or as far as his herds are grazing. Thus when he looks up from the entrance of his tent and sees three travelers approaching, Abraham must exercise his role as head of the household and its protector. He immediately goes out to them with the intention of defusing any potential threat and to gain the honor attached to such a display of correct social behavior (18:1–2).
2. Offer of hospitality: The offer consists of extending to the strangers the comforts of his household, which include water, foot washing, a shady place to relax, and food. It also contains a transparent assurance that Abraham has no intention of delaying them for any extended period and his expectation that the strangers will indeed move on once they are refreshed (18:1–5a).
3. Hosting begins: Once the strangers have agreed to honor Abraham's invitation (18:5b), the socially recognized roles of host and guest come into play, and both parties are tied into a code of behavior that places strict obligations on them. Thus Abraham carries out

Protocol of Hospitality
(based on Matthews 1991a: 13–15)

1. There is a sphere of hospitality that comprises a zone of obligation for both the individual and the village or town within which they have the responsibility to offer hospitality to strangers. The size of the zone is of course smaller for the individual than for the urban center.
2. The stranger must be transformed from potential threat to ally by the offer of hospitality.
3. The invitation of hospitality can be offered only by the male head of household or a male citizen of a town or village.
4. The invitation may include a time-span statement for the period of hospitality, but this can then be extended, if agreeable to both parties, on the renewed invitation of the host.
5. The stranger has the right of refusal, but this could be considered an affront to the honor of the host and could be a cause for immediate hostilities or conflict.
6. Once the invitation is accepted, the roles of the host and the guest are set by the rules of custom.
   a. The guest must not ask for anything.
   b. The host provides the best he has available—despite what may be modestly offered in the initial invitation of hospitality.
   c. The guest is expected to reciprocate with news, predictions of good fortune, or gracious responses based on what the host has given.
   d. The host must not ask personal questions of the guest.
7. The guest remains under the protection of the host until he/she has left the zone of obligation of the host.

his offer of food, but he garners additional honor by providing more than was initially offered to his guests, and while they eat, he stands ready to see that they are totally refreshed (18:6–8). At no time do the guests ask for anything to be given to them, since that would burden the host and dishonor him with the implication that he has not been a proper host.

4. Role of the guest: Having received the benefits of the host's hospitality, the guest is expected to reciprocate by providing news or entertaining stories that will benefit or amuse the host and his household. In 18:9–14 this takes the form of an annunciation story. One guest makes the unlikely prediction that this old couple will have a son within a year's time. Sarah's laughter as she listens in to their conversation from behind the tent flap is a break in the

protocol, since it questions the truthfulness of the guest. However, her lapse provides an opportunity for an etiology of Isaac's name (= "laughter") and to make the assertion "Is anything too wonderful for the LORD?" (v. 14).

5. Host's final obligation: When the strangers are prepared to depart, the host will "set them on their way" (v. 16) in order to assure them of his protection while they remain within his sphere of hospitality. Both parties remain under social obligation until they separate, and thus Yahweh's decision to inform Abraham about the fate of Sodom and Gomorrah falls within the hospitality protocol and gives Abraham the opportunity as gracious host to bargain for the lives of the people in those cities, including that of his nephew Lot (vv. 17–21).

Abraham has shown through his adherence to the hospitality protocol that he is righteous, and he calls on God to spare the cities if a few righteous people can be found there (vv. 22–33). His bargaining session with God over the value attached to righteousness has a number of echoes in Israelite tradition (Lundbom 1998: 140–45). Each example functions as a means of demonstrating God's just character and also reassures the audience that if they, like Abraham, are righteous, then God will spare them the punishment rained down on Sodom and Gomorrah.

A Final Test of Faith (Gen. 22)

The covenant promise of progeny had been fulfilled with the birth of Isaac (Gen. 21:1–7). With all other claimants to the covenant heirship eliminated, Abraham and Sarah have all of their hopes and expectations bound up in their only son. This then provides the background and the premise for a final, tension-filled episode in which God demands of them a final test of faith that seems too much for any parent to bear. The test begins with the command "Take your son, your only son Isaac, whom you love, and go to the land of Moriah, and offer him there as a burnt offering on one of the mountains that I shall show you" (22:2). There is a clear similarity in this command to "go to the land" and God's initial demand to Abraham: "Go from your country and your kindred and your father's house to the land that I will show you" (12:1). These two divine commands set off the entire narrative of Abraham's covenantal revelations, forming a distinct literary unit (Turner 1990: 87). This type of literary mapping is known as *inclusio*, wherein a text begins and ends with the same phrase or event.

Righteousness and a Just God

The emphasis placed in the Abraham narrative on his righteous behavior and his obedience to God's command is coupled with the assumption in Israelite legal and religious tradition that Yahweh by definition is a just God. This label differentiates Yahweh from the capricious gods of the other ancient Near Eastern cultures. Furthermore, since the covenant requires obedience to God's word, it also means that God cannot, without warning or reason, destroy the righteous. In this way a remnant may survive to restore the people and the nation (Matthews 2000: 41).

Noah—Prior to the great flood, God determines that Noah is "a righteous man, blameless in his generation" (Gen. 6:9). As such the obligation is for God to warn him of the impending disaster so that he can prove his righteousness by following divine instructions and thus save his life and his household.

Twelve Spies—Prior to their invasion of Canaan, Moses sends twelve spies into the land. All but two report the impossibility of conquering the well-fortified cities there. Moses is able to get Yahweh to forgive the people for their lack of faith, but God condemns the generation that had seen the divine signs of power at the Red Sea and in the wilderness to die without entering the promised land. Only the two faithful spies, Joshua and Caleb, will be allowed to leave the wilderness alive (Num. 13:17–14:24).

Jeremiah—During the prophet's trial for speaking out against the people's failure to obey the covenant and their false hope in the Jerusalem temple as a safe haven, the elders speak up and remind the court of how God spared the city from the Assyrians in Hezekiah's time. They say that Jeremiah's prophecies must be taken seriously in order to get God to "change his mind about the disaster" that the prophet has predicted (Jer. 26:17–19). Jeremiah later tells King Zedekiah that the only remnant that would survive the Babylonian siege would be those who surrender and accept God's punishment of Jerusalem (Jer. 21:8–10).

Marked Innocents—Ezekiel has a vision in which the only survivors of Jerusalem's destruction will be those who "sigh and groan over all the abominations" that its people have committed (Ezek. 9:3–10).

As was the case in 12:4, Abraham does not question God's demand (22:3). The emotions that one might expect of a father whose hope for the future has just been stolen away are absent. The only break in a silent three-day journey is an order to the servants to remain at the foot of Mount Moriah

(22:5) and a dismissive response to Isaac's question about the sacrificial animal (22:7–8; Sarna 1989: 153). Abraham shares nothing of God's command with his wife, his servants, or his son. He simply follows orders as if he were under a compulsion so strong that it could not be denied. Isaac, the potential sacrificial victim of the story, does not speak again to his father but is passively bound and placed on the altar for slaughter (22:9–10).

As the knife descends the tension is broken when God's angel calls out Abraham's name, and the faithful patriarch responds with the same phrase as he did when Isaac asked him for an explanation in verse 7: "Here I am" (v. 11). The collective gasp of the audience as they wait for tragedy to occur is transformed into a sigh of relief when a ram is substituted for the child as a sacrifice (vv. 12–13). One last time Abraham has demonstrated he is willing to give up anything (homeland, family ties, and his only son) in order to obey God's command.

What makes this story the appropriate climax to all the stories about Abraham and the covenant promise is this final precedent of total obedience. While it would not be easy to leave home, there is enough of the adventurer in most people to make this immigration to Canaan believable and understandable. Most could also accept the need to wait for God to fulfill the promise of children, though it would not be easy for an older couple. However, to have that long-awaited son snatched from them at this late date requires superhuman strength and catapults Abraham into the category of true founding figure—a cut above normal humans and able to abide by God's command, even when it seems the most devastating.

One could argue that this story is not a polemic against human sacrifice and that it has no relationship to the traditional myths and stories about child sacrifice from other ancient Near Eastern cultures (Sarna 1989: 153; Speiser 1964: 163). To be sure, human sacrifice is rarely mentioned in the biblical text. However, there are a number of similarities between the Genesis 22 account and two other instances of human sacrifice (Jephthah's daughter in Judg. 11:29–40; Moabite king Mesha's son in 2 Kings 3:27). This suggests awareness of both traditional stories and of this sacrificial practice by the Israelite audience (Levenson 1993: 26–37). For example, in each case it is the "only child" of the hero or ruler that is to be sacrificed. Certainly, the audience is being called upon to consider the implications of the loss of an only child and heir in all these stories. In Abraham's case, that potential for loss is heightened by his extreme old age and the number of times he has been disappointed in waiting for his son to be born. The solution to the question of how dependent Abraham's story may be on ancient Near Eastern traditions may lie in what is known as a "reflection story" (Zakovitch 1985). In this type of story the audience is given the opportunity to reflect on the implications of what would be to them an unusual, even frightening tale. The narrative itself could make use of familiar story elements but need not contain them all or even have the traditional ending (Boehm 2004: 152–56).

Thus in Abraham's story, the horrific ending involving the death of the child is set aside as anticlimactic. If Isaac dies, then Abraham and Sarah must start over and once again await God's promised child. Instead, the human sacrifice is halted at the last moment, and the covenantal history can continue on without further narrative detours. It also makes human sacrifice in all later stories a social and religious aberration (see 2 Kings 16:2–4) and certifies Abraham as both the model of obedience and the recipient of God's blessing through all generations. No better conclusion could be provided for the etiological narrative of God's covenantal relationship with the people of Israel.

Moses Leads the Israelites out of Egypt

While the establishment of the covenant with Abraham and his descendants was the first step in the salvation history of the Israelites, the story of the exodus from Egypt moves the relationship with Yahweh to a national scale and serves as the precedent for divine intervention in their affairs. Subsequent episodes in the history of the nation and much of the prophetic material use the escape from Egypt as the premise for obedience to God's commands and the covenant. The exodus narrative also features the first national Israelite figure, one who is the model for all future leaders (until David becomes king) and who becomes the model for the later prophetic figures. It should be understood that the exodus narrative not only serves as a chronicle of events that tell the story of the origin of Israel as a people but also sets out a series of precedents that form the basis for legal, religious, and social activities. Each event in the narrative and each legal or religious precedent will have a ripple effect on later Israelite tradition and history and will be cited repeatedly as the foundation of authority for practice or belief.

Moses' Birth Narrative

The exodus from Egypt is chronicled in an extended narrative that is designed to introduce and bolster the authority of Moses as the leader of the Israelite people. It begins with a miraculous survival story describ-

Miraculous Survival Story

1. Endangered infant is hidden by mother
2. Child is placed in basket and floated down river
3. Child is rescued from river
4. Child is raised by member of royal court
5. Adult is assisted by god and becomes great leader

ing how the infant Moses escapes the callous attempt by the pharaoh to reduce the threat of Israelite overpopulation (Exod. 1:8–2:10; compare Jesus' survival story in Matt. 2:1–18). In almost comic terms the two Israelite midwives trick the pharaoh's men and thus save many of the male infants decreed to be killed (Exod. 1:15–21).

Subsequently, Moses' mother is forced to leave her son's fate up to God by exposing him to possible death on the river. She places him in a reed basket that is floated down the Nile with the expectation that, if the child survives, it will be because of the intervention of God (Exod. 2:2–3). In microcosm, of course, this is exactly the situation for all the Israelite people. Their fate as they float helplessly within the sea of Egyptian bondage is also left up to divine intervention. Moses' first crisis is then resolved in a scene that is quite ironic. The daughter of the pharaoh who had ordered his destruction draws Moses up out of the Nile and gives him a place in the royal court (2:5–10).

Since authority in the ancient Near East is often based on the ability to draw on a precedent to certify a new event or a new leader, it is not surprising to find that the story of Moses' survival is a close match with an earlier Mesopotamian tale, the Story of Sargon of Akkad (see Redford 1967 for a list of thirty-two ancient parallels). This nearly legendary king, who ruled 2371–2316 BCE, also has a miraculous survival story associated with his birth. His ability to grow to adulthood is also based on his mother's actions to protect him, the assistance of a person associated with the royal court, and divine patronage.

A biblical echo of Moses' survival story is found in the prophetic metaphor of the redeemed child in Ezekiel 16 (see also Ps. 22:9–11). In this case it is a female child who has been left by her parents in a field. Because many families could barely feed and care for the healthiest members of their household, exposure of unwanted children became quite common in the ancient Near East, especially those infants who were malformed or female. Thus the prophet describes a well-known situation and one understood as a gesture on the part of the parents, offering the child to anyone who would choose to adopt her (Malul 1990: 98–101). This, of course, also includes God, and that is exactly the case in Ezekiel's example. Like Moses, the baby girl's fate is left up to God's decision, and in this case it is God himself who adopts the child (16:6–7). God provides all that is needed for the growing child and eventually marries her (16:8). All the clothing, jewelry, and food that are lavished on the bride stand in stark contrast to her infidelity (16:9–22), a metaphor for idolatry similar to that found in Hosea 2:5–13. In this instance, therefore, a familiar story line, the miraculous survival of an infant, is intentionally altered by the prophet to shock his audience and to emphasize how grave are the sins of Jerusalem and its people. One final twist is found in Ezekiel 16:20, where the once-abandoned child now sacrifices her own children to foreign gods or foreign powers (symbolized by her "lovers"), whose heavy taxes impoverish Judah.

The Burning Bush Theophany on Mount Sinai

Perhaps because of his mixed heritage (Egyptian court education and nurturing by his Israelite mother), Moses eventually breaks with the Egyptian culture and flees into the desert of Midian (Exod. 2:11–15). While living in this desert region as a shepherd, Moses takes the next major step toward his ultimate role: he experiences a theophany, a physical appearance and communication with God, and is called to return to Egypt to lead his people to freedom. It should be noted that each of these steps in Moses' career is an exact increment of forty years, a number later associated with the period of wandering in the wilderness and probably symbolic of the completion of a set period of time.

The Story of Sargon of Akkad

Call me Sargon. I am the child of a priest and an unknown pilgrim from the mountains. Today I rule an empire from the city of Agade.

Because my mother did not want anyone in the city of Asupiranu to know that she had given birth to a child, she left me on the bank of the Euphrates River in a basket woven from rushes and waterproofed with tar.

The river carried my basket down to a canal, where Akki, the royal gardener, lifted me out of the water and reared me as his own. He trained me to care for the gardens of the great king.

With the help of Ishtar, divine patron of love and war, I became king of the black-headed people and have ruled 55 years. (Matthews and Benjamin 1997: 85)

As he leads his sheep to pasturage on Mount Horeb (= Mount Sinai), Moses has an experience that will become the model for the call of prophets from this point on in the biblical narrative. Moses' call narrative provides the basic framework for those of many later prophets (especially Isaiah), and his subsequent career will be one measure upon which later prophets are determined to be authoritative (Habel 1965: 297–305). His call (Exod. 3:1–4:18) may be outlined in this way:

1. Moses' theophany occurs in the form of a "burning bush," a miraculous phenomenon that is designed to demonstrate Yahweh's mastery over creation and to catch Moses' attention (Exod. 3:2–3). No "call" can take place officially without this divine manifestation. It includes an identification of the god and a general reason for the occurrence, in this case "the misery of my people" in Egypt (Exod. 3:6–10).

2. Because of the belief that to see God "face to face" is deadly (see Gen. 28:16–17), Moses is overcome with apprehension at "seeing" God (Exod. 3:6), and this leads to a series of excuses for why he should not be the one called to perform the difficult task outlined by God. Moses is particularly adamant about this. He refers to himself as a nobody, but God quickly shoves aside that excuse as irrelevant since God will be with him (3:11–12). He delays by asking God's name and receives a response that is a wordplay based on the verbal root of Yahweh's name ("I AM has sent me to you"; 3:13–15). He asks for some means of proving he has the right to speak for God and receives the power to perform a series of miraculous "signs" (4:1–9). Finally, Moses declares that he lacks the skill to speak "eloquently" and even hints at a speech impediment, but God assures him that he will "be with your mouth" and give him the necessary words to speak (4:10–12). Still Moses tries one last plea to send someone else, and angrily God appoints Moses' brother Aaron to be Moses' "mouth" and spokesman (4:13–16). This final concession also forms the basis for the significant role of the high priest in later periods.

3. Once Moses has run out of excuses, God then provides resolution to the dramatic scene. Having dismissed Moses' many excuses, Yahweh simply instructs him to take up his staff, "with which you shall perform the signs," and get on with it (4:17).

4. Since no further argument is possible, Moses must now undertake the mission that God has outlined (3:16–22; 4:21–23). This brings to an end the theophany that began when Moses responded to his name by saying, "Here I am" (3:4).

Ripple Effect on Prophetic Literature

The precedents set in Moses' call narrative for encounters with the Divine are echoed in the encounters with God (theophanies) experienced by the major prophets in later Israelite history. Elijah, Isaiah, Jeremiah, and Ezekiel all have call narratives that resemble Moses' experience. It is unlikely that this is a coincidence. Indeed, it makes sense that Yahweh would manifest himself to humans in a similar way so that there would be no confusion about which god is present. After all, Moses had asked the name of the deity he had encountered (Exod. 3:13), and the social world of ancient Israel continued to be primarily polytheistic throughout their history. Thus the importance of distinguishing sights and words would reassure the people that Yahweh continued to care for them and to call their leaders to serve him in the name of the covenant between God and Israel.

The common element in each of these call narratives is the empowerment of the prophet during a time of crisis. Moses must aid his people to escape Egyptian bondage. Elijah speaks to Israel at a time when King Ahab and Queen Jezebel are actively persecuting the prophets of Yahweh (1 Kings 18:4, 13; 19:14). Isaiah experiences the fall of the northern kingdom of Israel (721 BCE) and the siege of Jerusalem (701 BCE) by the Assyrians (Isa. 36–37). Jeremiah's career encompasses the last days of Judah and the destruction of Jerusalem by Nebuchadnezzar and the Babylonians in 587 BCE (Jer. 21, 32, 39). Ezekiel, a priest and prophet living in the Babylonian exile after 597 BCE, must face the destruction of Jerusalem and its temple and the years of captivity for his people (Ezek. 9–10; 14; 33:21–33).

Call Narrative Pattern

Prophet	Theophany	Manifestation	Demur/Mouth	Submission
Moses	Mt. Sinai	Burning bush	Aaron speaks for Moses	"Here I am"
Elijah	Mt. Horeb (= Mt. Sinai)	Stillness after wind, fire, and earthquake	Elisha chosen as successor	"I have been zealous . . ."
Isaiah	Temple in Jerusalem	Earthquake and smoke	Hot coal on lips	"Here I am, send me!"
Jeremiah	Unknown place	Voice	Mouth touched	"I see . . ."
Ezekiel	In exile near river Chebar	Stormy wind, fiery cloud	Eats scroll	Falls on face

In each case, the prophet must both infuse courage into the people and remind them that their only hope of survival is faith in Yahweh to deliver them. That each prophet in some way is aided to speak and thus carry out his mission ties each of these narratives together and gives them a sense of common purpose and historical lineage. Thus when Moses says he is incapable of effective public speaking, God provides his brother Aaron to speak the words that God provides (Exod. 4:10–16). Elijah, who is hiding in the wilderness, claiming that only his voice remains to speak for Yahweh (1 Kings 19:14), is assured by God that seven thousand will remain whose "mouth . . . has not kissed him [Baal]" (1 Kings 19:18). In addition, the prophet is able to select Elisha as his successor who will continue to speak God's words to the people (1 Kings 19:19–21). In Isaiah's case, his excuse is that he has "unclean lips," a reference to the lack of ritual purity of a people who are not worthy to speak God's words (Isa. 6:5). This condition is rectified in the vision by the seraph taking a hot coal from the altar and placing it on Isaiah's lips. In this way they are spiritually cauterized and thus capable of serving God's purpose (Isa. 6:6–7). Similarly, Jeremiah, who claims that he is too young to speak with authority to the people, is reassured that God will provide him with the proper words, and he is empowered to speak when God places a hand on his lips (Jer. 1:6–9). Finally, while Ezekiel does not make any excuses for his inability to serve as God's prophet, he is given the power to speak his message by consuming a divinely provided scroll (Ezek. 2:8–3:3).

The Escape from Egypt: A Contest between Gods

There is no single story that is cited as often in the Bible as the exodus event. The phrase "I brought you up out of the land of Egypt" forms a common link among the prophets, who saw the exodus as the formative event for the nation and the basis for obedience to the covenant (see Jer. 2:6; Dan. 9:15; Hosea 11:1; Amos 2:10; Mic. 6:4; Hag. 2:5). The precedent that is set in the narrative of the escape from Egypt is Yahweh's ability to win any contest with other gods. Indeed, it is essential that these contest stories repeatedly appear in order to reaffirm the supremacy of Yahweh over the gods of Canaan, Egypt, and Mesopotamia, since Israel was for most of its history either influenced or controlled by these more dominant cultures.

The contest motif consists of the following elements: (1) endangerment of the covenant community, (2) intervention by Yahweh to remove endangerment, and (3) resolution of the problem demonstrating Yahweh's supremacy over all other gods.

Contest Motif Pattern

Contest	Endangerment	Intervention	Resolution
Wife/Sister (Gen. 12:10–20)	Pharaoh takes Sarai from Abram	Egypt afflicted with plagues	Pharaoh returns Sarai unharmed
Joseph interprets dreams (Gen. 41)	Famine	Yahweh aids Joseph to interpret	Pharaoh appoints Joseph to his court
Exodus from Egypt (Exod. 3–14)	Israelites in bondage in Egypt	Egypt afflicted with ten plagues	Israelites cross Red Sea unharmed
Mt. Carmel contest (1 Kings 18)	Ahab and Jezebel suppress Yahweh worship	Elijah challenges 450 Baal prophets	Yahweh consumes sacrifices and brings rain to end drought
Daniel interprets dreams (Dan. 2, 4)	Nebuchadnezzar holds Israelite exiles	Yahweh aids Daniel to interpret	Daniel appointed as high official

Interestingly, these contest stories tend to appear in situations when the Israelites face a major shift or turning point in their history. Thus the newly arrived Abram and Sarai can affirm that their God is more powerful than all the gods of Egypt, including the god-king pharaoh, when Yahweh intervenes on their behalf. This in turn sets a precedent for all future relations with Yahweh. Both Joseph and Daniel, who are subject to the will of a powerful ruler, represent a wisdom tradition capable of interpreting dreams and determining the path that will gain God's favor. When they are able to do this while the magicians and diviners of Egypt and Babylon fail, Yahweh is shown to be the people's divine champion even while they are slaves or exiles. Finally, the contest on Mount Carmel during the monarchy period serves as the most spectacular example of the contest motif other than the exodus event. Here Elijah stands up to the attempts of Ahab and Jezebel to suppress the worship of Yahweh, and God's flaming consumption of the sacrifice provides a graphic demonstration of who really is the source of power.

Within the story of the exodus, the plague sequence works on several levels of meaning (Zevit 1990). Individual plagues relate to aspects of life in Egypt that are dependent on the water of the Nile River (Exod. 7:17–25), that would contribute to a famine due to the devastation caused by swarms of locusts (10:4–19), and that would shatter the economy if their herds were afflicted by disease (9:9–11). Furthermore, the shifts in the basic ecology of the land, driving frogs from the polluted river and contributing to a huge increase in the number of stinging flies and gnats that carried disease (Exod. 8), would tip the balance from a marginally livable to an absolutely unlivable situation

Reuse of the Exodus Plague Rhetoric

It is only natural that later writers and storytellers would refer to the plagues of Egypt, weaving them into their accounts as warnings against violations of the covenant or as reassurance that God would continue to defend the people of Israel. In this way the cliché phrase, "I brought you out of Egypt," that is used so often to remind the people what they owe to God is defined better and perhaps had more impact.

Deuteronomy 28:27—Covenant breakers are warned that God will inflict them with "the boils of Egypt."

Joshua 24:5—Joshua recounts the exodus event during his covenant-renewal ceremony at Shechem following the conquest of Canaan.

1 Kings 8:37—Solomon lists potential plagues that the penitent ask God to relieve.

Psalm 78:43–51 and 105:26–36—The psalmist recounts the plague sequence as part of a recital of covenant history.

Amos 4:10—The prophet compares a pestilence in Israel to the one visited on Egypt.

in Egypt. Of course, the gods of Egypt were supposed to provide for their people, and sacrifices were made to prevent such disasters. The failure of the gods to respond and the inability of the pharaoh to stop the plagues stand in sharp contrast to the almost mechanical way in which Moses or Aaron predicts the coming of a plague and then calls on Yahweh to end it once the pharaoh pleads for relief (see, for example, 8:20–31). In this way the Israelites are taught to respect the power of Yahweh and to depend on their God to fight for them and provide for their needs.

The tenth plague, the death of the firstborn (Exod. 12:29), deprives the Egyptians of their heirs, throwing the inheritance of property into a legal maelstrom and raising the mounting level of despair to the breaking point. It also certifies the legal tradition that the Israelite firstborn belonged to God and were redeemed through their parents' obedience to God's command to place the blood of the lamb on their doorposts. The consecration of Israel's firstborn is first mentioned in the preamble to the recitation of the Passover ritual in Exodus 13:2. It is then mentioned again in the covenant legal code in 22:29 and 34:19–20.

Later legal reference to the role of the firstborn is found in Numbers 3:13, 41, and 8:14–16, where the Levites are accepted as "substitutes for all the firstborn." A return to the theme of God's destruction of Egypt's firstborn as part of salvation history is found in the numerous references in the Psalms (78:51; 105:36; 135:8; 136:10). Even a deuterocanonical work, the Wisdom of Solomon, contains a citation of Egypt's devastating loss in Wisdom 18:13. Clearly, this was considered the worst of the plagues since it endangered the future, throwing doubt onto all human planning and sense of power.

The apotropaic ritual of placing the blood of the sacrificial lambs on the doorposts spared the Israelite families from the ravages of the angel of death (Exod. 12:7, 12). The use of the doorpost as the physical symbol of the household is quite common in legal texts, such as Exodus 21:6, in which a debt slave becomes a permanent household servant by having an awl driven through his earlobe into the doorpost (see Matthews 1994: 129–30). It also is featured in religious texts like Ezekiel 45:18–19, which commands that blood from a sacrificial bull be placed on the doorposts of the restored temple and on the altar as part of a decontamination ritual (Block 1998: 661–62).

An even more interesting echo of the marking of the Israelite doorposts is found in Ezekiel's vision of the marking of the innocents (Ezek. 9). In that text, an example of the remnant theme of the prophet, six executioners and a scribe walk from one end of Jerusalem to the other, taking note of those few who "sigh and groan over all the abominations that are committed" in the city (9:4). The scribe is instructed to mark these righteous persons with the letter *tav* (which looks like an *X* in the ancient writing system). All others are to be slaughtered by the executioners (compare a similar "culling" process in the golden calf narrative in Exod. 32:25–28 in which the Levites carry out a slaughter of the unfaithful at Moses' direction).

The final step in the process of escape from Egypt is the crossing of the Red Sea. This episode, which is both a creation story and a climactic end to the contest-between-gods theme that has dominated the exodus events, showcases Yahweh's complete control over the elements of nature (see Batto 1984). Since the surrounding nations all had gods associated with creation (Marduk in Babylon; both Ptah and Amon in Egypt; El and Baal in Syria and Canaan), it was extremely important to the biblical writers to demonstrate Yahweh's role as a creator God. As a result, there are many creation stories found throughout the biblical text, all of which are designed to show both Yahweh's supremacy over other gods and a complete command over all of nature.

The escape account in Exodus 14 is quite dramatic in tone, raising the level of suspense as the Israelites are led by Moses into the desert while Pharaoh's chariots press after them. Since their route is not a direct one, the storyteller provides an explanation for their apparently aimless wandering in 14:3–4, noting that the contest with Pharaoh is

---

Creation Stories outside Genesis

Red Sea Crossing (Exod. 14)—Yahweh controls the waters, separating them from the dry land in a miraculous demonstration of power.

Creation Psalms—Many psalms contain creation themes or the recitation of the events of Yahweh's creation (Pss. 8, 19, 50, 104).

Divine Potter—Isaiah 64:8 and Jeremiah 18:2–6 refer to Yahweh as the potter, who has shaped all of creation, including humankind.

Breath of Life—Ezekiel 37:1–10 provides a new creation story featuring the rearticulating of skeletons scattered across an old battlefield. They are then given life through the infusion of the breath of God (compare Gen. 2:7 and Ps. 104:29).

---

not yet ended and that Yahweh will have one final opportunity to demonstrate to the Israelites and the Egyptians who really is God. It is in this extremity, with an imminent confrontation with Pharaoh fast approaching from one direction and the sea barring their path in the other, that the Israelites first engage in what will become the often repeated "murmuring motif" (Alexander 1995: 151–54; compare Num. 11:1–15; 14:1–12; 21:5–9). They complain to Moses that they have been brought here to die, and they call on him to allow them to return to their former servitude (Exod. 14:11–12). What this creates is an opportunity for the people to choose which master they will serve. Moses calls on them to "not be afraid, stand firm, and see the deliverance that the LORD will accomplish" (14:13). In fact, the Divine Warrior will "fight for you, and you have only to keep still" (14:14).

Within the Israelite social-world context, the power of Yahweh is often demonstrated over bodies of water, and in this way their God is shown to be free of rivals and the master of all creation. The actual crossing of the Red Sea has the effect of proving that the surging waters, so often related to the forces of chaos and disorder in ancient Near Eastern mythology, have no power over Yahweh. This stands in stark contrast to the Mesopotamian creation story (*Enuma Elish*), in which the gods are frightened by the threats of the watery chaos beast Tiamat and must wait for a champion, the Babylonian god Marduk, to confront and defeat this menace. Similarly, Baal, the storm god of ancient Ugaritic epic poetry, must struggle mightily against the god of the sea, Yamm, before gaining a temporary victory. What this reveals is the sense of eternal conflict that is at the heart of ancient Near Eastern religious belief. These people witnessed the crashing of lightning amid the storm clouds, the massive waves of the Mediterranean battering the coast, and the destructive floodwaters that submerged the land on many occasions.

The Song of the Sea, which celebrates the safe crossing of the Israelites and the destruction of Pharaoh's chariots (Exod. 15:1–19), may well be the oldest fragment of the story. In its very militaristic tone, like that found both in the Song of Deborah (Judg. 5) and in Psalm 98, it contains elements typical of a victory song (Hauser 1987: 266–79). This genre of victory song is also found in the celebratory monuments erected by the kings of the ancient Near East. For example, the Merneptah Stele (ca. 1208 BCE) provides a description of that pharaoh's campaign into Canaan and a list of his victories over cities, regions, and peoples, including Israel. It is possible that the inclusion of the song celebrating Yahweh's victory over the sea and over Pharaoh was designed to echo the familiar language of royal inscriptions while at the same time asserting the supremacy of Yahweh and the protected status of Israel's people.

Reassurance of Divine Intervention

It is remarkable how often divine reassurance is offered to the people and to kings throughout the biblical narrative. Based on this theme, an obedient and faithful nation can count on God to provide for them, even when they do not deserve it.

Joshua's promise—Following the defeat of a coalition of five kings, Joshua tells the people not to be afraid, for the Divine Warrior will continue to give them victories over their enemies (Josh. 10:24–25).

Psalmist reassurance—Psalms 37:5–7; 46:10–11; and 56:9–11 all state that there is no need to be afraid, for Yahweh will provide justice and victory.

Isaiah cautions Ahaz—In Isaiah 7:3–9 the prophet calls on the king to "be quiet" while the Divine Warrior deals with his enemies.

God's mercy—In Ezekiel 20:5–26 God recites the instances during the exodus and wilderness period when the people rebelled, but instead of destroying them Yahweh acted to meet their needs, saying this was done "for the sake of my name, that it should not be profaned in the sight of the nations."

Zechariah's postexilic promise—Zechariah 8:13–17 contains an assurance to the returned exiles not to be afraid, for God will bless them.

Use of Victory Songs
The elements most often found in victory songs include the following: 1. Repetition of the divine name: Exodus 15:1–3, 6; Judges 5:2–5; Psalm 98:1–2, 9 2. Stress of Yahweh's role in the victory: Exodus 15:2, 6, 11; Judges 5:3–5; Psalm 98:1–2 3. Use of the water motif as a prime element: Exodus 15:1–4, 10; Judges 5:4–5, 11; Psalm 98:7–9 4. Recording the enemy's failures: Exodus 15:1–2, 9; Judges 5:3, 28–30; Psalm 98:2–3 5. Divine justice for the enemy: Exodus 15:1, 4–5, 7, 10; Judges 5:24–27; Psalm 98:7–9

The Journey to Mount Sinai

Having escaped Egypt, the people then turn from the sea toward the mountain where God's presence had been revealed to Moses. A number of precedents will be set during this six-week trek through the Sinai wilderness, each reinforcing the Israelites' dependence on Yahweh to survive (Johnstone 1998: 244–46). During this period, as the people repeatedly complain about conditions, Moses functions as both a secular and a cultic leader. In both roles he has become the intermediary between the people and God.

Manna and Quail

Almost immediately the people set aside their celebration and return to their personal complaints. They miss the abundant food available to them in Egypt and cry out that they have been led into a wilderness where they will die of hunger (Exod. 16:2–3). Treating this as a test of their willingness to follow instructions, God provides for their needs with a curious substance called manna, which appears miraculously on the branches of the few bushes growing in the wilderness, and with a cloud of quail that can be caught in nets. The people are instructed to gather the manna before it is melted by the sun, and they are told that on the sixth day they must gather twice as much since they will not be allowed to work on the Sabbath (16:22–26). This is the first explicit mention of either the Sabbath celebration or the injunction to rest from their work once a week on that day. The Sabbath rest will be codified in the Ten Commandments (Exod. 20:8–11; 34:21), and it will become a sign of obedience to the covenant in the prophetic texts (Isa. 56:2; 58:13; Jer. 17:22–27). The provision of manna, celebrated as a sign of divine favor in later tradition (Neh. 9:20; Ps. 78:24), will continue throughout the wilderness wanderings and will end only when the people cross the Jordan River and begin the conquest under Joshua's leadership (Exod. 16:35; Josh. 5:12).

Water in the Wilderness

Another instance of the people's demands being met is found in Exodus 17:1–7 at Massah/Meribah. This time it is water that is in short supply (compare the similar story in Num. 20:1–13). The basic structure of the exodus murmuring motif is repeated, although this time Moses appears to be feeling the strain of leadership, telling God: "They are almost ready to stone me" (Exod. 17:4). What is raised here is the people's apparent willingness to "test the Lord" to be certain in every crisis that the Lord is truly with them. While this may seem curious given the pattern already set of divine intervention in times of need, the idea of repetition is useful as a didactic tool since the object of telling these stories is to reinforce Yahweh's covenant for later generations. The almost comic nature of these similar episodes also would play well with the audience and perhaps even be open to audience participation, shouting out responses or even making fun of these faithless ancestors.

The Divine Warrior and the Amalekite Threat

Up to this point, military actions for the Israelites have involved only the conflict with Pharaoh, and that was part of the contest-between-gods

---

Echoes of Miraculous Food

Like the provision of manna and quail in the wilderness, a number of biblical narratives include examples of miraculous food being provided by God.

Widow's cornucopia—Elijah aids the widow of Zarephath with a jar of meal and jug of oil that are not depleted until the three-year famine ends (1 Kings 17:8–16).

Elijah's cake—In 1 Kings 19:4–8 Elijah receives food from an angel while traveling in the wilderness to Mount Horeb (= Mount Sinai).

Elisha's feast—Elisha feeds one hundred people with only twenty loaves of barley, "with some left" (2 Kings 4:42–44; compare the feeding of five thousand in Matt. 14:16–21).

> ## The Underdog Theme and the Divine Warrior
>
> This theme features (1) an impossible situation that the Israelites cannot cope with, (2) unusual instructions in preparation for battle, and (3) complete military victory resulting from direct intervention by the Divine Warrior.
>
> **Fall of Jericho**—Joshua, the ark, and the people process around Jericho for seven days and then capture it with a shout and the crumbling of its walls (Josh. 6:1–21).
>
> **Gideon's victory**—Gideon is instructed to reduce the size of his army and then make a night attack, causing confusion with torches, trumpets, and shattered pots (Judg. 7:1–23).
>
> **Samuel's victory**—Frightened into putting aside their idols by the prospect of war with the Philistines, the Israelites are given victory when Yahweh's thundering voice confuses the enemy, allowing them to be routed (1 Sam. 7:3–11).

theme. Now, in Exodus 17:8–16, they face a people much like themselves, who are struggling to survive in the unforgiving environment of the Sinai desert. Their conflict over the scarce natural resources is quite understandable, but this battle clearly demonstrates the saving activities of the Divine Warrior and also transforms the Amalekites into a stereotypical enemy nation. Given that the Israelites have had no military training and probably have few weapons, they could not have competed successfully against the Amalekites. Thus this story is a perfect example of the premonarchic underdog theme, which features Yahweh saving an unprepared and inept people from acute physical danger.

Instead of avoiding conflict because the people lack military experience, Moses is ordered to take the people into battle. Curiously, the factor that determines the Israelite victory is Moses' ability to keep his arms raised in the air throughout the battle. Of course, Moses is elderly and cannot physically stand for long with his arms raised. He eventually has to sit down while Aaron and Hur hold up his arms throughout the remainder of the battle (17:11–12). Thus Moses' frailty is coupled with the inexperience of the Israelites to demonstrate conclusively that the victory is the direct result of the intervention of the Divine Warrior.

The potential for a ripple effect in later tradition is then voiced in verse 14, where Moses is ordered by God to record in a book the curse against Amalek. The Amalekites will be a threat and the subject of war for generations to come (17:16). This curse is repeated in Numbers 24:20 by the prophet Balaam, and it also appears in the Deuteronomist's injunction to destroy Amalek (Deut. 25:17–19), but

---

Amalek as the Enemy

Judges period—The Amalekites are listed as oppressors or raiders of Israelite villages in the Judges account (Judg. 3:13; 6:3, 33; 7:12).

Herem versus Amalek—Saul is ordered to carry out a "holy war" (herem) against the Amalekites in 1 Samuel 15:3, and his failure to complete the total destruction of these people is the basis for the end of the Saulide dynasty in Israel (1 Sam. 28:18).

David's conquests—Amalek is in the list of nations that David subdued (2 Sam. 8:12 and 1 Chron. 18:11).

Saul's death—Ironically, it is an Amalekite who claims to kill Saul at the battle of Gilboa (2 Sam. 1:6–10).

Mordecai's foe—Haman the Agagite (see Agag in 1 Sam. 15:9–33) plots to kill Mordecai and all the Jews in the Persian Empire (Esther 3).

---

the recurrent theme of Amalek as "the enemy" can be found in many later contexts.

The Events at Mount Sinai: Moses the Lawgiver

The product of the exodus was the creation of a covenant community. It was to be governed by a set of laws initially given at Mount Sinai in the form of the Ten Commandments and then expanded upon in the various legal codes found in Exodus 20:18–23:33 (Covenant Code); Leviticus 17–26 (Holiness Code); and Deuteronomy 12–26 (Deuteronomic Code). The central figure associated with the law is Moses, and as often as not the law is referred to as either the "law of Moses" (Josh. 8:32; 2 Kings 14:6; Ezra 7:6) or the "book of Moses" (2 Chron. 25:4; Ezra 6:18; Tobit 7:11–12). It is not surprising then that this final segment of the exodus narrative provides the origin story of Moses' traditional role as lawgiver. When the people complete the circle of events that began with Moses' theophany on Mount Sinai and return with him to that mountain of God, they are witnesses to Yahweh's miraculous actions on their behalf and are apparently ready to pledge themselves to the covenant.

Curiously, the first picture provided of Moses once they reach Mount Sinai is as an overworked magistrate, who cannot effectively organize his time and energies until his father-in-law, Jethro, makes a suggestion (Exod. 18:13–26). Placing Moses back into the role of the younger generation, even temporarily, does humanize his character. However, this is really the only time during this set of episodes that he appears to have the normal failings or weaknesses of average humans.

The need to appoint "lower court" judges for various groupings of the people (compare the military organization in 2 Sam. 18:1), who can take a large portion of the caseload off Moses, also appears in Numbers 11:10–30 and Deuteronomy 1:9–18. The Numbers passage, while precipitated by the need to obtain meat for the camp, provides the etiology of the seventy elders, who serve as officers over the people. In Deuteronomy Moses complains of the burden resulting from the growth of the Israelite population. The common denominator in these episodes is the recognition of the need for shared governance. It is quite likely that all these passages, as well as the appeals system outlined in Deuteronomy 17:8–13, are retrojections of judicial institutions that existed during the monarchic period (Wilson 1983: 239–40). Giving them an origin in the time of Moses gains a measure of authority for the judicial system and, of course, further solidifies Moses' dual role as mediator and lawgiver.

Moses' Second Theophany at Mount Sinai

The next two episodes in this narrative involve the formal renewal of the covenant with God. The first, in Exodus 19:1–9, lays out the theological underpinning of the exodus event and sets the stage for both the giving of the tablets of the law in Exodus 20 and the ritual certification of the people's acceptance of the substance of covenantal obligation in 24:1–8 (Childs 1974: 366–68). This theophany in Exodus 19 at least initially resembles the burning bush theophany of Exodus 3, with its emphasis on the revelation of God's presence and the appointment of Moses as the mediator between God and the people (Wells 2000: 33–34). It then takes on a more distinct character with a five-point pattern certifying Moses' role: Moses climbs the mountain; Yahweh speaks to Moses; Moses descends the mountain; Moses addresses the assembled people; and the people make a response to Moses (Chirichigno 1987: 460–61).

Even though it is Moses who "goes up" to speak with God, there is a greater sense here than in later episodes that the people are direct witnesses of God's voice speaking to Moses (compare the people's fear in Exod. 20:18–21). This may be a necessary element to demonstrate to later generations that Moses' words can be trusted and that the entire assembly was involved in this all-important theophanic event (Gammie 1989: 16).

What then becomes clear is the purpose for this encounter with God. The people, prior to receiving the law, are required to acknowledge the debt they owe Yahweh for releasing them from slavery. Further, they are to recognize the special obligations that are attendant to being God's chosen people: "You shall be a priestly kingdom and a holy nation" (19:6a). This concept of the Israelites as a holy nation is further defined in the formulation of the Holiness Code in Leviticus 20:26, as the premise behind the importance of ritual purity, and in Deuteronomy 26:16–19, which assumes that the law has been given and that the promise has been made to obey it. This translates into firm evidence of their being "a people holy to the LORD." The Deuteronomy reference also is intended to bolster the argument that Israel held divinely appointed superiority over other nations. It is further made clear that "Israel is commanded to keep the law because it is a holy people; not because it hoped to become one" (Wells 2000: 69).

The Ten Commandments

With the basis for their relationship laid out, the next step in this process of divine revelation is the giving of the tablets of the law. The Ten Commandments provide the legal foundation for all other legal pronouncements and explain what is expected of the people who have become a "holy nation" through God's intervention. This growing legal tradition is also characterized by the egalitarian principle, which commands that every head of household in the Israelite covenant community be treated equally under the law. This is based on the repeated statement that the Israelites remember that they were once slaves themselves (Deut. 5:15; 15:15) and thus must protect the weak and vulnerable (see the repeated reference to protected, vulnerable groups: Exod. 22:22; Deut. 26:12–13).

The first five laws in the Decalogue apply to the conduct of the entire nation and exemplify what differentiates Israel from its neighbors:

1. They are to worship only one God. There is to be no other god set "before" Yahweh. A careful reading indicates that this is not a statement of monotheism, which by definition must exclude the reality of other gods (compare Deut. 4:39; 1 Sam. 2:2; Jer. 16:19–20). Exodus 20:3 is an example of henotheism, which accepts the existence of other gods but chooses to venerate a particular one (M. S. Smith 2001: 152–53).
2. As an extension of the first commandment, they are forbidden to construct or worship idols. The elimination of images made Israel unique and increased the mysterious character of Yahweh. However, the number of references to idolatry in the prophets and elsewhere make clear that Israel had great difficulty ridding itself

---

Decalogue Cited in Later Tradition

Judges 3:4—God leaves enemy nations in Canaan in the
settlement period "to know whether Israel would obey the
commandments of the LORD, which he commanded their
ancestors by Moses."

Jeremiah 7:5–10—In his Temple Sermon Jeremiah lists most of
the Decalogue in his indictment of the people of Jerusalem.

Ezekiel 20:18–21—God reminds the people that their ancestors
had been commanded not to defile themselves with idols and
to hallow the Sabbath.

Hosea 4:1–2—Hosea equates the lack of "knowledge of God"
with the violation of five of the laws of the Decalogue.

Malachi 2:17–3:5—The prophet provides an assurance that God
will punish evildoers, including adulterers.

---

of these images (see Ps. 106:36–39; Isa. 2:8; Ezek. 6:5–6; Hosea
8:4).

3. The name of God was to be invoked with great caution. This injunction also appears in Near Eastern texts, but in the Decalogue
it is intended to reinforce the supremacy of Yahweh. In later Israelite tradition, God's name is not to be defiled (Ezek. 43:7), and
its power clearly demonstrates full divine supremacy (see Ps. 8:1;
Isa. 12:4; Dan. 2:20; Zeph. 3:12).

4. Keeping the Sabbath rest is recognition of Yahweh as the creator.
This is a huge sacrifice (one-seventh of total labor); it is unique to
Israel and becomes the hallmark of obedience to the covenant, es-
pecially in the postexilic period (see Neh. 13:15–22; Isa. 56:2–6).

5. There is legal precedent for honoring one's parents in the Sumerian law code (ca. 1800 BCE), but the injunction in Exodus 20:12
is designed to ensure that the aged will be taken care of and the
wisdom of elders will be respected. This emphasis on each generation caring for the other is tied into the concept of holiness
(Lev. 19:2–4), and it is both a source of honor (Prov. 10:1) and a
potential source of shame (Prov. 19:26).

The final five laws in the code are present in the legal traditions
of other cultures in the ancient Near East (as in Hammurabi's Code
from ancient Babylon) and are designed to maintain order and protect the rights of property owners. The one law in this group that is
most often cited in later tradition is the prohibition against adultery.
However, the prophets most often equate adultery with idolatry, since

both are violations of right behavior and are expressions of infidelity to the community and to God (Bosman 1988: 24–27; see Jer. 7:1–15; Ezek. 16; Hosea 1–3).

That portions of the Ten Commandments continue to be cited as the basis of obedience to the covenant indicates that they are an integral part of the education process for the Israelites and their children. It is inconceivable that the biblical writers and prophets would refer to the laws contained in the Decalogue if there was no chance that their audience would respond appropriately to the charge that they had failed to obey the law.

Covenant-Renewal Ceremony

Once the law is given to the people, it is necessary for them to pledge their obedience. This parallels God's command in Exodus 19:4–6 that they recognize their relationship to God under the covenant. Thus the collective cry "Everything that the LORD has spoken we will do" (19:8) is repeated verbatim as part of the covenant-renewal ceremony in 24:3b. It should be understood that this is not the initiation of the covenant between the people and Yahweh. That took place in the time of the ancestors (Gen. 12:1–3; 15:5–21; Fretheim 1991: 256). Here at Mount Sinai the stipulation that they must be obedient to the word of Yahweh is affirmed, and the event is solemnized with a massive sacrifice and the unusual step of flinging a portion of the blood onto the crowd (Exod. 24:6, 8). At this point, with the saving event of the exodus behind them and a land to take into their possession ahead of them, the staging of a covenant-renewal ceremony is essential. Without it they could expect no further divine aid. The covenant-renewal ceremony at Mount Sinai also later serves as a precedent for proper behavior when the nation faces similar crisis points (see Josh. 24:1–28; 2 Kings 23:1–3; Neh. 8).

As can be seen in the sidebar on the next page, each major epoch in Israel's history is defined by the recognition of the covenant made with the ancestors and the renewal of the people's understanding and willingness to obey the stipulations of that covenant. In the case of Josiah (622 BCE), there are political implications attached to the scene since it conjures up idealized images of the Davidic leadership, the hope of the restoration of all of Israel's former territories, and the hope for independence from the superpowers of Egypt and Mesopotamia. These aspirations had diminished by Ezra's day (ca. 400 BCE), with the emphasis now on maintaining the cultural identity of the Jewish people in the community around Jerusalem and in the exile. Their

---

Covenant-Renewal Ceremonies

Moses—Following the exodus from Egypt, at Mount Sinai the law is read to the assembly, the people affirm their willingness to obey, and a great sacrifice is made to confirm the covenant (Exod. 24:1–8).

Joshua—Following the conquest of Canaan, Joshua reads the law to the assembled tribes, they affirm their allegiance to the covenant, and a sacrifice is made at Shechem (Josh. 24:1–28).

Josiah—After discovering the book of the law in the temple, the king reads the words of the covenant to the people assembled in Jerusalem, they affirm their willingness to obey, and they celebrate the Passover Festival (2 Kings 23:1–3, 21–23).

Ezra—In postexilic Jerusalem, Ezra gathers the people, reads them the law, obtains their pledge of obedience, and celebrates the Feast of Booths (Neh. 8).

---

expression of renewal is based on ethnic and religious survival rather than political or territorial aspirations.

From this point on, the narrative, with the exception of the golden calf episode and the giving of the second set of tablets (Exod. 32 and 34), turns to preparations for departure from Mount Sinai. The tent of meeting and the ark of the covenant are created (Exod. 25–27; 36–40), a rudimentary priesthood is established (28:1–29:37), and the sacrificial rituals are initiated that will mark Israelite worship until the destruction of the Jerusalem temple in 586 BCE (29:38–30). Moses' role as leader and lawgiver will gradually diminish as Joshua is raised as his successor (Deut. 31:1–8, 14–29) and the conflicts associated with the grueling wilderness trek take their toll on his authority (Num. 12, 16, 20). The obituary in Deuteronomy 34 sums up Moses' importance, creating a mystery of his final resting place and setting the stage for future leaders and prophets who will have to measure up to the standard set by this seminal figure in Israelite history.

King David Makes
Jerusalem His Capital

In this survey of the critical moments in Israelite history, the next major event following the exodus from Egypt is the establishment of the monarchy and the creation of the political state of Israel in Canaan. The books of Joshua and Judges describe the period of initial settlement in the promised land, but the story that unfolds depicts a politically chaotic period. The Israelites find themselves in constant conflict with their neighbors, and, for the most part, they are unequipped to compete with the more established groups like the Philistines. In this chapter, the task is to provide some background on the political developments that eventually led to David's becoming king and the subsequent traditions associated with the Davidic monarchy. In addition, the role of Jerusalem as the political and religious capital of the nation is explored, especially in the Psalms and the Prophets.

Israel Becomes a Nation

Nations come into being in a variety of ways. For the Israelites living in the small villages of the central hill country of Canaan, that process began in the period after 1200 BCE when a group of invaders collectively known as the Sea Peoples disrupted the political stability of the ancient Near East and made it possible for new political units to emerge in Canaan (Schniedewind 1999: 18–21). Our current understanding of the archaeological record demonstrates that many new settlements were established in the central hill country between 1200 and 1050 BCE (Dever 2003: 75–100; Finkelstein 2003: 82–84). These unorganized farming villages were not much of a match militarily or economically for that segment of the Sea Peoples known as the Philistines, who settled along the coastal plain and in the rich Shephelah plateau. As the village population prospered and outgrew their holdings in the hill country, however, the inhabitants realized that they would have to break out of their isolated and environmentally limited area. They would have to challenge the peoples of the plain (Judg. 1:19) or die.

In the earliest period of the settlement, the tribal elders had to cope with the crises associated with farming the marginal areas of the central hill country in Canaan and the incursions of their hostile neighbors. As the tribal groups became somewhat more organized and their population began to grow, there was a transition period in their political development characterized by the rise of local war chiefs who were able to marshal the combined support of several tribes to deal with acute threats to their existence. However, eventually it became necessary to elevate a chief, who would be able to provide consistent and long-term leadership, thus allowing the Israelites to expand their territorial holdings and compete militarily and economically on a more even basis with the surrounding peoples.

It is this growing need, chronicled in the horrific stories found in the book of Judges (see Judg. 19–21) and voiced in the cry of the elders to the judge/prophet Samuel (1 Sam. 8:1–9), that eventually leads to the establishment of a coalition of the tribes under the leadership of Saul. Of course, not everyone would be happy to relinquish local and regional control to a central authority figure. The statement in Exodus 15:18, known as the Song of the Sea, may represent an expression of Yahweh as king when it says, "The LORD will reign forever and ever" (Roberts 2002: 676). But in the face of a growing threat to their continued existence, the people want a human king "like other nations" (1 Sam. 8:5). Putting a theological rationale on this demand, God tells the prophet/judge Samuel: "They have not rejected you, but they have rejected me from being king over them" (1 Sam. 8:7). In this way God both soothes Samuel's and perhaps the tribal leaders' anger and also voices the political and theological reality that accompanies the establishment of the monarchy in ancient Israel.

Based on the biblical account, one can say that initially a loose political arrangement is created that would always be in danger of collapse. Despite some initial victories (1 Sam. 11), Saul often finds himself in desperate straits as he prepares for each successive battle and sees his troops melting away at the least opportunity (1 Sam. 13:8). The continuing military crisis throughout Saul's reign keeps most of the tribes in line. However, it is clear that no real movement is possible at this time that would lead to the creation of the structures of government. As a result, Saul never fully controls the people and their resources as he struggles mightily to deal with the threats from surrounding nations.

As it becomes increasingly clear that Saul is unable to provide the type of leadership that will allow the nation to break out of its cycle of successive crises, the story shifts to David's career, from his being anointed by Samuel (1 Sam. 16:1–13), to his initial public success in slaying the Philistine giant Goliath (1 Sam. 17), to his marriage to Michal, the daughter of Saul (18:17–29). Each of these steps further legitimizes David's claim to the throne, and they function as part of the larger narrative that is often referred to by scholars as the "Apology of David." An apology is a literary genre designed to make a sympathetic case for a particular person or idea. For David, this means that his road to the kingship is filled with proper behavior and divinely sanctioned activities. Conversely, this apology makes the case, in a disqualification

Time Line Leading to the Israelite Monarchy

ca. 1200 BCE—**Sea Peoples** invade Near Eastern coastal areas: Ugarit destroyed (north Syria); Hittite kingdom ended (Anatolia); Egypt's control of Canaan significantly weakened; Philistines settle along coastal plain and in Shephelah of southwestern Canaan

ca. 1200–1050 BCE—**Settlement period**: hundreds of new hilltop settlements appear in central hill country of Canaan; emerging Israelite tribes compete with Philistines, Ammonites, Moabites, and other peoples for land, resources, and basic survival as a people

ca. 1050 BCE—**Saul** chosen first "king": coalition of Israelite tribes accept Saul as war chief to lead them against Philistines; first step toward nation building but without government structures or full cooperation

ca. 1000 BCE—**David** becomes king: following Saul's death and the murder of his son Ishbaal, Israelite elders offer David the kingship; Jerusalem is captured as new capital city; ark of the covenant brought to Jerusalem; first steps taken to create standing army and rudimentary bureaucracy to rule the people

ca. 960 BCE—**Solomon** becomes king: continues process to construct the apparatus of a state with national economy, improved infrastructure, functioning bureaucracy, and temple for Yahweh in Jerusalem story, justifying God's "tearing the kingdom" from Saul and giving it to his "neighbor" (1 Sam. 15:28–29).

What emerges from the text is the desire on the part of the biblical editors to strengthen David's position as claimant to the throne and to provide details of Saul's failures. Given the political reality that new chiefdoms are fragile political entities, it is not surprising that the elders could be persuaded to shift their allegiance to another leader if their current war chief was killed or proven to be powerless. Thus, an extremely important turning point in Israelite history occurs when Saul's last son, Ishbaal, is assassinated (2 Sam. 4:5–8), and the tribal elders have little choice but to come to David at his seat of local power in Hebron and offer him the kingship over the Israelites (2 Sam. 5:1–3). This marks the end of the short-lived Saulide dynasty and the emergence of a new ruling family.

Of course, this is not a particularly unusual event in the history of the ancient Near East. It has happened countless times in that turbulent region. In this case, however, it is not simply a shift in political power from one war-lord to another. Instead it marks a significant step in the evolution of the loosely bound Israelite tribal confederation that Saul had led into an emerging nation-state. For Israel to compete with the neighboring peoples and especially with the Philistine kings of southwestern Canaan, they have to have more than a war chief. They have to have the various accoutrements of government that would give them a national identity and make them a people, not just a group of loosely affiliated tribes. They need a more effective military organization (Weinfeld 1983: 77–78) as well as a political center from which consistent leadership could radiate, and they need the visible symbols of that power in the form of monumental architecture (palace, temple, city walls).

David as the Model King of Israel

The received account of the monarchy period that we have in the Bible is generally considered to have been produced by a group of editors collectively known as the Deuteronomistic Historian. This set of editors shaped the wealth of documents and oral traditions that existed about the Israelite monarchy between 1000 and 600 BCE, creating a chronological account that provides a summary of many of the accomplishments and failures of these kings. They also injected a particular theological agenda into the chronicle that assigned "good" and "bad" labels to each king based on his adherence to the covenant and his willingness to listen to the words of the prophets during his reign (see 1 Kings 11:6–13; 15:25–26; 16:29–30). Since this group of editors lived and worked at the end of the monarchy period, they had the luxury to look back at their

---

Judging Judah's Kings Based on the David Stereotype

Solomon—Despite his many accomplishments, including the construction of the temple to Yahweh in Jerusalem, Solomon is condemned: "For when Solomon was old, his wives turned away his heart after other gods; and his heart was not true to the LORD his God, as was the heart of his father David" (1 Kings 11:4).

Abijam—"He committed all the sins that his father [Rehoboam] did before him; his heart was not true to the LORD his God, like the heart of his father David" (1 Kings 15:3).

Asa—"Asa did what was right in the sight of the LORD, as his father David had done" (1 Kings 15:11).

Amaziah—"He did what was right in the sight of the LORD, yet not like his ancestor David; in all things he did as his father Joash had done" (2 Kings 14:3).

Ahaz—"He did not do what was right in the sight of the LORD his God, as his ancestor David had done" (2 Kings 16:2).

Hezekiah—"He did what was right in the sight of the LORD just as his ancestor David had done" (2 Kings 18:3).

Josiah—"He did what was right in the sight of the LORD, and walked in all the way of his father David; he did not turn aside to the right or to the left" (2 Kings 22:2).

---

own history. As they shaped the narrative, they could signal where they felt the nation had received proper leadership or where the people had been directed down the wrong path. At the same time, they apparently hoped to set some standards of behavior based on idealized images of the earliest kings of Israel (van der Toorn 1994: 227–28). Thus David, despite any faults he may have had, became a paragon in later tradition against whom all other kings would be judged.

Of course, David was not a perfect leader or, for that matter, a perfect person. The Deuteronomistic Historian could not totally disguise this, since the stories about his reign were undoubtedly too well known. Thus the editors do recount some of the negative details of his career, including the adulterous affair that he had with Bathsheba (2 Sam. 11:1–12:23) and the tumultuous relationship he had with his son Absalom (see episodes in 2 Sam. 13–16). Taken in context, these stories, like the trickster stories in the ancestral narratives about Abraham and Jacob (Gen. 12:10–20; 29–30), helped to create a human image of an important national leader. After David's death, however, it became standard (see the sidebar above) to speak of him as the king whom God loved (2 Chron. 6:42; Isa. 55:3) and as the model for proper mo-

David and Restoration

David is described as the embodiment of a postexilic, united monarchy matching the people's return to the land, to God, and to David. In this utopian image, Jerusalem becomes a sure resting place characterized by peace and ideal Davidic rulers (Weinfeld 1983: 103):

Isaiah 11:10—"On that day the root of Jesse shall stand as a signal to the peoples; the nations shall inquire of him, and his dwelling shall be glorious."

Isaiah 33:20—"Look on Zion, the city of our appointed festivals! Your eyes will see Jerusalem, a quiet habitation, an immovable tent, whose stakes will never be pulled up, and none of whose ropes will be broken."

Ezekiel 34:23–24—"I will set up over them one shepherd, my servant David, and he shall feed them and be their shepherd. And I, the LORD, will be their God, and my servant David shall be prince among them."

Ezekiel 37:24–25—"My servant David shall be king over them; and they shall all have one shepherd. They shall follow my ordinances and be careful to observe my statutes. They shall live in the land that I gave to my servant Jacob, in which your ancestors lived; they and their children and their children's children shall live there forever; and my servant David shall be their prince forever."

Zechariah 12:8—"On that day the LORD will shield the inhabitants of Jerusalem so that the feeblest among them on that day shall be like David, and the house of David shall be like God, like the angel of the LORD, at their head."

narchic behavior (Ezek. 34:23–24). The extent to which his memory is cleaned up can be found in the books of Chronicles, which date to the period after 500 BCE. These late accounts of Israel's history do not even mention the affair with Bathsheba, and they portray David as the sole engineer of all of the cultic activities and organizations in the Jerusalem temple (1 Chron. 23–26).

The extent to which David became identified with the monarchy and in particular the monarchy based in Jerusalem can be seen from references in the prophetic materials. For example, Hosea 3:5, in the late eighth century, speaks of an eventual restoration of the divided kingdoms after a period of punishment. The people of Israel, who had broken away from the southern kingdom of Judah around 940 BCE, "shall return and seek the LORD their God, and David their king." This

would, in the prophet's view, restore the surviving remnant of the northern kingdom to their proper covenantal relationship with Yahweh and to
their proper political allegiance to the Davidic monarchy (Stuart 1987:
68). This same pairing of a return to God and to David is also found
in Jeremiah 30:9. In each case, as well as those listed in the sidebar on
the previous page, these references to David reflect postexilic messianic
eschatology, which envisions a glorious restoration of the nation under
a David-like king at some point in the far future (Wolff 1974: 63).

David's Capture of Jerusalem

Second Samuel 5:6–10 (also 1 Chron. 11:4–7) recounts how David
takes his first step toward creating a seat of political power for the new
nation of Israel. This very short episode describes his capture of Jerusalem and its establishment as his capital city. Perhaps most important
in the minds of the editors, Jerusalem becomes the "city of David"
(2 Sam. 5:9). Jerusalem's history, part of which is chronicled in the
Amarna letters of Pharaoh Akhenaton, as a political center does reach
back into the mid–second millennium (Cahill 2003: 33), and its strategic
importance is found in its position guarding a north-south route in the
hill country (Dorsey 1991: 40–41). In the tenth century, however, most
of its population of perhaps two thousand persons would have been
engaged in agriculture, while a much smaller group of "elites" served
as artisans, priests, and administrators (Whitelam 2001: 114). It would
be some time before the city expanded beyond its initial boundaries
and acquired the architectural wonders associated with political power
(Whitelam 1986).

Given the importance that this action would have on the rest of Israelite history, it is surprising that we are not told more. It is unfortunate
that the curious details of the siege of Jebus involving the role of the
"blind and the lame" and the soldiers climbing through the water shaft
(2 Sam. 5:6–8) are not made clearer. Instead, the fundamental aspects of
this story remain enigmatic for modern commentators and archaeolo-
gists (Frolov and Orel 1999; Shanks 1999). All that can safely be said is
that from this point on Jebus/Jerusalem would serve as the focal point
of David's political career.

Despite this omission in the story, the editors make several important
points to show that David indeed has become king and that he will now
set in motion a series of actions that will solidify his hold on power.
These steps include:

1. Expanding the size of the city and its wall system: This allows for
   the construction of new housing for the Israelite people and for the

Jebusites who will become part of its mixed population (2 Sam. 5:9). A sign of a successful ruler is that he engages in construction projects that enhance his city. Some of the earliest political literature from the ancient Near East includes the recitation of a king's pride in strengthening and expanding his capital. This includes the ancient Sumerian king Gilgamesh, who calls on his companion to "Go up, . . . walk on the ramparts of Uruk. Inspect the base terrace, examine its brickwork . . . and if the Seven Wise Ones laid not its foundation!" (Pritchard 1969: 97). After David's time, the continued growth of Jerusalem becomes the task of his successors and a sign of their power (1 Kings 9:15, 24; 11:27). Furthermore, the tradition of the building of Jerusalem "as a city that is bound firmly together" (Ps. 122:3) also finds its way into a popular song in which a young lover can say that his beloved's slim neck is "like the tower of David, built in courses" (Song of Sol. 4:4).

2. King Hiram of Tyre sends cedar logs and artisans: David undoubtedly lacks these building materials as well as the skilled masons and architects needed to construct a royal palace in Jerusalem (2 Sam. 5:11). Hiram's aid is doubly important because it provides evidence of the recognition of David's kingdom by a foreign power, and it provides him with one of the major architectural necessities for kings—a palace. This sequence is repeated when Solomon constructs the temple in Jerusalem with Hiram's assistance (1 Kings 5:1–10), although in that case Solomon paid for the construction materials and artisans with large quantities of wheat and olive oil (5:11) and the ceding of twenty cities in the Galilee region (9:10–13).

3. David adds to his harem once he is settled in Jerusalem (2 Sam. 5:13): Royal marriages are a sign of the power and influence of the monarch since they create blood and political ties between the king and important families and foreign nations. David begins the practice of building his political fortunes when he marries Saul's daughter Michal (1 Sam. 18:17–29). After being expelled from Saul's court, David continues to build his harem even though he is an outlaw running from Saul's forces (1 Sam. 25:39–43). While he rules the tribe of Judah from Hebron, David recovers his former wife Michal as a way of restoring his link of legitimacy with Saul's family (2 Sam. 3:13–16). After he ascends the throne of Israel, the listing of David's children (2 Sam. 5:14–16) is an indication of how secure the Davidic dynasty will be with so many possible heirs to the throne. Certainly, Solomon takes this example to heart with his many wives and concubines (1 Kings 11:1–3), including a daughter of the pharaoh of Egypt. Later kings continue the pattern of

marrying the daughters of foreign rulers, most notably Ahab, who marries Jezebel, daughter of the king of Sidon (1 Kings 16:31).

4. David begins his reign in Jerusalem with two significant military victories over the Philistines (2 Sam. 5:17–25): Like Saul in 1 Samuel 11, David demonstrates his leadership to the people by protecting them from a traditional threat. The narrative here is also careful to note that David consults God to see if the Divine Warrior would provide a victory (5:19, 23). Saul had been cut off from communication with God (1 Sam. 28:6), and this had led to military defeat and his own death. Thus it is critical that in this first test of David's military ability God would play an active role. It will be a sign in later generations that those kings who are considered to have "walked in the way of David" are those who rely on divine help, generally through the words of prophets.

David Constructs the Institutional Character of the Monarchy

Having solidified his hold on power, with the sanction of the tribal elders and the acquisition of Jerusalem as his seat of office, David begins to build the institutional character of the monarchy so that it will become more acceptable to the Israelites as a whole. To do this, he must convince the people that the trappings of power associated with the kingship could be identified with his own family. This will be accomplished by two significant events. One he initiates himself (bringing the ark of the covenant to Jerusalem), and the other is provided by God's mandate (the everlasting covenant). This next section of his story contains extended discussion of each of these signal events.

David Brings the Ark to Jerusalem

Although the ark is a powerful symbol of God's authority and an aid to the people, David quickly recognizes that it must not be allowed to

---

Divine Aid Requested by Faithful Kings

Jehoshaphat—Labeled a "good king" in 1 Kings 22:43, he demands that he and King Ahab "inquire first for the word of the LORD" before going into battle with Syria (Aram) in 1 Kings 22:5.

Josiah—Labeled a "good king" in 2 Kings 22:2, he commands the priests to "inquire of the LORD for me, for the people, and for all Judah" regarding the words of the book of the law that had been found in the renovation of the Jerusalem temple (2 Kings 22:13).

compete with his public role as the sole leader of the Israelites (Matthews 2004a). In other words, the ark must be controlled and hidden from the eyes of the people so that from now on they will focus only on the person of the king. Ironically, as the ark disappears from public view, the Jerusalem temple emerges as the physical image of God's presence with the people. The kings will have to compete with it just as they did with the ark, and ultimately both the monarchy and the temple will come to an end at the same time in 587 BCE.

From the time of its construction in the Sinai wilderness (Exod. 25:10–22), the ark of the covenant both served as a repository for the tablets of the law and also represented God's presence with the people. Its power was made manifest when Joshua had the Levites carry it into the flooding Jordan River at Gilgal, allowing the people to cross on dry land (Josh. 3:6–17). It then became a sign of the Divine Warrior's power when it was taken in procession around Jericho, contributing to the conquest of that city (Josh. 6:6–21). After Joshua's passing, however, the Deuteronomistic narrative placed the ark in a shrine at Shiloh in the central hill country, where Eli and his sons served as officiating priests, making sacrifices and carrying out ritual duties in honor of Yahweh's presence (Halpern 2001: 289; 1 Sam. 4:2–4).

The greed and disrespect shown by Eli's sons, Hophni and Phinehas, to the people who made pilgrimage to Shiloh provided the backdrop to the demonstration that God's presence is not trapped within either the ark or the shrine at Shiloh (1 Sam. 2:12–17, 22–25). Thus when Eli's sons took the ark into battle against the Philistines, the Israelites were soundly defeated and the ark was captured by the enemy (4:10–11). The narrator explains that because Hophni and Phinehas had abused their power as priests, the ark had resumed its mundane character as a gold-encrusted box and was no longer capable of representing God's presence with the people. The disaster of losing the battle and the ark once again demonstrated that only obedience to the covenant and ritual purity brought positive results (see a similar military defeat caused by a breach of faith in Josh. 7:1–15).

Eventually, the ark was returned to Israelite territory by the plague-inflicted Philistines (1 Sam. 6:1–18), but the Israelites, who lacked anyone who could "stand before the LORD" (with Eli and his sons now dead), were unable to cope with this object of power that brought death to those who did not respect its properties (see 6:19). Without a priestly caretaker available, the ark was stored for a generation at Kiriath-jearim (6:20–7:2). This may explain why it was not a factor in Saul's career. However, it is also possible that Saul's failure to make use of the ark was simply another sign of his repeated difficulties with Samuel (1 Sam.

Danger Associated with Misuse of the Sacred

The biblical narrative is filled with examples of how dangerous it is to come into contact with sacred objects. They must be treated with great caution and respect or the divine forces that they contain or represent can wreak deadly havoc.

Joshua 7—Achan steals cloth, silver, and gold that had been dedicated to God during the *herem* that destroyed Jericho. For this he and his household are stoned to death (v. 25).

1 Samuel 5—The Philistines place the captured ark at the feet of the statue of their god Dagon to represent Yahweh's defeat. In the night, the statue is dismembered by Yahweh's power, demonstrating who really is God (vv. 1–4).

1 Samuel 6:19—Seventy men are killed at Beth-shemesh when they do not show proper respect for the returned ark (the Septuagint says they tried to look inside the ark).

2 Kings 5—Gehazi secretly demands payment for the cure received by the Syrian general Naaman. When Elisha finds out, Gehazi is inflicted with the leprosy from which Naaman had been purified (vv. 20–27).

Jeremiah 28—The prophet Hananiah breaks an ox yoke off the neck of Jeremiah to show that the "yoke of Babylon" would be broken and the exiles returned. Jeremiah confronts him wearing an iron yoke and predicts a long exile period and Hananiah's death—which occurs within a year (vv. 12–17).

Daniel 5—The Babylonian ruler Belshazzar uses the sacred vessels taken from the Jerusalem temple to serve his guests at a party. Divine handwriting appears on the wall that Daniel interprets as a prediction of doom for Babylon and its ruler.

13–15) and the priestly community (see the massacre of the priests at Nob in 22:6–19; van der Toorn 1994: 218–19).

Following the deaths of Saul and his sons (1 Sam. 31) and of his successor Ishbaal (2 Sam. 4:1–7), the elders at last offer David the leadership of all the tribes (5:1–3). Recognizing that he must control all the symbols of power in the kingdom, David first captures the Jebusite city of Jerusalem, thereby obtaining a politically neutral, well-defended, and more centrally located site for his capital city (5:6–10). Then, in order to gain tighter control over the official religion of Israel, David orders that the ark of the covenant be removed from its storage place and brought to Jerusalem (6:1–2).

When David retrieves the ark from its temporary warehouse in Kiriath-jearim, however, he makes a classic mistake. During the journey from Kiriath-jearim to Jerusalem, David chooses not to follow the established protocol for transporting the ark (see Exod. 25:12–15). Like the Philistines in 1 Samuel 6:10–11, he places the ark on a cart pulled by oxen (2 Sam. 6:2–4), and there is no explicit mention of Levites being present to accompany the ark. It is not surprising then that a tragedy occurs to remind David and the people involved in this triumphal procession, which is designed more to demonstrate David's power than that of the ark, that they cannot manipulate this powerful object without consequences (Carlson 1993: 18–22). This theme cautioning the careful use of sacred objects appears throughout the text as a warning that the power of God cannot be ignored or used for illegitimate purposes (see the sidebar on the previous page).

As the incautious procession enters the threshing floor of Nacon, one of the men accompanying the cart puts out his hand to prevent the ark from falling to the ground, and he is struck dead for this unauthorized contact with a sacred object (2 Sam. 6:6–7; see Num. 4:15 for the warning). At once angry and then fearful of the power inherent to the ark of Yahweh, David repeats the actions of a previous generation at Beth-shemesh, who had also been shocked by the way the ark was associated with sudden death (1 Sam. 6:19–7:2). He places it in the keeping of Obed-edom the Gittite for three months (a parallel to its previous period of rest at Kiriath-jearim). When it is determined that God's anger has subsided and that the Gittite's household has been rewarded by the ark's presence, David feels safe to resume the journey to Jerusalem (2 Sam. 6:8–12). However, this time the ark is carried by Levites and proper sacrifices are made to honor God along the processional route.

When the group approaches the gates of Jerusalem, David takes another step to demonstrate both his place among the people and his responsibility for "repatriating" this symbol of God and bringing it to the city (Halpern 2001: 292). He removes his garments and joins in the dancing with the other celebrants (2 Sam. 6:14, 20). A range of possibilities may explain David's choice of such minimal attire, consisting only of a linen ephod that is typically worn by priests (Exod. 28:42; Lev. 16:4; 1 Sam. 2:18; see McCarter 1984: 171). He may be doing penance for his inappropriate transport of the ark from Kiriath-jearim, which had already caused the death of Uzzah (2 Sam. 6:3–9). It also is possible that he is attempting to model proper behavior as a priestly figure as he brings this object symbolizing God's presence into Jerusalem. This would set a precedent of royal participation in ritual drama and enthusiastic worship. Certainly, there is ample mention in the Psalms of raising one's voice to the Lord and making a joyful noise (Pss. 66:1; 95:1; 98:4, 6; 100:1).

What may also be happening here, in addition to the above suggestions, is David's engaging in a visible manifestation of egalitarianism by "lowering" himself to the level of a common citizen so that all will see that he is their equal "before the Lord." This is the opposite of what Saul had sought to do in 1 Samuel 15:8–9, 15, 21, bringing the spoils and the king of the Amalekites back to Gilgal for a very visible sacrifice and celebration of his victory. Saul's disobedience led to God's rejection of his kingship and the symbolic "tearing of the kingdom" away from his dynasty when he ripped Samuel's robe (1 Sam. 15:27–28). In contrast, David refused to wear Saul's protective clothing/armor when challenging Goliath to single combat (1 Sam. 17). Doing this gave him greater freedom of movement and also allowed him to demonstrate that Saul's way was not David's way. Thus David's choice of attire in both of these episodes could be a conscious attempt to set a political tone for his reign that was very different from Saul's practice (Prouser 1996: 31). It also marks him as a figure willing to be vulnerable before the people and before God. Such an act does fit well into the later idealized image of the man whom God loved.

As for David's celebratory dance before the ark, this provides further evidence of a leveling of authority, with David joining the revelers who welcome the ark and Yahweh into the city (compare the dancers in Jer. 31:10–14). Although dancers are usually described as young women (Miriam and her women in Exod. 15:19–21; the daughter of Jephthah in Judg. 11; the women who celebrate Saul and David's exploits in 1 Sam. 18), that does not preclude the possibility of male celebrants as well.

Once inside Jerusalem, the ark becomes forever after associated with the Davidic monarchy, along with the other sacred icons and vestiges of the premonarchic, wilderness era (manna, the judges, the Divine Warrior; see van der Toorn 1994: 230). However, David's action in taking custody of the ark and installing it in his political center enhances the ark's importance over other regional or local objects, and it adds to the authority of Jerusalem as the place where God dwells (Miller and Roberts 1977: 9–17; Anderson 1989: 100). Solomon will complete this process when he constructs the temple within which the ark will be housed (see 1 Kings 5–7).

Clearly, for David's monarchy to be able to emerge and mature as an identifiable political entity, the person of the king, his "house," and his capital city must take precedence over all other political leaders and political centers. Thus David enhances the power and legitimacy of his regime by proving his ability to transport and make use of the ark and then physically places it in the background, where it cannot outshine or upstage him. This is then reinforced during Absalom's rebellion, when David orders the Levites who are evacuating the city with the ark

The Place Where God's Name Dwells

Since the name of God is synonymous with God's presence, the ark is referred to in 2 Samuel 6:2 as an object that is "called by the name of the LORD of hosts who is enthroned on the cherubim." Once it is installed in a shrine, then that place becomes the site where God's name dwells. However, this cannot be construed as a restriction on God's movements or physical presence. Just as the ark is abandoned and captured by the Philistines (1 Sam. 4:11), a place whose people have become disobedient or corrupt can be abandoned by God.

Deuteronomic Law—The late monarchic injunctions found in Deuteronomy 12:10–12 that justify Josiah's centralization of worship in Jerusalem (post–622 BCE) require that the Israelites bring all of their sacrifices, tithes and donations, and votive gifts "to the place that the LORD your God will choose as a dwelling for his name" (Deut. 12:11). All other shrines and high places are to be demolished so that neither they nor the gods who were worshiped there can compete with the Jerusalem sanctuary or with Yahweh (Deut. 12:2–4).

Shiloh—The ark and a group of Levitical priests led by Eli and his sons are housed in Shiloh during the settlement period. Their abuses of power cause God to abandon that place, and it is presumably destroyed by the Philistines (see 1 Sam. 3:11–14; 4:22; Jer. 7:12–14).

Solomon's Temple—Solomon completes the process begun by David's transport of the ark into Jerusalem by building a temple in the capital city as "a house for the name of the LORD" (1 Kings 5:2–5).

Jerusalem—As the Babylonians tighten their grip on Judah, Jeremiah predicts that Jerusalem will "be like Shiloh," a desolate ruin because of their violations of the covenant (Jer. 7:12; 26:9). Ezekiel, seeing the coming destruction of Jerusalem by the Babylonian army, recounts a devastating vision of God's presence actually departing the temple and disobedient Jerusalem (Ezek. 10:18–19).

to return it to its place (2 Sam. 15:24–25). In this way Jerusalem could retain its position as the place where God's name dwells and as a rallying point for David's forces to retake the city, which they eventually do. With these evidences of power, the political leadership of the nation and the presence of the ark of the covenant are exclusively associated with the house of David (Carroll 1986: 150).

Despite his efforts to fully control events, David is unable to take the final step and construct a temple to house the ark. He lacks the complete control of the natural resources of the nation and a period of peace to devote to such a monumental and costly project. It is left to his successor Solomon to complete the process of subjugating the ark, transferring it from "the city of David" to its new home on Mount Zion (1 Kings 8:1–9). This once all-important object is forever hidden from public view and replaced in the minds and sight of the people with a piece of monumental architecture associated with the dynasty of David. Although the ark is given a place of ultimate sacred honor within the holy of holies (Hurowitz 1994), it has been effectively removed from the world of the living and is never heard of again. The final mention of the ark of the covenant is as a thing of the past, no longer needed, not to be "missed," because Jerusalem has become the new "throne of the LORD" (Jer. 3:16–17).

Thus Israel's past is replaced and a new future is forged, creating new political and social understandings for Jerusalem, the temple precinct, and those who control both. But as God explains in 1 Samuel 8:11–18, the people also have traded away their personal freedoms and their allegiance to God as the divine warrior and provider in exchange for a very human and fallible "king . . . like other nations" (1 Sam. 8:5).

God Grants David an "Everlasting Covenant"

Even though David does not build a temple for Yahweh in Jerusalem, he does receive a gift far more precious to a reigning monarch. He is given divine assurance that his dynasty will continue to rule in Jerusalem forever. There is no better insurance against assassination than divine-right rule. As he explains to his followers, David himself had set a precedent for this when he had refrained from killing Saul in the cave at En-gedi (1 Sam. 24:1–7) because the king is the "LORD's anointed." To kill him would be to deny an act of God in choosing Saul as king. Furthermore, by assassinating a reigning monarch, David would have set a precedent that could be used against him and his successors.

Of course, a precedent had also been set with God choosing a successor to Saul who was not a member of Saul's royal family. A disqualification story is carefully crafted to explain this (see 1 Sam. 13–15, especially 15:10–35), hinging eventually on God's statement "I regret that I made Saul king" (15:11). This parallels God's attitude in Genesis 6:6–7, in which Yahweh is said to be "sorry that he had made humankind," signaling a divine decision to shift events in a new direction. However, Noah still must obey God's command to build an ark in order to save his life. And, significantly in the David narrative, Samuel must obey God's command

> ## "Shepherd = King" Metaphor
>
> **Lipit-Ishtar** of Isin (1934–1924 BCE) is referred to as the "humble shepherd of Nippur" (Thureau-Dangin 1907: 205).
>
> **Hammurabi** of Babylon (1792–1750 BCE) refers to himself as "the shepherd" in the prologue to his law code (Pritchard 1969: 164).
>
> **Cyrus**, king of Persia (550–530 BCE), is named "my shepherd" by God in Isaiah 44:28.
>
> **Jeremiah** (23:1–6) condemns the "shepherds . . . who have scattered my flock" and indicates that their right to rule the people has ended. Instead, God "will gather the remnant of my flock," bring them back from all of the lands, and finally "raise up for David a righteous Branch," who will rule over them with wisdom and justice.
>
> **Ezekiel** (34:2–24) echoes Jeremiah's condemning message against "the shepherds of Israel," meaning its king, his officials, and the priestly community.

to go to Jesse's house in Bethlehem and "anoint for me the one whom I name to you" as Saul's successor (1 Sam 16:3). Obedience, as always, is the key to positive results and divine assistance.

Once Saul's family is removed from the throne of Israel, it is absolutely necessary that David be portrayed as God's choice to serve as king. This will then authorize David's regime to claim the loyalty of the tribal elders and the people. The divine promise to bless David and his descendants is couched in terms of a personal relationship, a neat parallel with the personal relationship that God chose to establish with the Israelites when the covenant promise was offered to Abraham. The steps in the narrative that highlight David's rise to the kingship and conclude with the granting of an "everlasting covenant" consist of the following items:

1. Call narrative: God "took" David from his role as shepherd and chose him to be "prince over my people Israel" (2 Sam. 7:8). This is a statement of fact since David had been a shepherd for his father's flocks, but it also functions as a metaphor for his new position as Israel's king. The shepherd metaphor is often applied to God (Gen. 48:15; Ps. 23:1; Jer. 13:17), but it is also commonly used to refer to kings in the ancient Near East.

2. Recitation of past deeds: God reminds David of the Divine Warrior's past service to him, "cutting off" David's enemies (2 Sam. 7:9a). This rhetorical element is also found in the summary statement of the wilderness experience in Deuteronomy 2:7: "These forty

years the LORD your God has been with you." It is an aspect of the salvation history of the people and, in David's case, of a political success story.

3. Promise of a glorious future: Yahweh, whose name is intimately tied to the person and power of the Deity, now promises to make David's name great among the peoples of the earth, providing him with a dignity that will be a match for any other monarch (2 Sam. 7:9b–11). This promise includes a reaffirmation of a land for the people and a guarantee of peace and security (see previous statements in Gen. 13:15; 17:7–8, 19; 48:1). The significance of God's covenant with David is reiterated in Psalm 89:19–37 and placed into the cultic context of royal coronation language. According to this version in the Psalms, David has been adopted as God's son, and for this reason alone "no limits are to be set to his dominion either in space or time" (Weiser 1962: 592).

4. A dynasty is established: In addition to David becoming "a name," he is also to become "a house" (2 Sam 7:11b–16). This statement is a wordplay on David's original desire to construct a house for God. Instead, God turns it around and "constructs" a house of David. This could be compared with Jacob's request for the name of the being he wrestles with at the Jabbok River and how the request is turned around and Jacob is renamed Israel (Gen. 32:22–31). This dynastic promise is repeated for other kings, but it is qualified by the requirement that these monarchs must "walk in my statutes, obey my ordinances, and keep all my commandments," a proviso that previously had been imposed on the people as a whole when they arrived at Mount Sinai (Exod. 19:5; see also Lev. 18:4–5). Thus both Solomon (1 Kings 6:12–13) and Jeroboam (1 Kings 11:38) are cautioned that there are specific expectations for those who rule the people of the covenant.

Clearly, the covenant promise made to David and his successors shares the sense of obligation found in covenant statements made to the people of Israel (Weinfeld 1983: 88). Each involves obligations on the part of the participants. They must obey God's word and be willing to subscribe to the laws and ordinances established by God. Furthermore, they must accept that the inevitable failures to obey the stipulations of the covenant will result in sure punishment: "*When* he commits iniquity, I will punish him with a rod such as mortals use" (2 Sam. 7:14). However, God's "steadfast love" (Hebrew *hesed*) will remain a constant factor binding both the monarch and the people to Yahweh and the Deity to them (7:15).

Despite the obvious parallels between the covenants made to the people and to the house of David, the political result is an assurance that God will not take the kingdom away from them "as I took it from Saul," but their kingdom will remain "forever before me; your throne shall be established forever" (2 Sam. 7:16). This often-repeated promise (see Ps. 89:5; Isa. 55:3; Jer. 33:17–18) will remain intact for approximately four hundred years, although the northern tribes will break away under the leadership of Jeroboam (1 Kings 12:1–24). Davidic kings will reign over Judah from their Jerusalem capital without a break until the city is destroyed by Nebuchadnezzar's army in 586 BCE (2 Kings 25:8–10), and the last of the royal line dies in Babylonian exile (2 Kings 25:27–30).

The transformation of the everlasting covenant into the messianic expectation in the exilic and postexilic period will be examined in chapter 8 below. For now, it is enough to say that the origins of the Davidic ideal have their foundation in the succession narrative of the Deuteronomistic Historian that places David on the throne in Jerusalem and details how his son Solomon succeeded him (see Keys 1996: 43–70). In the process,

---

Covenantal Expectations for Successors

The covenant promise is made to the founding figures of the nation—Abraham, Moses, and David. Their successors will be offered a similar promise, but the expectation is that they will be as obedient to God's command as their "fathers."

Isaac—The covenantal promise of land and children is extended to Isaac if he is obedient to God's command to stay in Canaan. God promises to fulfill the oath made to Abraham "because Abraham obeyed my voice and kept my charge, my commandments, my statutes, and my laws" (Gen. 26:2–5).

Joshua—In order to obtain support for his leadership, Joshua is instructed to "be careful to act in accordance with all the law that my servant Moses commanded you" (Josh. 1:7).

Solomon—The new king is promised long life if he "will walk in my ways, keeping my statutes and my commandments, as your father David walked" (1 Kings 3:14). When he constructs the temple in Jerusalem, the proviso of divine blessing is repeated on the condition that he obey God's command (1 Kings 6:12).

Jeroboam—When the kingdom is divided and he is designated as "king over Israel," God promises Jeroboam that he will "build you an enduring house, as I built for David," if the king will "walk in my ways . . . keeping my statutes and my commandments" (1 Kings 11:37–39).

it sets a series of precedents for the monarchy's relationship with God and their right to rule the people. It will also provide a contrast with the political situation in the northern kingdom of Israel, which lacks a promise of everlasting fidelity to any one royal family and is quite unstable, marked by a succession of assassinations throughout its history.

Jerusalem Becomes Both the City of David and the City of Yahweh

The political process begun by David is solidified when Solomon succeeds his father on the throne of the united kingdom of Israel. All that David had accomplished is built upon, expanded, and transformed into a viable royal ideology centered on Jerusalem and the house of David (Monson 1999: 3). According to the narrative, Solomon's key act in completing the tasks of kingship begun by David is the construction of the temple in Jerusalem (1 Kings 5–7; see Ps. 132:13–14), but this can be seen as part of Solomon's larger vision of expanding Israel's and his influence beyond its borders economically and politically (Hopkins 1997: 308). His boast that he had built "an exalted house, a place for you [Yahweh] to dwell in forever" (1 Kings 8:13), separates Solomon from the incomplete heritage bequeathed by David and formalizes his claim to the throne (Knauf 1997: 82–86). This act also establishes the city as both a political capital and a temple city, the latter designation ultimately to be interpreted as a place of universal attention that will draw the nations to recognize Yahweh's majesty. The ancient temple cities of Mesopotamia (Nippur, Babylon, and Lagash) were heralded as "a place in which the oppressor and the wicked do not dwell, but in which righteousness and justice abide perpetually." Jerusalem and its sanctuary also adopt these attributes and gain worldwide fame (Weinfeld 1983: 105–11). Even after its destruction by the Babylonians, Jerusalem (often referred to as "Zion" in the prophetic materials) remains a place of hope and a repository of God's power and loving-kindness for the returning exiles.

The imagery that will be attached to Mount Zion includes (1) a dwelling place on a high mountain, (2) a life-giving source of water, and (3) a point from which the forces of chaos are conquered (Monson 1999: 7). In this way, Jerusalem supersedes all previous or rival mountaintop sanctuaries such as Mount Sinai, Shechem (Mount Gerizim), Shiloh, and Bethel (Levenson 1985: 89–96). The psalmists, in their effort to raise Yahweh worship above that of any of the gods of Canaan, impressed this image of Zion's supremacy over all other sites associated with the worship of other gods or symbolic of the power of other nations. The singular importance attached to Jerusalem is found in the numerous references to the city (seventeen) and to Zion (thirty-nine), and nearly all (with the exception of Ps. 132)

> ### Jerusalem, the Center of the Universe
>
> **Isaiah 2:2–3**—"In days to come the mountain of the LORD's house
>   shall be established as the highest of the mountains, and shall
>   be raised above the hills; all the nations shall stream to it. . . .
>   For out of Zion shall go forth instruction, and the word of the
>   LORD from Jerusalem."
> **Isaiah 60:14**—"The descendants of those who oppressed you
>   shall come bending low to you, and all who despised you
>   shall bow down at your feet; they shall call you the City of
>   the LORD, the Zion of the Holy One of Israel."
> **Ezekiel 5:5**—"This is Jerusalem; I have set her in the center of the
>   nations, with countries all around her."
> **Joel 3:17**—"So you shall know that I, the LORD your God, dwell
>   in Zion, my holy mountain. And Jerusalem shall be holy, and
>   strangers shall never again pass through it."

place their emphasis on God's decision to dwell in this place (Hoppe 2000: 24). Thus the theological significance of one more victory for Yahweh over other gods is found in Psalm 68:16, which taunts Bashan as envious of the mount "where the LORD will reside forever," and in Psalm 84:7, which exclaims that "the God of gods will be seen in Zion."

Conclusion

It is virtually impossible to separate the founding of the Israelite monarchy from the story of David and Jerusalem. Of course, Saul was the first king (better termed a "war chief" rather than a national ruler), but it is David who begins the process of creating the elements of monarchy: bureaucracy, capital city, central place of worship, more efficient army. Both David and Jerusalem become Israelite icons. They are not just a man and a city. David represents a dynasty of rulers over a four-hundred-year period, and his memory is idealized to the extent that all future kings are measured against him. Jerusalem, while continuously serving as the seat of power for the Davidic monarchs, outlives them and the institution of monarchy. Even though the city will be destroyed by Nebuchadnezzar in 587 BCE, the idea of Jerusalem or Zion lives on, becoming both a source of hope for the exiles and a promise of God's presence with the people after their return fifty years later.

What begins as a political move on David's part to provide a capital city for his newly formed nation becomes in the end an origin story for the presence of Yahweh in Jerusalem. Both David and Jerusalem will eventually become idealized icons within Israelite tradition. His rise to power marks the shift away from a tribal society to a central government. Furthermore, the "everlasting covenant" made with his dynasty creates a divine-right principle of leadership and sets the stage for the concept of the messiah when the monarchy comes to an end. Jerusalem serves as the physical capital city as well as the metaphorical perfect city, the place (i.e., the temple) where God caused his name to dwell, the place tied to the hope of return after the exile.

Jeroboam Leads the Secession
of the Northern Tribes

The history of every nation, including ancient Israel, contains examples of both exemplary and evil individuals. For the Deuteronomistic compilers of Israel's traditions, kings David, Jehoshaphat, Hezekiah, and Josiah were models of proper behavior and champions of the covenant. Ranged against these "good kings" were a group of villains, most of whom ruled the northern kingdom of Israel after the nation was divided. The worst of these were Manasseh of Judah and kings Jeroboam and Ahab of Israel. Since the Deuteronomistic Historian's account of the kings of Israel was most likely compiled and edited into a coherent form in the period after the monarchy had come to an end, it is not surprising to find somewhat exaggerated and biased portrayals of these rulers (Knoppers 2000: 129–33; Linville 1997). Despite the fact that the editors knew the basic elements of the story (preserved in court records and oral tradition), they chose to shape their account in such a way that it would be clear to the audience: (1) how the monarchy came into being, (2) how God established an "everlasting covenant" with the house of David, (3) how apostasy and political intrigue contributed to a division of the kingdom, and (4) how the rulers of both kingdoms responded to their obligation to obey God's covenant.

Jeroboam's role in the Deuteronomistic account ultimately becomes that of arch-apostate, and his record of covenant violations serves as a measure for all future kings (Cohn 1985: 25). Initially, however, Jeroboam, like Saul, is a sympathetic character. Like Saul and David, he is viewed as God's chosen and a man who has been promised a perpetual kingship for his family (McKenzie 2000: 140). Jeroboam, like David, is hailed as a talented young man who is forced by a jealous or misguided king to flee into exile (Frisch 2000: 17–18). The divine promise, "I will be with you" (1 Kings 11:38), is then withdrawn from Jeroboam as it was from Saul due to their failure to remain obedient to God's command (compare 1 Sam. 13:13–14 and 1 Kings 14:7–10).

It is these comparisons that can be made with David that serve as the narrative and theological backdrop to Jeroboam's up-and-down career. Both he and David come to the throne through the intervention of a prophet, and neither man is directly related to the ruling house of Saul (1 Sam. 16:1–13; 1 Kings 11:26). After a period of political exile, both are recognized by the people as their legitimate ruler. It is this easy comparison with David's early career that magnifies Jeroboam's evil reputation, since, unlike David, he does not become a champion of the covenant and in no way could be described as the king whom God loved.

Perhaps the most telling judgment of Jeroboam's God-given opportunity and his failure to measure up is found in the Deuteronomistic summary of Israel's history in 2 Kings 17:21–25 (Frisch 2000: 27). In these few verses the editors proclaim that when God divided the kingdom and "made Jeroboam son of Nebat king," it was Jeroboam's own policies that "drove Israel from following the LORD." Subsequently, "the people of Israel continued in all the sins that Jeroboam committed," and as a result "Israel was exiled from their own land to Assyria until this day."

Outline of the Jeroboam Narrative
(based on Cohn 1985: 24)

Introduction: relationship between Jeroboam and Solomon (1 Kings 11:26–28)
Ahijah's prophecy of Jeroboam as future king of divided kingdom (11:29–40)
Fulfillment of Ahijah's prophecy (11:41–12:24)
Jeroboam's sin (12:25–33)
Confrontation at Bethel with man of God (13:1–32)
Jeroboam's sin repeated (13:33–34)
Ahijah's prophecy condemning Jeroboam's house (14:1–16)
Fulfillment of Ahijah's prophecy (14:17–18 and 15:25–30)
Conclusion: narrative summary of Jeroboam's reign (14:19–20)

The Roots of Division

Although there are undoubtedly many unrecorded details behind the story of the division of the kingdom of Israel, it is certainly a major turning point politically and religiously for the Israelites, and it will be echoed throughout the Deuteronomistic History and in the Prophets. The biblical account indicates that the forces that contributed to the division of the Israelite kingdom are both internal and external (1 Kings 11:14–25). While the Transjordanian kingdoms of Edom and Aram to the south and northeast are mentioned as political rivals to Israel, the archaeological evidence suggests that only small clusters of village sites existed in Edom in this period (Edelman 1995: 177). We also lack extra-biblical tenth-century sources for the existence of a powerful kingdom in Aram (Syria). As a result, the tradition that these regions were able to pressure Israel's borders during Solomon's reign may actually be dependent on events in the eighth century that were projected by the biblical writers back into the period of the early monarchy.

A more likely political rival for Israel during the tenth century would be Egypt. Despite the story of Solomon's marriage to the daughter of the pharaoh (1 Kings 3:1), it is unlikely that either Egypt or Israel was a truly dominant power during this period. Instead, each would have engaged in the usual intrigues designed to weaken or undermine the influence of the other. This could explain why Egypt would feel it was to its advantage to harbor two political enemies of the Davidic dynasty, Hadad, ruler of Edom (11:17–22), and Jeroboam (11:40). This political maneuvering might contribute to an increase in Egyptian influence in Palestine (Edelman 1995: 179).

A further sign of growing Egyptian power is seen in the apparent ease with which the pharaoh Shishak/Shoshenq I moved his army through the Shephelah at the end of Solomon's reign. This indicates that Egypt was attempting to restore its political relations with the Philistines (Clancy 1999: 7–8, 19). It also marks a return, after a period of nearly two centuries, of aggressive Egyptian military and economic activities in this area (Weinstein 1998: 193–94).

Although the biblical editors create a picture of vast wealth and international influence during the reign of Solomon, it is ultimately his willingness to indulge his foreign wives' desire to have shrines for their gods and the resulting apostasy that are blamed for the political division of the kingdom (1 Kings 11:1–13). The Deuteronomistic Historian points to the growing influences of other cultures and the worship of other gods as the basis for the Israelites' failure to obey the covenant. For this reason God chooses to tear the bulk of the kingdom away from the house of David (11:11–13). Yahweh allows the Davidic rulers to retain control over Judah and Jerusalem, but the majority of the tribal territories are given to a political rival.

Ahijah and Jeroboam

The background theme of apostasy continues with the prophet Ahijah providing divine legitimacy to a new political figure, a public-works official named Jeroboam (Knoppers 1990: 428). Although the division of the kingdom will not occur until after Solomon's death, the text makes clear that the theological roots of political schism have already produced fruit (1 Kings 11:29–40). It must be a surprise to Jeroboam when the prophet Ahijah removes his robe (11:29–30), but he must have quickly recognized the advantage it would provide. The prophet is following instructions to seek out a new claimant to the throne of Israel, based on Solomon's apostasy, and when he meets Jeroboam along the road (possibly because of the danger associated with doing it in a more public place), he uses a symbolic divestiture to designate God's choice.

There is some ambiguity in determining who is actually wearing the "new garment" (salmah) in this passage. Since the verb for "to take hold" (wayyitpos), which also appears in the story of Potiphar's wife's seizure of Joseph's robe (Gen. 29:12), is generally used in passages where someone is seized or captured, it seems best to say that Jeroboam's robe is the object in question. This works best since the translation "take hold" would not fit the context when applied to oneself (Cogan 2001: 339). Thus Ahijah seizes Jeroboam's cloak from his shoulders and tears it into twelve pieces, instructing Jeroboam to take ten of them (1 Kings 11:30–31).

That this is called a "new garment" (salmah hadashah) suggests both its value as well as a new beginning for the nation that is about to be divided like the garment itself. Since it is torn apart by a prophet as a symbolic gesture or enacted prophecy (note the same verb qara' is used in 1 Sam. 15:27–28 when Saul tore Samuel's cloak), there is a measure of authority added to this cloth, which is being shared with the king-to-be, and it may be that the transformation of an item like this was a well-understood gesture in that culture.

It is unlikely that the investiture scene depicted in the Jeroboam narrative remained a secret (unlike what seems to be the case for Saul in 1 Sam. 10:1–8). In fact, the text indicates that Solomon subsequently tries to kill Jeroboam (1 Kings 11:40a). Furthermore, it is not surprising that Jeroboam would establish a relationship with the Egyptian king Shishak/Shoshenq (11:40b). The Egyptians, in sheltering a political enemy of Solomon, must have felt that they had much to gain from

---

Symbolic Gestures: Twelve Pieces

The story of how Jeroboam is chosen as Israel's king contains a political parallel with Saul's career. It is one of three stories involving the number twelve. It is possible that a political polemic is intended in all of these stories. Linking the scandalous behavior of the men of Gibeah with Saul further blackens his political memory, even though the military victory at Jabesh-gilead would be a high point in his career. In addition, there may be an intentional link between Jeroboam's moment of divine recognition and a gesture symbolizing the tearing asunder of the nation. The Deuteronomistic Historian's aim may be to establish a tie between Jeroboam and the failed dynasty of Saul (Matthews 2004b: 190).

Judges 19:29–30—When a Levite's concubine is assaulted in Gibeah (Judg. 19:22–26), the Levite cuts up her body into twelve pieces and sends them to each of the tribal territories to summon the leaders to a conference.

1 Samuel 11:7—In order to marshal an armed force to relieve the siege of Jabesh-gilead, Saul cuts up his oxen into twelve pieces and sends them throughout the tribal territories as both a signal for action and a threat against those who fail to respond. In addition to the number parallelism, 1 Samuel 10:26 states that Gibeah is Saul's home.

1 Kings 11:29–31—Ahijah removes Jeroboam's robe and tears it into twelve pieces as a symbolic gesture empowering Jeroboam to become king of the ten northern tribes.

---

serving as a political haven. In addition, Solomon obviously does not have the power to demand his extradition.

A Kingdom Divided

Another factor in the emerging crisis for Solomon and Rehoboam is the problems associated with hereditary monarchy. Initially, it appears that concerns over the succession have at last been settled. The smooth transition of power from Solomon to Rehoboam is evidence of the maturing of Israel's monarchy. There is no struggle for power, no elimination of the family members of the previous dynasty, and no rival claimants from the Davidic ruling family. The narrative merely records that Rehoboam succeeded his father, but that simple statement (1 Kings 11:43) indicates that sufficient preparation had been made during Solomon's reign so that an orderly political transition could take place. However, the forces of secession quickly draw Rehoboam into a confrontation that would provide the crisis leading to the division of the kingdom.

The alliance between Jerusalem and the various tribal leaders that had been engineered by David and Solomon proves to be too fragile to survive the forces of division that assert themselves when Solomon's weak son, Rehoboam, comes to the throne (Master 2001: 130). In the face of Rehoboam's inability to negotiate successfully with the tribal leaders, the former political structure (a loose confederation of tribal groups) reasserts itself. When the cry to separate the northern tribes, first heard during Sheba's revolt in David's time (2 Sam. 20:1), rings out again, it spells the end of any further attempts to unite all of the Israelite tribes under a single leader.

> What share do we have in David?
> We have no inheritance in the son of Jesse.
> To your tents, O Israel!
> Look now to your own house, O David.
>
> (1 Kings 12:16)

Only when a general assembly of the people is called at Shechem does the text begin to indicate that all is not well politically in Israel (1 Kings 12:1). This meeting, called by the tribal elders and to which Rehoboam is summoned, stands in stark contrast to the gathering of the tribal leaders in 2 Samuel 5:1–3, when the elders came to David's stronghold at Hebron to anoint him as their king and to pledge their allegiance to him as their ruler. Instead, Rehoboam must travel to the northern tribal center at Shechem and face an assemblage of the people who are already in a rebellious mood (1 Kings 12:1; Tadmor 1982: 252–54).

What makes this even more difficult for Rehoboam is the presence of Jeroboam, who is ready to take power should the tribal elders not receive a favorable response to their demands for greater local autonomy (1 Kings 2:3a, 12; 2 Chron. 10:2; T. Willis 1991: 42–43). Indications in the description of Solomon's administrative policies (1 Kings 4:7–19) are that the king had heavily taxed the tribal districts (Ash 1995). Their call for less interference by the central government and fewer demands for labor service is symptomatic of the growing pains for new states.

When, after three days, Rehoboam chooses to listen to his younger advisors rather than to more experienced men, the northern tribal leaders have little choice. They are unwilling to bend to Rehoboam's blustering attempts to intimidate them, and they "vote with their feet" (Matthews 2002: 58–59). It is therefore possible to charge that Rehoboam's "evil deeds," emphasized in the Septuagint version, are the basis for the division of the kingdom (Schenker 2000: 233–34). The story has aspects of a wisdom tale in which the young king has the opportunity to display his wisdom but fails to do so (compare Solomon's wisdom in 1 Kings 3:16–28; Dillard 1987: 85). Ultimately, however, in both the Kings and Chronicles versions, the text makes clear that the actual division of the kingdom is the result of a decision made by God, not just by the tribal leaders (Machinist 1995: 117–20).

Of course, the narrative has already indicated in 1 Kings 11 that God has made the decision to divide the kingdom and has sent the prophet Ahijah to designate the ruler of a northern kingdom of Israel. As a result, Rehoboam's role in the drama may add further evidence for why the division should take place, but it is not the ultimate cause (Boer 1996: 154–55). Ahijah's divinely directed actions, which grant to

---

Promise and Fulfillment Motif

Abraham and Sarah—God repeatedly promises the ancestral couple "land and children" and ultimately fulfills that promise by directing them to Canaan and by providing Isaac as their heir (Gen. 12:1–3; 21:1–7).

Moses—God calls on Moses to lead the people out of Egypt, pledging to fulfill the covenant promise made to Abraham and guaranteeing the people's safety during their journey. To fulfill this promise, God directs them to Mount Sinai and provides manna, quail, and water along the way (Exod. 6:1–8; 15:1–18; 16–17; 19:1–6).

Joshua—God promises to be with Joshua during the conquest of Canaan. This promise is fulfilled in the victories over the peoples and cities of Canaan as long as the Israelites are obedient to God's word (Josh. 1:2–9; 7:11–15; 11:16–23).

Saul and Jeroboam—God promises these men that they will rule Israel and that their families will rule after them as long as they obey God's command. Their failure prevents this promise from being fulfilled (1 Sam. 10:1; 12:13–15; 15:26–28; 1 Kings 11:31–39; 14:7–16).

David—God promises the kingdom to David and his house as an everlasting covenant. However, Solomon's apostasy causes this promise to be altered so that David's descendants will rule only Judah (2 Sam. 7:11b–16; 1 Kings 11:9–13).

Jeremiah 31:31–34—God promises to make a "new covenant" with the returned exiles and write the law "on their hearts." Their iniquity then will be forgiven while they enjoy the benefits of fertility for their families and their land.

Ezekiel 36:8–12—God promises the barren and depopulated land of Israel that it will be restored to fertility and productiveness and that it will once again be filled by the returned exiles.

Jeroboam the right to rule the northern tribes, can be seen as part of a common literary pattern of promise and fulfillment. This same pattern is found throughout the Bible, especially in those cases where the covenant promise is a central feature or in which God chooses to take a personal interest in human endeavor. A similar pattern of promise and fulfillment will continue in the prophetic material as God calls on the people to return to their covenantal obligations and promises them that they will eventually return from exile and restore the promised land (Leene 2000: 172–75).

Politically and realistically, the division of the kingdoms weakened both of these small states. Whether the Egyptian pharaoh Shishak/ Shoshenq had a free hand to invade and raid Judah and Israel is uncertain from textual and archaeological evidence (Kitchen 1986: 296–300; Clancy 1999: 18–19). It is quite possible that Rehoboam was forced to pay heavy tribute to the Egyptians, but any great hopes of restoring an Egyptian empire in Canaan were dashed by Shishak's death (Ussishkin 1990: 73–74). As a result, Israel and Judah will find themselves to be pawns in the game of international intrigue played by the Egyptians and Assyrians over the next three centuries (Gitin 1998: 162–63).

Jeroboam's Sin

Jeroboam's attempt to create a separate identity for the new northern kingdom of Israel, especially his establishment of alternative shrines to the Jerusalem temple at Dan and Bethel, came to be known as the "sin of Jeroboam." Naturally, this is not the term that Jeroboam or most of the people of the northern kingdom would have applied to his policies. However, the account in 1 and 2 Kings was produced by the Deuteronomistic Historian (a group of editors from the southern kingdom of

---

Jeroboam's Sin (1 Kings 12:26–32)

- Royal shrines are created at Dan and Bethel to rival Jerusalem as the sole cultic center.
- Golden calves are placed in these shrines as substitutes for the ark of the covenant.
- High places (*bamot*) are tolerated or even encouraged in local village culture.
- Non-Levites are appointed to serve as loyal priests for the northern kings.
- The religious calendar is revised to keep people away from Jerusalem during major festivals.

Regnal Formula Statements

Nadab—"Nadab son of Jeroboam . . . reigned over Israel two years. He did what was evil in the sight of the LORD, walking in the way of his ancestor and in the sin that he caused Israel to commit" (1 Kings 15:25–26).

Baasha—"Baasha son of Ahijah . . . reigned twenty-four years. He did what was evil in the sight of the LORD, walking in the way of Jeroboam and in the sin that he caused Israel to commit" (1 Kings 15:33–34).

Ahaziah—"Ahaziah son of Ahab . . . reigned two years over Israel. He did what was evil in the sight of the LORD, and walked in the way of his father and mother, and in the way of Jeroboam son of Nebat, who caused Israel to sin" (1 Kings 22:51–52).

Ahaziah—Ahaziah son of Jehoram, king of Judah, "reigned one year in Jerusalem. His mother's name was Athaliah, a granddaughter of King Omri of Israel. He also walked in the way of the house of Ahab, doing what was evil in the sight of the LORD . . . for he was son-in-law to the house of Ahab" (2 Kings 8:25–27).

Judah). It would have been impossible for the kings of Israel to receive an unbiased review by these southern editors (Cross 1973: 279–81; Donner 1977: 388). This can be seen by comparing the variances between the Hebrew text and what appears in the Greek Septuagint version as well as its supplement, 3 Kingdoms 12:24a–z. The latter text actually downplays Jeroboam's responsibility for the division of the kingdom and instead places this political disaster squarely on the shoulders of Solomon's son Rehoboam (Shaw 1997: 56–57).

The official version produced by the Deuteronomistic Historian comprises an "ideology of the founder" (Mullen 1987: 213). In effect it provides an explanation for Israel's eventual downfall in 721 BCE and Judah's temporary survival until 587 BCE (Ash 1998: 23). According to this ideology, because Jeroboam, the northern kingdom's first king, was evil, his dynasty is doomed to failure, and for purposes of comparison his "sin" will be used as the means of judging the character of all future kings. If they continue to perpetuate "Jeroboam's sin," then they are by definition evil and are subject to the same condemnation that Jeroboam's family faced (see Mullen 1987: 230–31). This criterion is also applied to the kings of Judah, although the Deuteronomistic Historian vilifies those, like Ahaziah, who had direct family ties to the kings of Israel (Boshoff 2000: 28). The regnal formulas that appear at the beginning

Echoes of Jeroboam's Sin

The biblical writers and prophetic figures repeatedly cite "Jeroboam's sin" as the basis of God's displeasure with the people. Kings are condemned for continuing these policies, and the people are cast adrift because they have ignored God's command to worship God only in the place where "his name dwells"—Jerusalem (Deut. 12:5–7).

2 Kings 10:28–31—In his regnal formula, Jehu, a king of Israel who "wiped out Baal" from the nation, is faulted because "he did not turn aside from the sins of Jeroboam son of Nebat, which he caused Israel to commit—the golden calves that were in Bethel and in Dan." Even though he was given God's promise that "sons of the fourth generation shall sit on the throne of Israel," he "did not turn from the sins of Jeroboam," and this ultimately led to the fall of his dynasty and of the kingdom.

2 Kings 17:1–18—The description of the fall of Israel to the army of the king of Assyria includes an indictment based on idolatry (vv. 7, 10, 12, 15–17), use of high places for worship (vv. 9, 11), ignoring the warnings of prophets (v. 13), and making "cast images of two calves" (v. 16).

Hosea 10:15—In his prediction of Israel's destruction, Hosea, who is most likely a Levite and therefore unable to participate in the priesthood in Israel, condemns Bethel "because of your great wickedness," referring to its use as a royal shrine.

Amos 3:14—In his oracle against Israel, the prophet states God's decision that "on the day I punish Israel for its transgressions, I will punish the altars of Bethel."

Tobit 1:5–6—The second-century BCE writer of the deuterocanonical book of Tobit has the main character state: "All my kindred and our ancestral house of Naphtali sacrificed to the calf that King Jeroboam of Israel had erected in Dan and on all the mountains of Galilee. But I alone went often to Jerusalem for the festivals, as it is prescribed for all Israel by an everlasting decree." Thus the Deuteronomic tradition of Jerusalem's sole supremacy as a cultic site was accepted by at least a segment of the second-century Jewish community.

and end of each monarch's narrative contain the standard language used by the Deuteronomistic History to express the editors' judgment of these kings. While their continued appearance in the narrative provides a sense of continuity for the monarchy, their harsh judgments suggest that punishment for the nations is only postponed and that it cannot be set aside forever (Boer 1996: 148–49).

Royal Shrines in Dan and Bethel

In the view of the Deuteronomistic Historian, the most important step taken by Jeroboam is to establish two royal shrines at either end of his newly formed state. Both Dan (see Judg. 17–18) and Bethel (see Gen. 28:19; 31:13; Judg. 21:2–4) had previously served as regional religious centers. However, his favoring them with "official" royal status is seen as a betrayal of those who considered Jerusalem the only proper place for cultic activity (see the divinely ordained caution in Deut. 12:13 that the people "take care that you do not offer your burnt offerings at any place you happen to see"). What Jeroboam accomplishes in setting up these rival shrines is to provide his people with two conveniently located religious centers, and this helps to wean them away from any religious dependence they may have had on Jerusalem.

In subsequent narrative and in prophetic speech, Dan and Bethel are condemned because of their association with Jeroboam's sin. This is perhaps most graphically seen in the confrontation between the prophet Amos and the priest in charge of the "king's sanctuary" at Bethel (Amos 7:10–17). This non-Levitical appointee challenges Amos, who is from Tekoa in Judah, saying he has no right to prophesy at Bethel, "a temple of the kingdom" (v. 13). Amos responds that he has been called to speak by Yahweh and cannot be told to be silent by Amaziah. Amos's response is an illustration of an "irreconcilable conflict" between the north and south (Andersen and Freedman 1989: 734). In prophesying disaster for Amaziah's family and the coming exile of the people of Israel, Amos demonstrates his own legitimacy as the true representative of Yahweh.

Golden Calves

Jeroboam's placing images of golden calves in each of these royal shrines is an interesting move. One could argue that Jeroboam wanted to provide the people with an iconic substitute for the ark of the covenant, whose lid featured the wings of the cherubim and functioned as a pedestal or throne for Yahweh. The golden calves also could be seen as divine pedestals, perhaps not as unique as the ark but still serving as recognizable substitutes. Despite the arguments that can be made for the political wisdom of Jeroboam's decision, some scholars go so far as to define his actions as a form of "original sin" for the northern kingdom and its monarchy (Hoffmann 1980: 132). Certainly the Deuteronomistic Historian makes the case that Jeroboam's aim is to draw the people into idolatry in strict violation of the covenantal ideal of "constraining them from idolatry" (Lasine 1992: 144–45).

Whatever his motives, it is unlikely that Jeroboam's actions represent a religious innovation since many Israelites accepted cult images and were familiar with calf symbolism (Cross 1973: 73–75; E. Stern 2001b). However, the Deuteronomistic Historian has no intention of making excuses for Jeroboam. Instead, the king is soundly condemned for leading his people into idolatry and promoting false worship practices (Knoppers 1995: 101–3).

Echoes of the Golden Calves

Moses—There are clear parallels between Jeroboam's story and Exodus 32, where Aaron shapes a golden calf to pacify the frightened Israelites at Mount Sinai. However, there is also a real contrast between these two events. In Exodus 32 Moses quickly moves to put an end to their idolatry and commands the Levites to "cleanse" the camp by slaying three thousand offenders who had bowed down to the idol (32:27–28). Jeroboam (930–909 BCE) never repents of his actions, and there is no indication that he ever takes steps to remove the golden calves from Dan and Bethel. Jeroboam uses a dedication formula similar to that found in Exodus 32:4, calling on the people to recognize the calves as images of "your gods . . . who brought you up out of the land of Egypt" (1 Kings 12:28). In this way the Exodus story provides a model for corrective behavior, while Jeroboam's story has only negative images.

Jehu—Even though this king of Israel (842–815 BCE) systematically destroyed the images and the temple to Baal in Samaria, he "did not turn aside from the sins of Jeroboam son of Nebat, which he caused Israel to commit—the golden calves that were in Bethel and in Dan" (2 Kings 10:25–29).

Hoshea—The last king of Israel (732–722 BCE) saw his country invaded and depopulated by the Assyrians. The Deuteronomistic Historian then provided a theological explanation for this disaster, charging Israel with multiple violations of the covenant, many of which were attributable to Jeroboam's sin (2 Kings 17:9–16). They built "high places" and made offerings to other gods there (vv. 9, 11), and they "made for themselves cast images of two calves" (v. 16).

Hosea—In his oracles predicting God's punishment of the northern kingdom of Israel, the prophet proclaims that the people of Samaria will find no comfort or protection in the "calf of Beth-aven" (Hosea 10:5), and he is outraged that "people are kissing calves" instead of calling on Yahweh for help (13:2).

Non-Levitical Priests

The remaining elements of Jeroboam's reforms seem to be blatantly political in nature. His decision to employ non-Levites as priests in his shrines indicates that he is aware of the mixed loyalties of the Levites, and he values the political loyalty of his appointees over the religious orthodoxy of the hereditary priesthood. These newly appointed men owe their jobs to King Jeroboam, and it could be expected that any decisions they make on ritual practice and the education of the people would be in line with the government's position. Frankly, all ancient governments made use of the priesthood to promote their agenda. The prophets took exception to this position, reminding the kings that they were not exempt from God's law and that they had no special privileges beyond those granted to every member of the covenantal community. Any exercise of royal power that oppressed the people or led to idolatry was met with harsh criticism by angry-voiced prophetic figures.

The disgust with which the prophets view the actions of priests and kings can be seen during the final years of the nation of Israel's existence, when Hosea laments that "my people are destroyed for lack of knowledge" and states that God rejects the priests appointed by Jeroboam, for they "have forgotten the law" (Hosea 4:6). One of the primary tasks of the priests would have been instructing the people on the law, and their failure to do this spells doom for the people (Birch 1997: 51–52). Hosea goes on to warn the people and their leaders: "Hear this, O priests! Give heed, O house of Israel! Listen, O house of the king! For the judgment pertains to you" (5:1). He tells them that God has taken away their king "in my wrath" over their failure to obey the covenant (13:10–11).

Promotion of High Places

In promoting the use of high places and by constructing a "bamot-house" in Bethel, Jeroboam once again chose to maintain current religious practice rather than institute any innovative schemes. The high place was a familiar facility in both the village culture and in the cities of ancient Israel (see Nakhai 1994: 20–22 for a summary of biblical citations in the premonarchic and early monarchic period). While the high places (bamot) served as a focus for cultic activity, the architecture or lack thereof associated with these sacred precincts is unclear and may have varied from one site to another (Whitney 1979: 147; Barrick 1996: 641–42). Most likely the high place consisted of a platform with various cult objects and an altar that provided a place for the sacrificial offerings of individual households (Nakhai 1994: 19). Local harvest festivals and celebrations would be staged within the boundaries of this recognized sacred space (see Deut. 12:2–3).

False Shepherds

One of the favorite metaphors used by the prophets to condemn kings and priests who had failed in their responsibilities to correctly lead the people is the "false shepherd."

Isaiah 56:11—Isaiah places the blame for Israel's problems on its "shepherds" who have "no understanding." These corrupt rulers "have all turned to their own way, to their own gain, one and all."

Jeremiah 23:1–4—In a theodicy explaining the exile of the people and predicting their eventual restoration, Jeremiah points to the "shepherds who destroy and scatter the sheep of my pasture." Their unfaithful stewardship required God to "gather the remnant of my flock . . . and bring them back to their fold," and God will then "raise up shepherds over them who will shepherd them."

Ezekiel 34:2–16—The prophet lists the crimes of the "shepherds of Israel," including "feeding yourselves . . . but you do not feed the sheep"; they have not ministered to the sick or to strays, "but with force and harshness you have ruled them," allowing them to be scattered, "with no one to search or seek for them." Again God must take up the task of shepherding the flock, bringing them back to the fold, and performing the role of the Good Shepherd.

Zechariah 10:3—Having first condemned the people's reliance on idols and diviners rather than calling on God to bring rain in its season (10:1–2), the prophet proclaims: "My anger is hot against the shepherds, and I will punish the leaders; for the LORD of hosts cares for his flock, the house of Judah."

To deny the people the right to use these traditionally sanctioned high places was a dangerous undertaking, as Hezekiah discovered in 701 BCE during the siege of Jerusalem by the Assyrians. The enemy ambassador, "the Rabshakeh," included in his charges against Judah's king that Yahweh had sent the Assyrians to punish Hezekiah because he had removed God's "high places and altars," telling the people they must "worship before this altar in Jerusalem" (2 Kings 18:22). It is possible that the Assyrian diplomat was addressing his charges to the many "northerners" who had escaped the destruction of Samaria and who would have had a greater attachment to the high places that they had known in Israel (Barrick 1996: 638–39). If the Rabshakeh's remarks were effective at the end of the eighth century, it seems quite likely that two hundred years earlier Jeroboam's decision to sanction the use of traditional altars and places of worship was a wise political move designed to obtain the loyalty of the people, most of whom lived in small villages (Zevit 2001: 449). He must have realized that as long as his government was not overly aggressive in imposing change upon the daily lives of the people, they would support him and his new government (Knight 1995: 105–7).

Of course, political expediency was not a sound argument for the Deuteronomistic Historian or for the prophets, who regularly condemned the use of high places. For them, Jerusalem was the place where God's name dwelt, and no other shrine was acceptable as a center for worship. Any king who did not subscribe to their view that Yahweh is the only God and that Yahweh had chosen Jerusalem as the only sanctioned place where the Deity could be worshiped (see Solomon's dedicatory speech

High Places Condemned

Deuteronomy 12:1–7—The ideal of proper Yahweh worship is set by the Deuteronomistic Historian. The people must "demolish completely all the places where the nations . . . served their gods, on the mountain heights, on the hills, and under every leafy tree." They must not worship in these places, but instead bring their sacrifices to "the place that the LORD your God will choose . . . to put his name there" (that is, Jerusalem).

Jeremiah 2:20; 3:6—Jeremiah charged the people with bursting their covenantal bonds, serving other gods: "On every high hill and under every green tree you sprawled and played the whore." As is so often the case, idolatry is equated with infidelity.

Jeremiah 17:1–4—The prophet warns the people of Judah that by their own decision to construct horned altars and sacred poles "on the high hills" they have condemned themselves and negated their covenantal heritage.

Ezekiel 6:2–6—Ezekiel is instructed to prophesy against the high places, saying God will destroy them, leaving their altars desolate and their incense stands broken. He will heap corpses up before their idols, and their towns and high places shall be ruined.

Hosea 10:8—The prophet predicts that "the high places of Aven, the sin of Israel, shall be destroyed. Thorn and thistle shall grow up on their altars."

Amos 7:9—Having determined the extent of Israel's sin, God promises that "the high places of Isaac shall be made desolate, and the sanctuaries of Israel shall be laid waste."

in 1 Kings 8:16–21) was a failure and a source of evil for the nation as a whole (Boshoff 2000: 26).

Revised Religious Calendar

By changing the religious calendar, Jeroboam's intention may have been (1) to forestall the people's desire to make their religious pilgrimage to Jerusalem and (2) to increase his popularity by adjusting the cultic calendar to better reflect the realities of the agricultural year in the northern kingdom. The climactic conditions were slightly different between the northern and southern portions of the country, and as a result farmers could find that they were required to travel to Jerusalem with their "firstfruits" for the Festival of Sukkot before the appropriate moment had arrived for them to harvest their fields. Jeroboam's decree "freed the northern cult with its agricultural holidays from the southern agricultural season" (Zevit 2001: 450). In addition, by adjusting the dates for major harvest festivals like Sukkot and calling on his people to come to Bethel instead (see Amos 5:5 and 8:14 for the use of alternative shrines), Jeroboam enabled the people to fulfill their cultic obligation without having to set foot in Judah or Jerusalem (Fleming 1999: 172).

Jeroboam and the "Man of God" from Judah: 1 Kings 13

One final scene in the Jeroboam narrative that needs to be analyzed is the confrontation between the king and an unnamed prophet from Judah. The scene in 1 Kings 13:1 follows quite smoothly from 12:33, which mentions Jeroboam's intention to go up to Bethel to burn incense. It also encompasses all that the king had done on his own initiative to separate the northern kingdom from Judah and Jerusalem: dedication of a royal shrine and the determination of the time for the Sukkot festival (Toews 1993: 100–101). As the king revels in his exercise of power, a confrontation occurs when the "man of God" from Judah appears and conducts a desecration ritual aimed at the Bethel shrine. His oracle is directed at the altar and is a snub of Jeroboam's cultic role. By initially ignoring the king, the narrator employs one aspect of a "motif of opposition" to Jeroboam's kingship (Walsh 1989: 358). However, the prediction of the altar's destruction in Josiah's reign can easily be separated from the rest of the narrative (vv. 2–3, 5). This section is most likely an editorial intrusion designed to justify Josiah's demolition and desecration of the cultic site as he attempted to revive Israelite nationalism in the reaction to the demise of the Assyrian Empire (2 Kings 23:15–20; De Vries 1985: 170; Dozeman 1981: 383).

It is only when Jeroboam stretches out his arm in verse 4, gesturing at the prophet, that the audience is drawn into the human confron-

Confrontations at Cultic Sites

In analyzing the effect that a speech has on its audience, one of the most important factors to consider is where it takes place (Lincoln 1994: 7–9). Many of the confrontations that take place between a prophet and a king are staged at cultic sites. Thus Jeroboam's confrontation with the prophet from Judah gains greater significance from its setting at the royal shrine of Bethel. This clearly ties their conflict to obedience to the covenant and calls on God as a witness to the proceedings.

Elijah—To graphically display for the people who truly is their God, Elijah confronts King Ahab and successfully challenges the 450 prophets of Baal and the 400 prophets of Asherah to a contest on Mount Carmel (1 Kings 18:17–40). Since this story is set in the northern kingdom, it is not surprising that the contest is staged on a "high place" that had an "altar of Yahweh" (v. 30) on its summit.

Jeremiah—In order to more effectively challenge Jerusalem's people to return to the covenant and not rely on the temple to save them from the Babylonians, Jeremiah stands in the gate of the temple (Jer. 7 and 26). He later has his friend and scribe Baruch read a scroll of his prophecies within the temple precincts, further tying the fate of Jerusalem and its temple to the people's willingness to "turn from their evil ways" (36:1–10).

Amos—The prophet is sent from Judah to Israel to condemn Bethel and to warn the people to end their oppression of the poor and weak. He has a confrontation with the priest Amaziah for prophesying words of doom for King Jeroboam II and Israel within the precincts of the temple at Bethel (Amos 7:10–17).

tation. Like Amaziah, the priest of Bethel who is irritated by Amos's message in the eighth century (Amos 7:10–13), Jeroboam is outraged that his dedicatory ceremony at Bethel has been interrupted. His peremptory gesture is probably just a signal to his guards to remove the troublemaker. The miraculous withering of the king's arm (v. 4b) is the direct result of Jeroboam's discounting the prophet's words. This parallels the pattern of events found in the Elijah/Elisha cycle of stories in which a person (or persons) who fails to give proper respect to the Lord's representative is slain or wounded (see 2 Kings 1:9–16; 2:23–24; 5:19b–27).

Stunned by the power displayed by the prophet, Jeroboam pleads with him to pray to "the LORD your God" to heal his arm. This is an acknowledgment of the prophet's authority and a curious response by Jeroboam, who, presumably, had been about to offer incense on the altar to Yahweh. Perhaps in this way the Deuteronomistic Historian is able to further portray the Israelite king as both an idolater (the golden calves in 1 Kings 12:28) as well as a "foreigner," someone cast out of the covenantal community (Van Winkle 1995: 110; Cohn 1985: 31). It also echoes the pleas of the pharaoh during the plague sequence in Exodus when he calls on Moses to "pray for me" in order to end the devastating plagues in Egypt (Exod. 8:8, 28; 9:28; 10:16–17; 12:32).

When Jeroboam's arm is healed, he is grateful and is also obligated to reciprocate for this kindness. He invites the prophet to "come home with me and dine, and I will give you a gift" (1 Kings 13:7). This invitation fits well into the protocol of hospitality (see Gen. 18:3–5; Matthews 1991a: 13–15). The protocol, however, does allow the "guest" to refuse an invitation without infringing on the honor of either party, if there is a need to move on or some abiding reason that transcends the granting of the favor of acceptance (Matthews 1991a: 14). In this case, the prophet bases his refusal on a previous command from Yahweh that he "not eat food, or drink water, or return by the way that you came" (1 Kings 13:9). As is made clear later in the chapter, the prophet's response is an expression of the need for absolute obedience to the command of God (Gross 1978: 129) and is a further reinforcement of the magnitude of Jeroboam's sin (Van Winkle 1995: 106, 112). The force with which the prophet refuses Jeroboam's hospitality, however, does seem a bit excessive: even "if you give me half your kingdom, I will not go in with you" (v. 8). What could be the reason for such a firm and categorical refusal?

One possible explanation for the prophet's statement may be an unwillingness to become a partner in Jeroboam's gift-giving strategy (Matthews 1999: 99–100). The king has already been shamed in a public ceremony, maimed, and then forced to plead with the prophet for assistance. He has been so severely dishonored by these events that it will be nearly impossible to recoup his losses. If, however, Jeroboam can get the prophet to come to his house and accept his hospitality, it will be a public demonstration of his generosity and his willingness to transform an enemy into a guest. It is also possible that within the public mind the power manifested by the prophet's words and his healing ability could then be associated with Jeroboam's regime. This would actually legitimize the king's cultic actions at Bethel and give a political boost to the separatist northern kingdom. Then the road between Bethel and Jerusalem would be open for travel, and both cultic sites would be legitimized in the eyes of all the people (Boer 1996: 174).

By so firmly turning down Jeroboam's gift of hospitality, the prophet obeys God's command and publicly discounts Jeroboam's political ambitions. Like Daniel, who refused Belshazzar's offer to be elevated to a "rank third in the kingdom" (Dan. 5:16–17), the "man of God" will not in any way sanction this illegitimate shrine or Jeroboam's rule. He will not allow himself or Yahweh to be used in this manner, and thus it is mandatory that he refuse to "break bread" with the king (Walsh 1989: 358). The prophet, who had proven his status as a "true prophet" by healing the king, is safe in doing this according to the principle of prophetic immunity (see Jer. 26:12–15). Furthermore, according to the protocol of hospitality, Jeroboam cannot refuse to let him go on his way. Unfortunately, the prophet later comes to a bad end when he ignores his instructions and accepts the invitation of the prophet of Bethel to share a meal (1 Kings 13:11–32). This companion episode, however, has more to do with the prophet's disobedience to God's command than to the political fortunes of Jeroboam.

Succession by Assassination

Despite being condemned by a prophet for his actions, Jeroboam, like Saul, is not immediately removed from his throne. However, because the northern kingdom does not have the benefit of an "everlasting covenant" to protect the monarchs from rebels and assassins, the history of Israel from 900 BCE until its destruction by the Assyrians in 721 BCE is filled with political intrigue and unrest. The prediction of the prophet Ahijah in 1 Kings 14:7–11 provides the political backdrop to the elimination of many of its kings through violence. It is the first of several similar examples of a prophet designating God's choice of successor in the northern kingdom and the subsequent removal of a ruling family from the throne (see the sidebar on the next page).

What is particularly telling in these narratives about Israel's kings is the lack of hesitation on the part of individuals who hope to supplant them on the throne. David was quite adamant when he had the opportunity to slay Saul that he would not harm the "Lord's anointed" (see 1 Sam. 24:4–7; 26:5–12), and he was equally consistent in punishing those who raised their hands against Saul or his sons (see 2 Sam. 1:12–16; 4:5–12). In the northern kingdom, any general who felt he had sufficient control of the army could, and often did, rebel against his master.

The frequency of this rebelliousness is justified to an extent in the account as fulfillment of the curses prophets heaped on unfaithful kings. In each case, God uses a prophet to declare judgment on the offending royal house. They are all accused of "walking in the way of Jeroboam" and are threatened with the horrible curse of lying unburied and having their entire household murdered by their successor. The language is so similar in each of these cases that it is obviously standardized as part of the scribal shorthand used in the summaries of the kings. It also serves to reinforce the political and theological message of the Deuteronomistic Historian that (1) the only legitimate royal house is David's and (2) only the temple in Jerusalem can function as the legitimate seat of Yahweh's power and cult (Holder 1988: 27–28).

Political Unrest in Israel

Ahijah—When Jeroboam's infant son is brought to the prophet, Ahijah accuses the king of failing to be "like my servant David, who kept my commandments" (1 Kings 14:5–8). He exclaims that because the king has done evil, including casting idols and thrusting God's word "behind your back," God will "consume the house of Jeroboam," allowing their bodies to lie unburied as food for dogs and birds (14:9–11). Subsequently, a conspirator named Baasha kills Jeroboam's son Nadab in battle and then kills all the members of Jeroboam's house, fulfilling Ahijah's prophecy (15:27–30).

Jehu son of Hanani—This prophet received God's word of judgment on Baasha, saying the king had been "exalted out of the dust and made leader over Israel" and yet had "walked in the way of Jeroboam." For these crimes, God "will consume Baasha and his house," again leaving their bodies to be eaten by dogs and birds (1 Kings 16:1–4). Fulfilling the prophecy, a chariot commander named Zimri kills Baasha's son Elah and all of Baasha's household (16:8–13). Zimri, however, survives only seven days and is overthrown in turn by another army commander named Omri (16:15–19).

Elijah—After Jezebel obtains Naboth's field for her royal husband Ahab by having Naboth executed on false charges, Elijah confronts the king with the now familiar curse that God will "cut off from Ahab every male," making his household "like the house of Jeroboam and the house of Baasha," leaving their unburied bodies to be eaten by dogs and birds (1 Kings 21:17–24).

Elisha—To fulfill Elijah's curse against Ahab, Elisha sends one of the "sons of the prophets" to an army commander named Jehu. He is to anoint Jehu in the same manner that Saul and David had been anointed king and announce that Jehu is to "strike down the house of your master Ahab" in order to make it "like the house of Jeroboam . . . and the house of Baasha" (2 Kings 9:1–10). Jehu accomplishes this task by killing Joram in battle (9:14–15) and then massacring all of Ahab's descendants (10:1–7).

Conclusion

Whether all of Jeroboam's actions actually represent new reforms or play upon already existing conditions in Israel cannot be readily proven. Some suggest that Jeroboam simply takes advantage of religious traditions that already existed in Israel and shapes them to fit his political aims (Ash 1998: 24). If this is the case, then the Deuteronomistic Historian is condemning idolatrous and cultic practices in Jeroboam's day while actually aiming vitriol at an audience in the late seventh century BCE. The argument is also made that the Deuteronomistic Historian is using an ancient Near Eastern motif of the "evil ruler," whose crimes are the cause for the destruction of his own dynasty and the nation (Evans 1983). Whatever the case, the stamp that the editor puts on the royal annals displays a clear theological and political agenda designed to strengthen the position of the Davidic monarchy and Jerusalem.

Taking into account the various versions of these events that must have existed during the period of the monarchy and afterward, the Deuteronomistic Historian subsequently judges the reigns of all kings, of both Israel and Judah, on whether they continued the "sin of Jeroboam." In their editing of the material, the king's shrines in the northern kingdom at Dan and Bethel as well as the local high places, the non-Levitical priesthood, and the revision of the festival year celebrations are condemned, and Jerusalem as the place where God's name dwells is given even more prestige. Nearly all political events in the northern kingdom are minimized or polemicized despite the historical, political, and economic importance of the north in relation to Judah on the ancient world scale. Of course, the northern kingdom will also be conquered and destroyed in 721 BCE, providing the basis for the claims that "following the way of Jeroboam" can lead only to God's wrath and national oblivion.

Samaria Falls to the Assyrians

Tis is the story of the death of a nation. One might envision a bold headline in the Jerusalem newspaper heralding the terrible message: "Samaria falls to the Assyrians!" Some would see this event as a potential threat to Judah and Jerusalem, since the Assyrians had already put a heavy burden of tribute payments on them, and the rampaging nature of the Assyrian army was well known to the people of the ancient Near East. Judah could easily be next on the Assyrians' list of conquests. At the same time other voices, prophets among them, explain Samaria's fall as a direct result of the "sin of Jeroboam." According to their interpretation, that king's policies had allowed Israel to engage in idolatrous practices and ignore their covenantal obligations.

The fall of Israel's capital city to the Assyrian king Sargon II in 721 BCE raises other questions: What lasting effect will this have on the remaining kingdom of Judah? With the majority of the people from the northern kingdom deported and settled into some other portion of the vast Assyrian Empire, who will inhabit the territory of the former kingdom of Israel? Certainly this event and the potential for demographic change mark a critical point for the people as a whole. They now must realize that nations can die, even if they have been part of the covenant community.

How is this event explained by prophets, priests, and kings? Did Yahweh fail to protect a people who are part of the covenant community, or have they been justly punished for their disobedience? What are the implications for the southern kingdom of Judah? Its leaders and people have also been charged by the prophets with failure to uphold the covenant. Will they respond to the call to take heed and return to obedience to God, or will they trust in the presence of the temple in Jerusalem to save them?

Historically, Samaria's fall also represents the beginning of what is known as the Diaspora, the "scattering" of the Israelite people. Many of the exiles will be assimilated into the new cultures that surround them. For those who choose to remain loyal to their God and to the covenant, the transformations in their national identity that will occur as a result of this displacement will lead to the next stage in their cultural development.

Historical Overview

About 800 BCE the Assyrian Empire conquered and absorbed Israel's chief political and economic rival, Syria, but then the Assyrians temporarily stopped their advance while they consolidated their gains (Matthews 2002: 70–75). As a result both Israel and Judah took advantage of the situation and expanded their economic interests in Transjordan. This provided a period of prosperity for the nobility and the merchant class during the first half of the eighth century BCE, but given the charges made against "those who feel secure on Mount Samaria" (Amos 6:1), it apparently also created a false sense of security.

Political unrest rose to new levels when King Jeroboam II of Israel died in 750. His immediate successors, Zechariah and Shallum, were assassinated after reigning just six months and one month, respectively (2 Kings 15:8–14). The next king, Menahem, was forced to pay heavy tribute to the Assyrian monarch Tiglath-pileser III in 738 BCE to "help him confirm his hold on the royal power" (15:19–20). When Menahem's successor, Pekahiah, was assassinated after only two years by one of his military commanders, Pekah, Israel was obviously slipping into political chaos and would soon succumb to the military might of the Assyrians, despite efforts to ally with Egypt (Hosea 7:11–16).

Compounding the political tensions in this period was a struggle for power during the 730s between Israel and Judah, sparked by the ambitions of the re-emergent rulers of Syria (Aram) to break away from the Assyrian Empire. The instability caused by what became known as the Syro-Ephraimite War, described in Isaiah 7:1–9 and 2 Kings 16:5–9, is further evidence for the claim that almost continual border disputes

Annals of Tiglath-pileser III (744–727 BCE)

They overthrew their king Pekah and I placed Hoshea as king over them. I received from them 10 talents of gold, 1,000 (?) talents of silver as their tribute and brought them to Assyria. (Pritchard 1969: 284)

occurred from the time of the division of the kingdoms to the end of the eighth century (Tomes 1993: 70). Thus when Judah's King Ahaz was pressured by the political ambitions of Israel and Syria, he appealed for assistance to the Assyrian emperor Tiglath-pileser III. Quick to deal with the potential threat of a general revolt by these border states, an Assyrian campaign against Damascus relieved the pressure on Judah. One could even say that the heavy tribute Ahaz paid for Assyrian assistance saved his people from aggression by his neighbors and therefore could be termed an effective diplomatic maneuver by both sides (Parker 1996: 220). However, the biblical account suggests that the Edomites took advantage of the situation to regain control of Elath, the vital trade link to the Gulf of Aqabah (2 Kings 16:6). It is also quite likely that Judah was bled dry by Assyrian demands for tribute.

Meanwhile Israel continued its spiral into political chaos. The Assyrian Annals contain a record of Israel's final years. The Assyrian king Tiglath-pileser III deposed Pekah for his disloyalty to the empire and placed Hoshea on the throne (2 Kings 15:29–30). The heavy burden of tribute payments stripped Israel of much of its resources and may have made them desperate enough to revolt in the 720s. These periodic revolts seem misguided in retrospect, but few nations envision their own demise. As Isaiah 9:8–10 reports, the people of Samaria were overconfident in believing in the indestructibility of their nation. They relied on Yahweh to save them no matter the circumstances and took no heed of the warning signs. In their pride, they boasted about rebuilding and replanting without attention to their covenant violations (Schmitt 1995: 362; see Amos 6:1 for another attack on this attitude).

The military campaigns that brought an end to the northern kingdom of Israel and its capital of Samaria are recorded in various Assyrian documents, the Babylonian Chronicle, and 2 Kings 17:3–6 and 18:9–12. The last king of Israel, Hoshea, was confirmed on Israel's throne by Tiglath-pileser III about 732 BCE, and he remained loyal until about 723, when the Egyptians convinced him to revolt (2 Kings 17:4). The Assyrian emperor Shalmaneser V then responded to his rebellion, as recorded in the Babylonian Chronicle, and "ravaged Samaria" (Grayson 1975: 73).

Assyrian Annals of Sargon II

The ruler of Samaria, in conspiracy with another king, defaulted on his taxes and declared Samaria's independence from Assyria [2 Kings 17:4–6]. With the strength given me by the divine assembly, I conquered Samaria and its covenant partner, and took . . . prisoners of war [2 Kings 17:23; 18:11]. . . . I conscripted enough prisoners to outfit fifty teams of chariots. I rebuilt Samaria, bigger and better than before. I repopulated it with people from other states which I had conquered, and I appointed one of my officials over them, and made them Assyrian citizens. (Matthews and Benjamin 1997: 175)

In 722 Hoshea was captured by the Assyrians and held hostage throughout the remaining two years of the siege of the city of Samaria. There is no record of a new king of Israel being crowned during the siege, and it is likely the Assyrians had already begun the administrative changes designed to transform Israel from a vassal state into a province (Hayes and Kuan 1991: 164–66). The length of the siege of Samaria was prolonged by the death of Shalmaneser V in 722 and the multiple revolts throughout the Assyrian Empire at the accession of Sargon II. Despite this regime change, the Assyrians did not withdraw from their positions (Hayes and Kuan 1991: 162) but remained in place, blockading Samaria and slowly starving it until the defenders could no longer resist and the city fell in 721 BCE.

Unlike many of the cities conquered by the Assyrians during this time, the archaeological record at Samaria has not, to this point, provided evidence of a total razing of the city (Younger 1999: 474–75). While such a demonstration of Assyrian power would have been awe inspiring, the most important aspect of this conquest was the deportation of the people and the political demise of the northern kingdom. The survivors of the siege were taken prisoner, and eventually much of the Israelite population was taken as exiles to a faraway portion of the Assyrian Empire. Extrabiblical accounts of these events indicate that the biblical record compressed what was actually a series of political decisions and separate deportations into a single, devastating departure for the Israelites (Younger 1998: 215–19). The deportation of a large segment of Israel's population also served as the origin story of the "Ten Lost Tribes of Israel," as these people disappeared from history over the next two centuries.

The Israelites who were deported by the Assyrian king were scattered throughout the empire, into both urban and rural settings (2 Kings 17:6). They were resettled as part of an imperial policy to eliminate future revolts by removing rebels from their homeland and mixing them with other exiled groups and the indigenous population (Becking 1992: 82). This policy aided the Assyrian economy by reopening arable land to cultivation in previously devastated areas. It also helped to bolster the population in cities crucial to the protection of the empire's borders (Oded 1979: 67–74). The exiles' presence in Mesopotamia is confirmed by lists of West Semitic names found in Assyrian economic documents (Becking 1992: 80–83; Oded 2000: 92–99). In fact, Israelite names continue to appear in Assyrian economic and military documents throughout the seventh century (Zadok 1988: 304), and there are "Samarian" members of the Assyrian army listed in Sargon II's records (Younger 1998: 219–21; Dalley 1985: 41). These records indicate that some Israelites resisted assimilation to Mesopotamian culture, at least to the extent of retaining their West Semitic personal names. The memory of these people remained alive for several centuries (see the mention of Israelite exiles in the deuterocanonical book of Tobit), but there is no way to trace whether any returned to their homeland.

One can surmise that Judah received reports and even eyewitness accounts of the fall of Samaria from survivors who fled south. The event coincided with King Hezekiah's sixth year (2 Kings 18:10) and may have strengthened his resolve to find a better solution to the Assyrian crisis. He was accorded the honor bestowed on very few kings of having done "what was right in the sight of the LORD just as his ancestor David had done" (18:3). As a result, he gained the respect of both the Deuteronomistic Historian and the prophet Isaiah.

What Hezekiah faced was the transformation of Samaria into an Assyrian province. It was repopulated with new groups from elsewhere in their empire, who mixed with the few remaining Israelites in the area (Oded 1979: 66; 2 Kings 17:24). A fair assumption is that many of the people of Israel fled south during the last days of the kingdom, taking with them their traditions and their memories of the shocking events that had destroyed their homeland. Presumably, the tales told by these fleeing refugees of the invincibility of the Assyrian troops were confirmed by those who actually had seen the destruction wrought by these fierce plunderers (Broshi 1978: 12). This must have impressed the people and rulers of Judah and suggested to them that they were also in grave danger (Machinist 1983: 722). Events throughout the rest of the eighth century would prove this to be a correct assumption as Judah struggled to stay alive. Hezekiah would have his hands full protecting what he could of his nation, and his successors, particularly Manasseh, would be forced into quiet submission to Assyrian rule (2 Kings 21:1–18).

The Case against Israel

The roots of Israel's demise, according to the Deuteronomistic Historian and several of the prophets, are planted in the division of the kingdom and in "Jeroboam's sin" (2 Kings 17:21–23; see chap. 5 above). The effort on the part of the first king of Israel to create rival shrines for Yahweh worship within his own kingdom and thus to diminish Jerusalem's importance as the central cultic site could never be forgiven by his critics in the south. Furthermore, his willingness to sanction the use of images, such as the golden calves installed at Dan and Bethel, provided the basis for charges of infidelity and clear violations of the covenant (1 Kings 12:25–33). This will become a common theme in the prophets, who equate idolatry with infidelity (see Hosea 2:2–13). Finally, the use of non-Levitical priests, whose appointment was based on loyalty

---

Terms Used for the Northern Kingdom

The prophets employ a number of different terms for the northern kingdom of Israel. Modern readers should be aware of them and be able to make the same connection that was clear to the ancient audience.

Israel—a political term used after the division of the united monarchy and prior to the fall of Samaria for the northern kingdom (1 Kings 12:20–2 Kings 17:23). After 721 BCE, "Israel" is used as a collective term for all the Israelites once again, whether they come from the north or the south (Ps. 81:8; Isa. 43:1; Mal. 1:1).

Joseph—as Jacob's favorite son, the tradition of the Joseph tribes (his twin sons Manasseh and Ephraim) as politically equivalent to all the northern kingdom occurs a number of times (Ezek. 37:16; Amos 5:6; Obad. 18).

Ephraim—twin son of Joseph whose name becomes synonymous with the northern kingdom, presumably because this tribe came to dominate all the others (Isa. 7:8; Hosea 9:8).

Jacob—since ten of the tribes descended from Jacob made up the northern kingdom and the southern kingdom was associated with Jacob's son Judah, this usage makes sense geographically and politically (Isa. 2:5–6; 10:20; Mic. 2:12). There is evidence after 721 BCE of its usage for all Israelites (Ps. 14:7; Nah. 2:2; Mal. 3:6).

Samaria—as the capital of the northern kingdom, Samaria is also used to designate the entire nation (Galil 1995: 54; Isa. 36:19).

to the king rather than adherence to the law or allegiance to Jerusalem, created antagonisms with the displaced Levites in the northern kingdom and led to numerous condemnations of kings and priests (see Amos 7:10–17). All of these factors combined with the natural jealousies that existed between the two states (especially with the relative wealth and prosperity enjoyed by Israel with its kinder climate, greater abundance of natural resources, and proximity to international trade routes) to create tensions that led to periodic border disputes and a rivalry in which each would claim to be "God's chosen."

Negative Rhetoric

A prime example of the negative rhetoric employed in the account of Israel's kings is found in the description of King Ahab (1 Kings 16:31–34). The long list of charges made against him far outweighs those of all other kings of Israel, except for Jeroboam (Schniedewind 1993: 651–53). Thus Ahab not only is said (1) to "walk in the sins of Jeroboam son of Nebat," but also (2) he marries Jezebel, the daughter of the king of Sidon, thereby repeating Solomon's error of marrying foreign women (1 Kings 11:1–13), who bring their own culture and religion to Israel, and (3) he acquiesces in worshiping her god Baal by erecting an altar to Baal "in the house of Baal, which he built in Samaria," and also by putting up a sacred Asherah pole, which provokes God's anger (see its prohibition in Deut. 16:21). Not content with labeling him as the worst of "all the kings of Israel," the editor goes on to say that Ahab activated the ancient curse that Joshua had laid on anyone who rebuilt the gates of Jericho (see Josh. 6:26). The intent of the passage is to so utterly condemn the king that it would be a relief to the people to see him defeated and slain for his evil deeds (see the regnal summary in 1 Kings 22:37–40). The implication is also clear, however, that the nation will be punished for the sins committed by Ahab and the other kings of Israel who had disdained their responsibility to God and the covenant.

A more complete analysis of the fate of the northern kingdom than that contained in the list of sins provided in Ahab's regnal summary is found in 2 Kings 17. After a terse account of the events of 722–721 (17:5–6), there is an extensive list of the infractions committed by the unnamed northern kings, which serves as the basis for the defeat of Israel by the Assyrians (17:7–22). It is possible that this narrative developed over time as a succession of editors drew upon their own explanations for this devastating event (Brettler 1989: 281). Since this narrative unit also mentions Judah's demise (17:13, 19–20), its final editing and insertion into the chronicle took place in the postexilic period (Becking 2000: 216).

An Indictment of the Nations

In an extended indictment of the nation and its leaders in 2 Kings 17, the Deuteronomistic Historian provides a list of charges against the people of the covenant that justifies their destruction at the hands of the Assyrians and Babylonians. Prophets and postexilic editors repeat these same charges in later indictments. The arguments made here are designed to present a progression from God showing favor to God expressing wrath (Becking 2000: 219).

1. Despite God's efforts to rescue them from Egypt, they had chosen to worship other gods (2 Kings 17:7). Compare similar charges in Jeremiah 2:4–8.
2. They walked in the customs of the nations that the Lord had driven out before the people of Israel and in the customs that the kings of Israel had introduced (2 Kings 17:8). Compare the warning in Jeremiah 10:2–5.
3. Despite God's blessings, they secretly built high places at all their towns (2 Kings 17:9). See Hosea 4:13; 10:8; and Amos 7:9 for the condemning of high places.
4. They set up pillars and sacred poles "on every high hill and under every green tree" (2 Kings 17:10). See the parallel expression in Jeremiah 2:20 and 3:6.
5. They made offerings on these unsanctioned high places in the manner of other nations (2 Kings 17:11). See similar charges in Jeremiah 1:16; 7:18; 10:2.
6. They violated the Decalogue (Exod. 20:4–5) by worshiping idols (2 Kings 17:12). See Jeremiah 7:9 and Ezekiel 8:6–12.
7. They would not heed the words of warning from God's prophets to turn from their evil ways and keep the commandments (2 Kings 17:13–14). Compare Jeremiah 6:17; 26:5–6; and Ezekiel 3:7.
8. Despising God's commandments, they worshiped false idols, "followed the nations," cast images of two calves, made a

The obvious redundancy of this passage in 2 Kings 17 is typical of what is referred to as "resumptive repetition," in which single ideas or thoughts are expressed and then made a refrain or repeated in summary form. What is interesting to note is the way in which the ideology of the nation's fall is formulated, based on events that begin with the division of the kingdom and that encompass the policies and practices of kings like Ahab of Israel and Manasseh of Judah, who brought destruction on their nations. Throughout this narrative the editors clearly contrast the graciousness of God in relation to the sinfulness of the people (Viviano 1987: 550).

sacred pole, worshiped "the host of heaven," and served Baal (2 Kings 17:15–16). This indictment closely parallels the one made against Manasseh (21:2–9). No similar list exists in the records of the northern kings (Brettler 1989: 275), but some of these charges are made against Ahab in 1 Kings 16:32–33.

9. They "made their sons and their daughters pass through the fire; they used divination and augury; and they sold themselves to do evil in the sight of the LORD" (2 Kings 17:17). Compare the similar charge made against Manasseh (21:6) and Jeremiah's indictment of false worship practices (Jer. 19:4–5).

10. They broke away from Davidic rule, making Jeroboam their king, and then continued in all of his sins (2 Kings 17:21–22). This contrasts with 1 Kings 11:11–13, in which God acts to tear the kingdom away from Solomon's son and appoints Jeroboam (Brettler 1989: 278). It is also suggestive of Hosea's complaint that the people "make kings, but not through me" (Hosea 8:4).

The generally negative evaluation of Israel's kings in the Deuteronomistic History is tempered occasionally, but only because of a humbling or submissive act by one of the kings. Thus even Ahab receives a temporary reprieve when he impresses God with his abject repentance after being condemned for benefiting from the "judicial murder" of his neighbor Naboth (1 Kings 21:27–29). In this instance, however, the editor employs a literary device known as the "king's call to justice," which demonstrates that kings are not above the law and that they will be judged by a sovereign God, who will determine their fate and the fate of their dynasty (Matthews 1991b: 206).

An example of the mixed evaluations given to kings is found in the story of King Jehoahaz of Israel (2 Kings 13:1–9). This portion of the royal annals is reminiscent in tone of the "Judges cycle" and the episodes found in Judges 3–16 (also an editorial creation of the Deuteronomistic Historian). The Judges cycle provides a common literary framework for the otherwise unrelated stories in Judges (Matthews 2004b: 8–9). The basic structure of the framework follows this sequence: (1) disobedience to the covenant, which (2) causes God to allow the Israelite tribes to be oppressed by their neighbors, which in turn is followed by (3) repentance on their part. This then (4) causes God to raise up a judge, who relieves the people of their oppressors, but (5) when the judge dies, the people once again fall into disobedience, and the cycle begins again.

A rather transparent example of this pattern appears in the Jehoahaz narrative. The king is first condemned in the typical fashion as a ruler who "followed the sins of Jeroboam" (2 Kings 13:2). This, in turn, "kindled" God's anger against Israel, allowing them to be harassed repeatedly by King Hazael of Aram and his son (13:3). When Jehoahaz prays for God's assistance, Yahweh acknowledges their need, "for he saw the oppression of Israel" by Aram. The reassuring idea of God seeing the people's need can be compared to the story of Moses' call (Exod. 3:7), in which God tells the Israelite hero: "I have observed the misery of my people. . . . I know their sufferings." In each of the instances found in Judges and Kings, the theological message is that God has justly punished the people but will not abandon them forever. Either God will take a hand directly, as was the case in the exodus event, by giving "Israel a savior" (2 Kings 13:5a), or God will provide the needed military leadership when the people acknowledge Yahweh's ability to help them (see this same theme in Isa. 19:20).

With God's assistance, Jehoahaz is able to lift the "hand of the Arameans" from his people, and they are allowed to live in peace for a time (2 Kings 13:5). That was not the end of the story, however. The narrative pattern continues, even in the face of this evidence of divine blessing, for Jehoahaz did not "depart from the sins of the house of Jeroboam," for the "sacred pole also remained in Samaria" (13:6).

Perhaps it is the inability of the rulers of Israel to break away from the "sins of Jeroboam" that eventually makes it impossible for God to withhold the punishment they so richly deserve. A growing sense of frustration is voiced in the words of the prophets during the eighth century. While some, like Hosea, still plead with the people and suggest that there is time to repent, others, like Amos, see little chance for change and instead concentrate on justifying the coming disaster.

Prophets in Judah also lay out the case for Israel's destruction. Among them is the late-eighth-century, rural prophet Micah. He is quite explicit

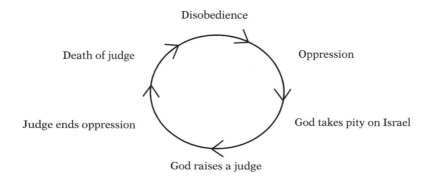

Eighth-Century Prophetic Voices

Amos—This prophet comes from Judah to the king's sanctuary at Bethel and engages in a series of scathing attacks against the rulers and priests of Israel. One can sense that Amos sees the absolute need for strong measures that will wipe away the causes of the people's disobedience.

Amos 3:9–15—Since the rulers of Israel "do not know how to do right," the prophet calls on the Assyrian garrisons in Ashdod and the Egyptians to be witnesses to the ravaging of the land and the plundering of its strongholds, which will leave only a sad remnant of the people to scavenge amid the ruins (Andersen and Freedman 1989: 373–74). Their "altars of Bethel" will be broken in pieces (3:14), and the proud "houses of ivory" owned by the wealthy will be torn down (3:15). The complacency of the ruling class is further denounced in Amos 4:1 and 6:1 for their elitist practices and inattention to the words of the prophets (Schmitt 1995: 358).

Amos 6:1–7—One ploy used by prophets suggests to their audience that they "go and see" what God has done to other cities or nations as an example to them of their own fate (see Isa. 20:6; Jer. 7:12–15). Amos warns Israel that its cities are no better than those in Syria that have already been destroyed by the Assyrians.

Hosea—Though he has more sympathy for the fate of his own people in Israel than Amos did, Hosea is still quick to condemn their unfaithfulness, especially their idolatry.

Hosea 4:15–19—The prophet charges Israel with "playing the whore" and with being "a stubborn heifer" that is "joined to idols" and blind to its drunken, unmindful display. Condemning them for the "sin of Jeroboam," Hosea predicts that they will be shamed because of their altars and false worship. Direct references to the cultic use of a calf image are found in Hosea 8:5: "Your calf is rejected, O Samaria"; and 10:5: "The inhabitants of Samaria tremble for the calf of Beth-aven."

Hosea 5:3–9—Citing Israel's pride and Ephraim's whoring, Hosea charges that because the people "do not know the LORD" (5:4), God "has withdrawn from them" (5:6). As a result, "Ephraim shall become a desolation" (5:9).

Hosea 7:1–11—In a series of baking metaphors, Hosea details the corruption and false dealing of Ephraim's officials and kings. The conspirators who regularly plot to overthrow "our king" (7:7) are like the walls of an oven heated to the point that bread will bake without further stoking (MacIntosh 1997: 258–59). These "hotheads" (a common image in Egypt, whose Wisdom literature condemns the unthinking, "hotheaded" man) are unmindful of their danger; and unwilling to call on God, they will be devoured by foreigners.

> ## Isaiah's Stages of Israel's Decline
>
> **Yahweh's action**—"sent a word" by a prophet against Jacob "and all the people knew it—Ephraim and the inhabitants of Samaria" (Isa. 9:8–9a). This could be a reference to the message of Amos to Israel (Blenkinsopp 2000: 217–18).
>
> **Israel's reaction**—pride and arrogance led them simply to rebuild and replant without a thought for the cause of destruction (Isa. 9:9b–10; possibly a reference to the earthquake of Amos 1:1).
>
> **Yahweh's action**—"raised adversaries" and "stirred up enemies" from Aram and Philistia to ravage borders and appropriate territory (Isa. 9:11–12; see 2 Kings 14:23–28).
>
> **Israel's reaction**—"did not turn to him who struck them or seek the LORD of hosts"—either not recognizing the source of their troubles or not repenting (Isa. 9:13; compare Amos 4:6–11).
>
> **Yahweh's action**—struck down those in Israel who had led them astray (elders, leaders, and false prophets) and did not take pity on the people, "for everyone was godless and an evildoer" (Isa. 9:14–16).

in his charge that "the transgression of Jacob" is Samaria (Mic. 1:5–6). To cleanse the land of the people's transgressions and their idols (1:7), God will utterly destroy the city, transforming it into a "heap of stones" that will serve as a warning to all who see it (R. L. Smith 1984: 18). Micah's concerns are also with the fate of Judah, since that nation will also be subject to invasion by the Assyrians at the time that Samaria is destroyed. By pairing Samaria and Jerusalem as the cause of the nations' plight, this rural prophetic voice points to the foreign idols installed and worshiped in these cities as the source of the people's and their leaders' folly (Mays 1976: 46–47). Micah's prophetic contemporary, Isaiah, echoes that prophet's condemnation of idolatry. In Isaiah 10:9–11 he lists several destroyed cities, including Samaria, calling them "kingdoms of the idols" and saying, "Shall I not do to Jerusalem and her idols what I have done to Samaria and her images?"

Isaiah also provides a postevent analysis of the stages of Israel's final destruction in his oracle in chapter 9. He portrays God's attempt to warn the nation through the word of the prophets, to jog them into a proper response by causing minor disasters and political troubles, and finally to punish them so severely that there could be no doubt that Yahweh had chosen to end their relationship (without the hope of reconciliation offered in Hosea's marriage metaphor—Hosea 2:14–23).

This pattern of divine intervention is based on the idea that a just God must warn the people so that the righteous remnant among them will be able to respond and survive to restore the nation after it has been punished. In his "poem on divine anger" (Isa. 9:8–21; Blenkinsopp 2000: 215–19), the prophet eventually concludes that all the people are "godless" and evil and therefore God's "anger has not turned away, his hand is stretched out still" (Isa. 5:25; 9:12, 17, 21; 10:4b). Isaiah uses this refrain to tie together the pieces of his oracle, concluding that it is the people's disregard for God's outstretched hand that condemns them to their fate (Brown 1990: 437–39).

Furthermore, in referring to Assyrian aggression during that period, Isaiah points to Israel's failure to maintain the covenant with Yahweh. These unscrupulous judges and officials apply the law in such a way that they oppress the needy, rob the poor, and impoverish the widow (Isa. 10:1–2). These were the protected classes of people in Israelite society (Deut. 26:12–13), and to treat them in this way was a total reversal of covenantal obligation. Figuratively shaking his head at their actions, the prophet asks them: "What will you do on the day of punishment? . . . To whom will you flee for help, and where will you leave your wealth?" (Isa. 10:3; Childs 2001: 86–87). Having judged these people to be without merit, Isaiah explains that Assyria's conquests are simply the "rod of God's anger" (10:5), punishing the unruly and unfaithful. This form of theodicy, or religious justification for God's actions, serves best as a warning to Judah, since Israel's fate is already sealed by this time.

Narrative and Poetic Echoes of Samaria's Fall

Whatever the political, economic, or religious reasons for Samaria's fall at the end of the eighth century BCE, the ripple effect on later traditions (prophetic, historical, or poetic) is enormous. The biblical text contains a range of reactions to this event. Some appear to take the form of accusations centered on the "sin of Jeroboam." For instance, Psalm 78 may, at least in part, have been used in cultic practice to retell the story of Samaria's fall while providing an account of Israel's salvation history. Attempts to date the composition of this psalm to the period of the nationalistic reforms of Hezekiah or Josiah (eighth–seventh century; Junker 1953: 493–98) are problematic, as are those dating it to the postexilic period (Kraus 1989: 124). Since the psalm does not mention the fall of the Jerusalem temple but refers only to the shrine at Shiloh (v. 60), a postexilic date seems less likely (P. Stern 1995: 44–45).

What concerns us here is the statement, in verses 9, 67–72, that God had "rejected the tent of Joseph, he did not choose the tribe of Ephraim." Instead, divine blessing is extended to Mount Zion and to "his servant David" (see this same claim in Ps. 87:2). This could be interpreted as an attempt to discredit the northern kingdom's rulers and its sanctuaries based on their lack of trust in God's direction of the people (Gosling 1999: 513). However, this charge could be made quite effectively during the early history of the northern kingdom or in later periods (see Goulder 1996: 111–12). Certainly, it bolsters the argument that Zion is the only proper place for Yahweh's temple and cultic community to operate. With that in mind, I would suggest that although the text was probably composed during the period of the divided monarchy, the psalm's use in cultic performance during the postexilic period could be based on the efforts being made by the Samaritans to obstruct the rebuilding of the Jerusalem temple (Ezra 4:1–5). In other words, the story of Ephraim's rejection and demise lives on in later contexts.

A certain degree of shock at what seems like a betrayal or failure by God to protect Israel is found in the text as well. Surely there would have been a sense of dread among the people based on their realization of their physical and spiritual vulnerability.

One particularly interesting use of the story of Samaria's demise as a terror tactic is contained in a speech by the Assyrian ambassador, the Rabshakeh (2 Kings 18:19–35). When he stands before the walls of Jerusalem and confronts King Hezekiah's advisors, his evaluation of their dire situation is quick to include the Assyrian victory over Samaria. Of course, his message is a piece of political propaganda designed to intimidate Assyria's enemies. The Assyrians were famous for their psychological ploys, which included massacring entire city garrisons (see the mass grave at Lachish; Ussishkin 1997: 321), piling up corpses, impaling prisoners, and engaging in other atrocities (Bleibtreu 1991). They also boasted of their victories over nations and their gods in their annals and, based on Isaiah 36:16–20, in their negotiations. Thus the Rabshakeh lists a series of points, some of which are designed to taunt Jerusalem's weak military position. He also includes as part of his argument that Hezekiah and Jerusalem should surrender to the Assyrian army (701 BCE), an invitation for them to consider that none of the gods of other countries, including Samaria (Isa. 36:19), "have saved these countries out of my hand," and therefore they should not trust Yahweh to save Jerusalem. Hezekiah's advisors are frightened by the Rabshakeh's arguments and ask him to speak in the diplomatic language of Aramaic rather than the common Hebrew vernacular (Isa. 36:11).

These advisors must have realized that the people of Jerusalem were aware of their danger and were not content to rely on Yahweh to save them. It is not surprising then to find in both the biblical and the Assyrian accounts of the siege of Jerusalem that Hezekiah is forced to pay a huge ransom in order to get the Assyrians to spare Jerusalem (2 Kings 18:13–16; Cogan and Tadmor 1988: 241–44). The parallel

---

Jerusalem Is Warned

Over a century after the fall of Samaria, the prophets pointed to it as a prime example of what an unrepentant Jerusalem would have to face.

Jeremiah 7:14–15—Jeremiah's Temple Sermon condemns the false assumption that God will be forced to save Jerusalem from the Babylonians because of the presence of the temple. The people's violation of the covenant and failure to "amend their ways" means that God will "cast them out," just as Shiloh and the "offspring of Ephraim" have been destroyed.

Jeremiah 23:13–15—Jeremiah compares the prophets of Samaria, who served Baal and "led my people astray," with the false prophets of Jerusalem, who "commit adultery and walk in lies" and whose "ungodliness has spread throughout the land." Judah's failure to learn from Samaria's mistakes means that she "shall drink from your sister's cup" (23:32–34).

Ezekiel 23:5–10—Using the name Oholah for Samaria, the prophet describes the nation's downfall as the result of "lusting after her lovers the Assyrians," accepting their political governance, and worshiping foreign gods. For this, "judgment was executed upon her, and she became a byword among women" (compare Ezek. 16:46, Samaria "the evil sister").

---

account in 2 Kings 19 and Isaiah 36–37 does not include Hezekiah's capitulation but instead focuses on God's intervention to save the city. This is probably a Deuteronomistic addition intended to provide a more theological explanation of these events (Childs 2001: 271–72). It is based in part on the actual events twenty years after the siege of 701 (Blenkinsopp 2000: 475), including Sennacherib's forced recall to Nineveh to put down a political uprising by his sons. However, the theological intent in the parallel story is to present Hezekiah as a contrast in leadership with his father, Ahaz. Unlike his father, who did not follow Isaiah's advice (Isa. 7; 2 Kings 16:5–9), Hezekiah takes the proper step of consulting Yahweh's prophet Isaiah and subsequently receives divine assistance. Furthermore, the mention of the fall of Samaria in Isaiah 36:19 ties the defeat of the northern kingdom to its persistent idolatry and equates Israel with other "foreign" nations (Blenkinsopp 2000: 473). This after-the-fact theological judgment is consistent with the Deuteronomistic Historian's view of the northern kingdom.

Prophetic Voices on the Return

Deuteronomy 30:1–10—Set in a speech by Moses to the Israelites prior to their entrance into the promised land, this seventh-century voice of the Deuteronomistic Historian follows up on the curses laid out in Deuteronomy 29:22–28, assuming that the punishment has already occurred. He then predicts in this passage how God will eventually return (Hebrew *shub*) the scattered peoples from every land, based on their repentance (vv. 8, 10), and restore them to their heritage (Nelson 2002: 346–47).

Amos 9:7–15—In a summary statement that concludes the prophet's set of visions, he reiterates that Israel's claim to election as the people of God does not protect them from divine justice (compare Amos 3:2; Jeremias 1995: 164). God's determination is to destroy the sinful within the kingdom of Israel (vv. 8a, 10), but the Lord also pledges not to "utterly destroy the house of Jacob" (v. 8b). This seemingly contradictory statement takes into account the utter destruction of the nation of Israel but allows for a restoration of a remnant of the exiles (Noble 1997: 338–39). Amos then describes his vision of the restoration of David's kingdom (i.e., the united monarchy), the destruction of Edom (v. 12), and the creation of an Eden-like paradise in the promised land that is marked by widespread fertility and good fortune for "my people Israel." They will rebuild their cities, plant vineyards, and enjoy the fruits of their gardens. Once this occurs, God pledges to "never again" (compare Gen. 9:11) pluck them up "out of the land that I have given them" (vv. 14–15).

Once the destruction of Samaria becomes a historical event rather than a recent disaster, it serves as a warning signal to Jerusalem and the inhabitants of Judah as they face their final trial with Nebuchadnezzar and the Babylonians in the early sixth century. Both Jeremiah (3:8–10) and Ezekiel (16:15–47) employ the marriage imagery of Hosea 1–3, describing Yahweh's stormy relationship with two wives, Jerusalem and Samaria (Schmitt 1995: 361). This is an acknowledgment of the political situation during the divided monarchy, and it serves to remind their audiences of earlier prophetic warnings. Hosea's assertion in 14:1 that "Samaria must bear her guilt, for she has defiled her god," would justify the divorce/destruction of Israel as a nation and would add a sharper edge to Ezekiel's comparison between the two wives who will share similar fates.

Isaiah 11:10–16—As he does in naming his son Shear-jashub, "a remnant shall return" (Isa. 7:3), the prophet voices this theme again, describing how God "will assemble the outcasts of Israel, and gather the dispersed of Judah from the four corners of the earth" (11:12). This future reunification sets aside the conflicts between the two nations described in 9:21 and maintains the ideal of a single state that is also found in Ezekiel's vision of the "two sticks" (Ezek. 37:15–28; Blenkinsopp 2000: 268).

Jeremiah 31:1–9—Perhaps influenced by the common Mesopotamian literary theme of "a gathering of scattered peoples" by their patron deity (Widengren 1984: 234–37), the prophet describes how God will cause singing and dancing to break out (v. 4) as the "remnant [Hebrew *she'erit*] of Israel" (v. 7) return. In this way Ephraim, God's "firstborn" (v. 9), is guided on "a straight path" beside "brooks of water" (compare Ps. 23:3; Isa. 43:19), displaying to the nations that the God "who scattered Israel will gather him" (v. 10). This "new Israel" will form a "new covenant community" (Thompson 1980: 569).

Ezekiel 37:15–28—In his vision of the "two sticks," Ezekiel provides the ultimate expression of the reunification theme. He clearly describes how both kingdoms, referred to as "the stick of Joseph" and "the stick of Judah," will be transformed into a single stick (v. 19). They will be gathered from the nations where they are scattered, and "one king shall be king over them all" (v. 22). Tying these acts together is the twice-voiced promise by God once again to "be their God" (vv. 23b, 27). A general return to fertility is marked by the establishment of "an everlasting covenant with them" (v. 26), and all this serves as a sign so "the nations shall know" that Yahweh is truly God (see Block 1998: 394–95).

Echoes of Israel's Fall and the Promise of Return

The story of Israel's fall to the Assyrian horde continued to be told for centuries after it occurred. As noted above, it served as a warning to Judah prior to its own destruction by the Babylonians in 587 BCE. The preexilic prophets made good use of Israel's demise as an indicator of improper behavior and its consequence (Isa. 10:9–11; Jer. 23:13). Also characteristic of these prophecies is the tradition of a remnant that would survive the catastrophe and would, with the aid of God, return to the land (Widengren 1984: 240–41). Once Judah's people had survived the Babylonian captivity (598–538 BCE) and the call to return was heard (see Isa. 40:1–5), the story of fall and restoration would be voiced yet again.

In their vision of a restoration for a remnant of God's people, prophetic voices consistently included the exiles from both the northern and southern kingdoms as part of their vision of a future when the peoples would return to the promised land. This image of a reunited people was also included in the apocalyptic visions of prophetic figures who represented the very end of the Old Testament period, with their descriptions of an ingathering of all of the people of the covenant into an idyllic environment.

There is a strict theological logic for why the prophets and later editors chose to include this image in their message. In the early expressions of these beliefs, the prophets were speaking for the benefit of the Israelites and their descendants who had escaped south from the Assyrian rampage, giving them hope that their relatives, who had been taken into exile after 721, would eventually find their way back to join in a newly revived nation. The concept of a reunited nation is also an expression of the Deuteronomistic Historian's ideology that the northern kingdom was politically illegitimate. Thus by right all of its territory and its people should and would return to their allegiance to the house of David.

The theodicy that explains the divine punishment of Israel and Judah and the theme of God's ingathering of the exiles will be examined once again in chapter 7 on the fall of Jerusalem and its temple. The intent of this present chapter has been to demonstrate how Israel's fall became the precedent for all subsequent recitals of God's judgment on the nation. It will be the southern editors from Judah, however, who have the final word on the way in which that story is told. As a result of the work of the Deuteronomistic Historian, the "sins of Jeroboam" will never be expunged from the people's memory, but a promise of reconciliation is possible if the remnant of the northern kingdom returns to their God and to the sovereignty of the house of David.

7

Nebuchadnezzar Destroys Jerusalem and Deports the People of Judah

The fall of Samaria and the stories told by the survivors of the northern kingdom should have reminded the people of Judah that cities and nations are vulnerable to outside invasion. Despite all that had happened to Judah and Israel during the eighth and seventh centuries, however, the one abiding belief of the people and their leaders was that Jerusalem would remain sacrosanct because it contained the temple where God had "caused his name to dwell." While towns and villages throughout the kingdoms were ravaged by the armies of Assyria, Jerusalem continued to stand as a beacon of hope that God would relent and would allow the people to survive. This was made particularly clear when Sennacherib did not capture the city. In the century after 701 BCE, however, as Judah became increasingly subservient to Assyria, the likelihood of its continued survival amid the storm of international conflict became less clear. Then, as the Assyrian Empire faded and a new Mesopotamian superpower emerged, centered once again in Babylon, Judah faced an even more uncertain future.

This uncertainty may have contributed to an ill-founded alliance with Egypt by Josiah's successors. When the Babylonian king Nebuchadnezzar drove the Egyptians out of most of Syria-Palestine in 603 BCE, the rulers of Jerusalem never reconciled themselves to their new political masters. What followed was a political and social tragedy that

143

ended with the capture of Jerusalem in 598 BCE and the transport of
an initial group of hostages to Babylon. A decade later, again as a result
of Egyptian plotting and a failure to judge the political situation correctly, Jerusalem fell a second time, and at this point it was substantially
destroyed, and a large proportion of its people were taken into exile.
Yet the history of the people of the covenant did not end here. Despite
the dislocation of the exile, the story of ancient Israel continued. This
chapter explores the importance of the Zion tradition, the events that
led up to the capture of Jerusalem, and the ways in which the story of
Jerusalem's fall continues to be told for generations.

Zion Tradition

Like many significant places in the ancient Near East, the city of
Jerusalem has a long history. Some aspects of this history have been
discussed in chapter 4 on David's choosing Jerusalem as his political
and religious capital. What is of particular importance in the context of
this chapter are the traditions behind the veneration of Jerusalem and
its connection with what will be referred to here as the Zion tradition.
Specifically, it is critical to understand how the God who confronts Abram
in Haran and brings him to Canaan with the covenant promise relates
to the God of Mount Sinai, who brought the Israelites out of Egypt and
gave Moses the Ten Commandments, and to the God associated with the
everlasting covenant that was made with the house of David. Is there a
trail that leads from Mount Sinai to Mount Zion and Jerusalem?

To express the question another way, are these divine manifestations
in various sacred places part of the evolution of Israelite religion as the
community enlarges and becomes more complex? Is there a process,
as Israel emerges as a nation capable of competing with its neighbors,
that allows for the merging of these traditions? Does the Israelite God
then absorb divine associations that are tied to specific places and other
gods as the people's understanding of a universal rather than a localized
deity takes root?

The Sinai/Zion Connection

Although the biblical text generally portrays the end of the process
leading to the supremacy of Jerusalem, there are still references to Sinai
that suggest that its authority and importance in Israelite tradition are
never totally supplanted. For example, there is an elaborate festal calendar
that is embedded in Numbers 28, dating to the period of Ezra in the fifth
century (Davies 1995: 307), that contains a reference in verse 6 to the
"regular burnt offering ordained at Mount Sinai." This demonstrates a
continuing requirement in the cultic community to draw on the authority

of Sinaitic tradition long after the people had left the wilderness behind and established themselves in Jerusalem (Ashley 1993: 564).

Another attempt to draw on the Sinai to Zion/Jerusalem journey through a recitation of the salvation history is found in the processional hymn in Psalm 68 (Schaefer 2001: 164). Here a triumphant Yahweh, "the God of Sinai" (v. 8), provides for the people while scattering their enemies (vv. 9–14). Reference is then made to "the mount that God desired for his abode, where the LORD will reside forever" (v. 16). In Jerusalem (v. 29) the God of Sinai assumes his place after leading the Israelites from their captivity (J. Willis 1997: 299). All the tribes and the kings of the nations will come to this sacred place in solemn yet joyous procession, bearing gifts and singing God's praises "in his sanctuary" (vv. 24–35; compare 46:5).

The biblical narrative is careful to delete any mention of other deities that may have been associated with Mount Sinai or for that matter with Mount Zion, even though Jerusalem was a Canaanite and Jebusite city before it became David's capital. However, there are some hints that we can examine. One place to begin our analysis is with the story of Abram's dealings with Melchizedek, the so-called priest-king of Salem in Genesis 14, and the possible identification of Salem with Jerusalem. There are some difficulties with this identification, since Jerusalem is never referred to in extrabiblical texts as Salem (e.g., fourteenth-century BCE Amarna texts). In addition, during the time of David's siege of the city, Jerusalem is referred to by yet another name, Jebus (2 Sam. 5:6–10; 1 Chron. 11:4–9). Compounding our problem is the route Abram takes after his victory over the invading forces of Chedorlaomer (Gen. 14:14–16). It seems unlikely that he would have detoured as far north and west as Jerusalem (Margalith 2000: 508).

Despite these problems there is a clear association of Jerusalem and Salem in Psalm 76:2: "His abode has been established in Salem, his dwelling place in Zion." In this triumphant hymn, "God penetrated history through Abraham" and "chose a geographical center where he could approach the people, Salem, . . . Zion" (Schaefer 2001: 187). This suggests that regardless of geographic difficulties or political associations found in extrabiblical documents, a strong biblical tradition grew up that did make this equation.

A further design on the part of the storyteller in Genesis 14 may be to provide a stark contrast between Sodom and Salem. The king of Sodom, whose people had been rescued by Abram's forces, shows neither respect nor thanks to his savior, and he simply demands that Abram return his people to him (14:21). Melchizedek, king of Salem, who stood to gain nothing from Abram's military exploits, is gracious, bringing out bread and wine and blessing the victorious leader while asking for nothing (14:18–20). As representatives of their cities, these kings stand as polar

Convergence of Divine Traditions

Israelite poetry often makes use of divine titles and imagery that formed part of the cultic language of the Canaanites and the people of Ugarit. This allowed the Israelites to superimpose Yahweh's supremacy over all other gods while applying the familiar attributes of power of these deities to their God (M. S. Smith 1990: 21).

Deuteronomy 33:26–27—employs the storm language typically applied to Baal and the epithet of "the ancient god" applied to El: "There is none like God . . . who rides through the heavens to your help. . . . He subdues the ancient gods, shatters the forces of old."

Psalm 18:13–15—depicts Yahweh in the guise of a master of the forces of the storm in much the same way that Baal is often described: "The LORD also thundered in the heavens. . . . And he sent out his arrows, and scattered them; he flashed forth lightnings, and routed them."

Psalm 86:6–7—demonstrating Yahweh's role as the head of the divine assembly (a role reserved in Ugaritic literature for El), Yahweh judges the gods of the other nations, calling them the *bene ʿelyon* ("sons of the Most High"), a title similar to that applied to the god of Salem in Genesis 14:19–20.

opposites—a message that later editors would relish as Salem is equated with Jerusalem and with the Davidic monarchy (Frisch 1994: 80–81).

The entire episode would have certainly served the purposes of the Davidic monarchy, tying their capital city back to the time of the ancestors and augmenting its sacred history (Emerton 1990: 70). Furthermore, since the story also contains a scene in which both Abram and Melchizedek acknowledge the role of El Elyon in providing Abram with his victory, there seems to be an attempt to combine a Canaanite deity, El Qoneh, "El, Creator of the earth," with Elohim/Yahweh of the Israelites (Röllig 1999: 281). This epithet is often found in the description of the Canaanite and Ugaritic high god El, as well as in a Hittite text (M. S. Smith 1990: 11). It is therefore quite possible that the tradition surrounding the god of Salem, in whose name Abram is blessed (Gen. 14:18–20), is simply added to that of Israel's God, and this again strengthens the ties between Jerusalem and Yahweh.

Davidic Association with Zion

Although the narrative in Samuel–Kings highlights the Davidic connection with Jerusalem, it is quite likely that a Zion tradition was associated with Jerusalem prior to David's time. Psalm 46:4–7, which a number of scholars identify as originally a Canaanite cultic song (Clements 1980: 77; Kraus 1988: 461), clearly ties God to the city, naming it "the holy habitation of the Most High," but there is no mention of David or the monarchy in this hymn (Renz 1999: 85). Similarly, in Psalm 48:1–2 God's "holy mountain" is identified as Mount Zion, and an invitation is offered to other kings and nations to "walk about Zion . . . count its towers, consider well its ramparts" as a physical symbol of God's presence and protection (48:12–14). The antiquity of this challenge to compare the city of God with all others is seen in a parallel passage from the Mesopotamian Epic of Gilgamesh, in which the semidivine hero calls on his companion to "walk on the ramparts of Uruk" and be amazed at his great city (Pritchard 1969: 97).

Given this separate, pre-Israelite tradition, it would have been useful for the emerging Davidic monarchy to push all previous divine associations in Jebus/Jerusalem to the background or to merge them with the attributes of the Israelite God (Stuhlmueller 1990: 20). In this way, greater legitimacy would be achieved for David's rule as Yahweh's "earthly regent in Jerusalem" (Roberts 1973: 340–42).

The initial point in the narrative connecting Zion to Jerusalem and to the Davidic monarchy occurs when David brings the ark of the covenant to Jerusalem and thus installs Yahweh's presence in that formerly Jebusite city (2 Sam. 6:1–19). To be sure, the covenant made at Mount Sinai in Moses' time is not set aside by this action. However, the people had emerged from the wilderness and settled in the promised land and are now on the verge of taking a major step toward nationhood. At this point in their history, looking back to Sinai consists of acknowledging God's role in their release from Egyptian slavery and their being accepted under the covenant as a "kingdom of priests" (Exod. 19:6) and as the chosen people. Their decision to ask for a king (1 Sam. 8:4–5) is an attempt to look forward to life within the promised land, and it is therefore essential that God's dwelling place be in that land as well.

Of course, there are other sacred places in Canaan such as Shechem, Bethel, Beer-sheba, and Hebron that have associations with Yahweh dating back to the ancestral narratives. However, each of these places also has political baggage that may cloud the importance attached to centralizing worship and elevating the position of Yahweh as a national God. Thus Jerusalem, a Jebusite city, makes sense politically as a neutral site. If it can also be paired with earlier Yahweh traditions or at least with an essentially sacred character, then its acceptance as the eventual temple site is strengthened. It is even possible that David and his successors were able to draw on a Jerusalem tradition that dates back to the fourteenth-century BCE Amarna period. In one of the many letters sent by provincial officials, the pharaoh is described in a letter

---

Similar Phrases and Story Lines

Genesis 24:1 and 1 Kings 1:1—Abraham/David "was old and advanced in years": In each case a narrative involving the purchase of land is followed by this phrase, which marks the transition to the story of the next generation. The editor either borrows the phrase from the earlier ancestral narrative or chooses to use it in both places as a means of indicating to the audience that a new story is about to begin.

Genesis 23:3–20 and 2 Samuel 24:18–25—transactional dialogues: Abraham negotiates with Ephron the Hittite for the cave of Machpelah as a burial place for Sarah and subsequently most of the ancestors. David negotiates with Araunah the Jebusite for his threshing floor in order to build an altar and make a sacrifice marking the end of a plague that had devastated the nation. Although in each instance the land is offered as a gift, the Israelite character insists on purchasing the property. As a result, in both cases the land deal provides official title to a piece of the promised land and marks the transition away from Hittite or Jebusite presence in this place (a fulfillment of God's promise to drive out the inhabitants of the promised land—Exod. 34:11; McDonough 1999: 129).

---

from Abdi-Heba, the governor of Jerusalem, as the protecting deity of Jerusalem, who had "placed his name" (possibly a royal statue as well) in that city and therefore was committed never to abandon it (Ockinga 1988: 59–60; Amarna text 287:60–63).

At issue then is how the Davidic monarchy and the later editorial work of the Deuteronomistic Historian were able to tie the preexisting, sacred nature of Mount Zion to Jerusalem and the monarchy. One example of this may be found in the story of David's census in 2 Samuel 24. This remarkable narrative caps off David's active career as king and sets the stage for the succession of Solomon to the throne and the eventual construction of the temple in Jerusalem. It also contains two story elements found in the ancestral account of Abraham: (1) immediately following the story of the census, the editor provides a distinctive catchphrase marking the end of David's career in the same words that are applied to Abraham, he "was old and advanced in years" (Gen. 24:1; 1 Kings 1:1); and (2) both Genesis 23:3–20 and 2 Samuel 24:18–25 contain a transactional dialogue in which the Israelite character purchases a piece of land (McDonough 1999: 128–29).

The story of David's census also functions as a sequel to the account of how Joab successfully suppresses two revolts against David's rule by his son Absalom and the Benjaminite leader Sheba (2 Sam. 16 and 20). The census serves the political purpose of reclaiming sovereignty over previously disputed territory. It also represents the practical royal motive of surveying the resources in the most northern portions of the king's domain (Halpern 2001: 382). Taking a census was never a popular act in the ancient world, however, since it was direct evidence of the central government's desire to tax the people and draw on their resources for public works projects and service in the military. For example, in the eighteenth-century BCE administrative documents from the northern Mesopotamian city of Mari, a local governor writes to the king that when the villagers in his area heard about a census, the young men all fled into the hills so they could not be recorded (Dalley 1984: 143–44).

Whether or not David's census was a proper political step to take immediately after two civil conflicts, the Deuteronomistic Historian focuses on God's reaction to it and divine anger with the king. In response to David's presumptuous act of ordering a census of his people, God sends the prophet Gad to order David to choose what punishment will be laid upon him and the nation. Demonstrating that it is his prerogative as king to determine the form that the punishment will take, David chooses a plague rather than an invasion that might cost him his throne (Wyatt 1990: 360). An angel carries out the destruction until it reaches Jerusalem, and God then commands that the avenger "stay his hand" (compare the slightly different version in 1 Chron. 21:16).

Once the plague has run its course, David humbles himself before God, and then he negotiates the purchase of the threshing floor of Araunah as the site for his propitiatory sacrifice. In this way, David acknowledges God's overlordship, both accepting the necessity of the punishing plague and then taking on the weight of guilt himself as he pleads with God to relent. The building of an altar and the sacrifice create a precedent for sacred activity on this spot later referred to as Mount Zion, which will eventually become the site of Solomon's temple—firmly attaching the Israelite and Davidic claim to Zion in perpetuity (Wyatt 1990: 354).

Yet another sign of this process of association may be found in the work of the Deuteronomistic Historian, which never actually mentions Jerusalem by name but makes clear that God chose this place for his name to dwell. In this way the editor ties God's choice of Israel, of their king (Deut. 17:15), and of the priests who will guide them (18:5) to the covenant promise of land and children for God's chosen people (McConville 2002: 219–20). If this is then coupled with David's adoption of Jerusalem as his

Psalms and the Zion Tradition

It is quite likely that the tradition that Yahweh personally chose Zion as the holy mountain, Jerusalem as his dwelling place, and David as his faithful servant is an innovation of the Solomonic court designed to strengthen the authority of the rulers of the Davidic dynasty, even in the face of the division of the kingdom (Roberts 1973: 343). This tradition, similar to that found in Ugaritic and Canaanite religious expression, is then used by later writers to fit the needs of their social and religious context. It also serves to reinforce the tradition of the inviolability of Jerusalem/Zion, since its divine protector would never allow it to fall (Hayes 1963: 424).

Psalm 78:54–55—In this long recitation of salvation history, a psalmist of the divided kingdom initially describes how God brought the people "to his holy hill, to the mountain that his right hand had won," and from there he aided them in driving "out the nations before them." The psalm then continues with the description of the people's disobedience, the abandoning of the shrine at Shiloh (v. 60; compare Jer. 7:12), and then at verses 67–68 picks up with the division of the kingdom and the choice of Judah and Mount Zion as the place where God's sanctuary is "founded forever." The initial mention of God's "holy hill" separate from Zion may be synonymous with the promised land as a whole (compare similar language in Exod. 15:17).

Psalm 132:8–18—A postexilic psalmist makes no mention of previous divine dwelling places for Yahweh. Instead, the story begins with David's transporting the ark of the covenant to Zion, the place Yahweh "has desired for his habitation" (compare 1 Chron. 28:2). In this favored place, God resides and blesses its people, its priests, and the offspring of David. Clearly, this post–500 BCE writer selectively draws on the early history and traditions of Israel to add authority to the community that served the second temple in Persian-period Jerusalem (Patton 1995: 650–51).

political capital and the special status achieved by the house of David as the recipient of the "everlasting covenant" (2 Sam. 7:1–17), then a firm foundation is established for the tradition of Jerusalem's dual function as the national political and religious center (see Levenson 1985: 98–99).

Playing off this theme of Jerusalem's unique political and religious position, Isaiah 2:2–4 goes so far as to describe Zion as the place to which nations will be drawn and from which God will send forth instruction and judgment between the nations and peoples of the earth (see J. Willis

1997: 295–96). This functions as a unifying tradition that brings support to the Davidic monarchs, who are closely associated with Yahweh through the everlasting covenant. It also magnifies Jerusalem's place in the political and religious consciousness of the people.

The process is then completed by Solomon's subsequent construction of the temple for Yahweh in Jerusalem (1 Kings 5–7). This central act, coupled as it is with the desire of the kings to demonstrate their power through monumental architecture (Whitelam 1986), further solidifies the sense of God's presence in that place by creating a magnificent house like those built for the gods of other nations. Perhaps as a cautionary note, Solomon muses in his dedicatory prayer on whether God would "indeed dwell on the earth" when "even heaven . . . cannot contain you" (1 Kings 8:27). But, drawing on the theme expressed in Deuteronomy 16:11, the king urges God to keep a perpetual watch on "the place of which you said, 'My name shall be there'" (1 Kings 8:29).

Indeed, the traditions concerning Solomon's reign are intimately associated with his construction and furnishing of the temple. Subsequent segments of his royal chronicle begin with stock phrases taking note of the temple's building and completion. In addition, the actions of later kings of Judah, for good or bad, often center on "Solomon's temple," and the community of priests who serve the temple take their very identity from that place.

Jerusalem and Cultic Responsibility

From the time of the establishment of the Davidic monarchy, Jerusalem came to be known as the city where God had chosen to make his name dwell—the veritable center of the universe (Ezek. 5:5–6; Renz 1999: 86–87).

Deuteronomy 12:5–11—As the preface to the Deuteronomic law code, the people are enjoined to "seek the place that the LORD your God will choose . . . as his habitation to put his name there" (v. 5). It will be here that they are to bring their offerings and sacrifices, tithes, donations, and gifts "to the place that the LORD your God will choose as a dwelling for his name" (v. 11). This injunction regarding offerings is repeated in Deuteronomy 14:23.

Deuteronomy 16:2, 6, 11—In its description of the Passover celebration, the people are required to offer their sacrifice "at the place that the LORD will choose as a dwelling for his name."

The Tradition of the Invulnerability of Jerusalem

With so much attention given to Solomon's construction of the temple in Jerusalem, it would eventually become difficult to think of Yahweh's presence in any place other than the Jerusalem temple, and it would be equally inconceivable that God would allow this favored city to fall no matter the odds. Thus the city of Jerusalem, the institution of the monarchy, and the temple of Yahweh were transformed into political and religious icons for the people of Judah. Each was considered a visible sign of God's presence with the people and a guarantee that they would always be God's people (Ps. 46:4–7). In fact, the city of Jerusalem, referred to as Zion in many of the Psalms (Pss. 48, 78, 125, 132, 137), was even equated with God's person as a means of reassuring the people that they (the city and God) would continue to provide a sure refuge (Ollenburger 1987: 74–75).

The tradition of Jerusalem's invulnerability continues to hold up even during the period of Assyrian hegemony (750–620 BCE). For some it is reinforced when the capital of the northern kingdom, Samaria, falls in 721 BCE to this voracious invader. They are reassured because Hezekiah of Judah is able to withstand a siege in 701 BCE and eventually to purchase the safety of Jerusalem with a huge ransom payment to the Assyrian emperor Sennacherib (2 Kings 18:13–16; Cogan and Tadmor 1988: 241–44). This belief, at least among the people of Jerusalem, is strengthened even though the countryside of Judah is ravaged by the Assyrian army and many of its cities are destroyed. All that seems to matter is that Jerusalem continued to hold out, and this solidifies the belief that Yahweh would never allow his dwelling place to fall.

The prophet Isaiah adds weight to this tradition, first predicting the demise of the Assyrian ruler and the shattering of his yoke of oppression (Isa. 14:24–25), and then proclaiming to the messengers of enemy nations (possibly the Philistines) that "the LORD has founded Zion, and the needy among his people will find refuge in her" (14:32; Blenkinsopp 2000: 289–90). Similarly, in 31:4–5 Yahweh the Divine Warrior is credited with descending to do battle on Mount Zion and protecting and delivering Jerusalem. It should be noted, however, that Isaiah does demand faith in Yahweh as the condition for the Divine Warrior to protect the people. They must not trust in foreign alliances (31:1) or human resources to preserve them. It is only "in returning and rest" that "you shall be saved" (30:15; Hayes 1963: 425–26).

Invulnerability Negated and Jerusalem Destroyed

The historical events that eventually led to the fall of Judah and the destruction of Jerusalem may have their roots in this tradition of Jerusalem's invulnerability and in the nationalistic efforts of Hezekiah to

The Fate of the Nation and Solomon's Temple

The construction of the temple in Jerusalem by King Solomon serves as a high point in the history of the nation. Its importance to the people is often mentioned in subsequent accounts. However, signals in the text indicate that the building's importance and sanctity as God's dwelling place depend on the people's adherence to the covenant.

1 Kings 9:1–5—Following the statement that Solomon had finished all that he "desired to build," God again appears to Solomon (see 1 Kings 3:5–14 for the first appearance). This is then followed by God's certification of Solomon's work, a consecration of this house where God will "put my name there forever" (v. 3), and a restatement of the everlasting covenant made with David (vv. 4–5).

1 Kings 9:15—In describing Solomon's activities to strengthen the defenses of his kingdom, the action begins with reference first to his having built the temple. No project ever supersedes it in importance or prestige.

2 Kings 21:2–7—The Deuteronomistic Historian chronicles the evil that Manasseh inflicted on Judah through his construction of high places, erection of altars to Baal and the "host of heaven in the two courts of the house of the LORD," and worst of all his placing of a "carved image of Asherah" in the temple. What makes this particularly villainous is the reference in verse 7 to God's promise to David and Solomon that in this house and in Jerusalem "I will put my name forever." In this way, the endangering of the people is clearly tied to a king who ignored the obligations of the covenant and set aside the central importance of God's designation of Jerusalem as his dwelling place (Levinson 2003: 29).

2 Kings 25:8–17 and Jer. 52:12–23—These parallel accounts describe the systematic looting of Solomon's temple by the Babylonian commander Nebuzaradan. The degree of detail in this passage serves as a reversal of that found in 1 Kings 6:14–36 and 7:15–50, where Solomon and Hiram of Tyre constructed and placed the treasures and sacred implements in the Jerusalem temple. The impression is a stripping of the building of all that had made it Yahweh's temple. A metaphorical parallel to this is found in Ezekiel 16:35–40, where God strips his unfaithful bride (Jerusalem) of her fine clothing and leaves her naked to be abused by the crowd.

Ezra 2:58 and Neh. 7:60—The list of returning exiles (post–538 BCE) includes 392 of the descendants of Solomon's "temple servants." Despite the fact that the temple had been destroyed fifty years earlier, these men continued to claim their status and personal identity from their ancestors' association with the temple and the sacrificial cult.

Jerusalem/Zion in the Psalms

There are numerous references in the Psalms to God's choice of Jerusalem and the Davidic monarchy. It is likely that many of these were composed by members of the royal court or by priests who wished to glorify the line of kings who had constructed the Jerusalem temple.

Psalm 68:16—The psalmist affirms that the Jerusalem temple and Mount Zion are Yahweh's chosen dwelling place, "where the LORD will dwell forever."

Psalm 78:56–72—In a recitation of the nation's salvation history, the psalmist chronicles that God had "utterly rejected Israel" (the northern kingdom) and "abandoned his dwelling at Shiloh." After God "rejected the tent of Joseph . . . he chose the tribe of Judah, Mount Zion, which he loves," where his sanctuary is built, and then "chose his servant David," who tended the nation as he had his flocks. This idealized view of history up to the time of David serves the political purposes of his descendants after the fall of the northern kingdom and sets the monarchy and Jerusalem at center stage.

Psalm 84:5–8—Pilgrims are encouraged along their way to Zion with assurances that they will be strengthened during the journey, their obstacles will be removed, and they will experience the presence of the Lord in that holy place (compare the postexilic call to return to Jerusalem and God's presence in Isa. 40:3–5).

Psalm 125:1–2—The psalmist assures the people that "those who trust in the LORD are like Mount Zion, which cannot be moved, but abides forever" (compare Ps. 21:7).

assert a larger degree of independence for Judah during the final years of the eighth century. The king's reforms included cleansing the temple of its foreign influences (2 Kings 18:4). However, this was undoubtedly viewed by the Assyrians as a violation of their vassal treaty with Judah. Even though the Deuteronomistic Historian applauded Hezekiah, stating that "there was no one like him among all the kings of Judah after him" (2 Kings 18:5), his actions led to the mass destruction of many of Judah's towns and villages by Sennacherib's Assyrian armies (see Micah's complaints about Samaria's and Jerusalem's policies in Mic. 1:5–6). Even more important, however, was the total subjugation of Hezekiah's successor, Manasseh, to the control of the Assyrian kings. During the period immediately after 701 BCE, Judah's economy was badly weakened, and many of its people, like those captured during the fall of Lachish, were taken into exile (Na'aman 1991: 55).

Archaeological surveys of seventh-century Judah indicate a shift of population into the hill country, including an increase in the area around Jerusalem and in the Beer-sheba valley (Finkelstein 1994: 177–78). While Judah struggled to rebuild its economy, there is significant population growth and prosperity in the area immediately north of the Shephelah and in Philistia (Finkelstein 1994: 173). Among the Philistine cities, Ekron became the center of the lucrative olive oil trade (Na'aman 1993: 114). Thus the actual borders of Judah during the seventh century shrank as a result of Sennacherib's transfer of portions of the Shephelah to "more reliable" vassals, leaving a small "heartland" that included "the Judean mountains, Benjamin, the Judean desert, and the biblical Negev" (Kletter 1999: 28).

Fueling Judah's continued desire to break away from Assyrian hegemony was the internal turmoil that weakened Assyria during the late seventh century (Miller and Hayes 1986: 381–85). These political stresses, coupled with incursions by the Scythian tribes from the steppes north and east of the Black Sea (Na'aman 1991: 37–38) and the difficulties of maintaining order in all parts of their far-flung empire, made it more difficult to launch major military campaigns (Brinkman 1984: 93). However, there would be no change in Judah's political fortunes until after the death of the Assyrian emperor Ashurbanipal in 627.

The outbreak of a civil war between Assyrian claimants to the throne provided the opportunity for young King Josiah to launch a reform after 622 BCE similar to that of his great-grandfather Hezekiah and to try to expand Judah's territory and influence (2 Kings 22:3–23:24; Na'aman 1991: 38–41). Some elements of the story of Josiah's reform are very similar to other biblical narratives. For instance, covenant-renewal ceremonies also occur in Exodus 24:4–8; Joshua 24:1–28; and Nehemiah 8:1–12, and each marks a major transition in the history of the people. More important, however, were the destruction of all sacred objects associated with foreign gods, the centralization of worship in Jerusalem highlighted by the renewal of the Passover Festival, and the deposing of the priests who officiated at the local high places (2 Kings 23:4–9). In this way, he restored the supremacy of Jerusalem as the central cultic site for the worship of Yahweh and reinvigorated the concept of the city's invulnerability.

Unfortunately, Josiah's reforms could not survive the ambitions of the superpowers in Egypt and Mesopotamia. Their struggles to carve up the former Assyrian Empire and to control the vital land bridge of Syria-Palestine led to Josiah's death in 609 BCE at Megiddo (2 Kings 23:29–30). Without his leadership, Judah was thrown into a period of turmoil in which the weak rulers of Jerusalem would eventually cause the destruction of the city and the exile of many of their own people.

Prophetic Warnings against Jerusalem

The eighth-century prophets Amos and Hosea had repeatedly warned the kings of the northern kingdom that Samaria, Dan, and Bethel would all be destroyed as centers of covenant violation. This theme is then reprised by Micah during the Assyrian invasion of Judah in 701 BCE, when he proclaims that "Zion shall be plowed as a field" (Mic. 3:12). However, the strongest arguments against the people's false hopes in the inviolability of Jerusalem and its temple are found in Jeremiah, who invites the people to go to Shiloh and see what has become of a place where God once made his name to dwell (Jer. 7:12; see also Ps. 78:59–61).

Amos 5:21–24—Hollow worship is unacceptable to God: "I hate, I despise your festivals, and I take no delight in your solemn assemblies."

Hosea 4:1–3—Lack of the knowledge of God: "Hear the word of the LORD, O people of Israel; for the LORD has an indictment against the inhabitants of the land. There is no faithfulness or loyalty, and no knowledge of God in the land. . . . Therefore the land mourns."

Micah 3:1–7—Unjust rulers and false prophets are condemned: "You who hate the good and love the evil, who tear the skin off my people. . . . The LORD . . . will hide his face from them at that time, because they have acted wickedly."

Micah 6:6–8—Useless sacrifices bring no blessings: "Shall I come before him with burnt offerings, with calves a year old? Will the LORD be pleased with thousands of rams, with ten thousands of rivers of oil?"

Jeremiah 7:3–11—Only right behavior can save Jerusalem: "Amend your ways and your doings; and let me dwell with you in this place. . . . Has this house, which is called by my name, become a den of robbers in your sight?"

Ezekiel 10:18–19—After detailing how the Jerusalem temple has been thoroughly corrupted by the worship of other gods (Ezek. 8:5–17), the prophet describes how "the glory of the LORD" physically departed the temple, abandoning it and the city to the destructive forces of the besieging Babylonian army.

Prophetic Warnings and the End of Many Things

Throughout the history of the divided monarchy, the implicit dangers of an unconditional, blind faith in Jerusalem's invulnerability were assailed by several prophets who pointed out that temples, shrines, altars, and priestly communities could not withstand God's wrath. They lose their sanctity when they are used for the purpose of worshiping other gods or to assuage the conscience of merchants or political leaders who oppress the people in violation of the covenant. It does no good to publicly make costly sacrifices or devote huge sums to building projects in the temple precinct, if there is no commitment to the terms of the covenant with God. As is explicitly detailed by the Deuteronomistic Historian in Moses' closing speech to the people on the plains of Moab, "All who hear the words of this oath and bless themselves, thinking in their hearts, 'We are safe even though we go our own stubborn ways'" (Deut. 29:19), can only expect to see the source of their false confidence destroyed before their eyes.

Dismantling the hope of Jerusalem's invulnerability, however, could not be accomplished by prophetic warnings. In the desperate days of the siege of Jerusalem, Jeremiah uses a familiar Deuteronomic formula, pleading with the people that it is within their own ability to "choose life" when making decisions based on the commands of the Lord (Deut. 30:15–20; Nelson 2002: 349). He tells the frightened people of Jerusalem that their fate depends on choosing between "the way of life and the way of death," but there is no record that any followed his instruction to "go out and surrender to the Chaldeans" (Jer. 21:8–9). In fact, during Jeremiah's trial for speaking out against the temple as a false haven, a group of the "elders of the land" cite Micah's prophecy against Jerusalem in Hezekiah's time (Mic. 3:12) and note that when the king did not execute the offending prophet, God "changed his mind" and spared the city (Jer. 26:17–19). Thus the story continued to be told of the sure mercy of God, ignoring the dire warnings they heard until the walls of Jerusalem fell down around them.

Lament for the City of God

When Jerusalem, the temple of Yahweh, and the Davidic monarchy all were destroyed by Nebuchadnezzar's army in a single calamitous event in 587 BCE, the shock must have driven many of the people to despair. Compounding their loss was the physical transportation of many of the survivors into an exile that wrenched them away from all that was familiar. The emotions expressed in Psalm 137 of depression, resolution, and a desire for retribution speak of the complexity of what had happened and point to new solutions like that expressed by Jeremiah in his letter to the exiles offering them the opportunity to worship Yahweh outside Judah (Jer. 29:1–23).

One natural reaction to the disaster was to compose and recite communal laments. These are common in the Psalms (12; 44; 60; 74; 79; 80; 83; 85; 94:1–11; 126; and 137), and their general purpose is to lament the fate of the nation (usually as a result of political and military disasters) and to call upon Yahweh to deliver them from their pitiful condition (Day 1990: 33). They would have been used in temple worship and may have involved the use of sackcloth and other forms of physical mourning (see Jon. 3:6–9; Judith 4:9–15). There is some evidence of public mourning immediately after the destruction of Jerusalem (Jer. 41:5), and this became a regular feature of the postexilic religious calendar, with mourning and fasting prescribed during the fifth month (Ab) in Zechariah 7:3–5 (Hillers 1972: xl). The liturgical use of communal laments followed a pattern set in Mesopotamia in the second millennium BCE in which a group known as the *gala*-priests regularly recited canonized lamentations to prevent a repetition of the destruction of cities and temples by the gods (Cohen 1988: 14).

It is quite likely, therefore, that the Israelite reaction to the destruction of Jerusalem continued this practice of public lament, although it is doubtful that they borrowed directly more than a few of the standard phrases or expressions found in ancient Mesopotamian texts (Hillers 1972: xxx). Their petitions to the Deity represented a form of collective repentance designed to draw the Deity's attention to their plight and to accept their humble supplication. In this way, they hoped to eventually be restored to God's favor, and they looked for a better day when they and their city would be rebuilt.

The book of Lamentations provides an extended example of Judah's reaction to the destruction of all that they held dear. The book contains four communal laments (chaps. 1, 2, 4, 5) and a central chapter with an individual lament. In this way, the nation's story as well as the suffering of the individual are recounted. It may be that this book also represents a new form of the literature of suffering. Certainly, the events of 587 BCE were unprecedented in the history of Israel, and this may have required the composition of a poem that went beyond the standard lament form in the Psalms and even attempted to represent the unsettled minds of the devastated people (Salters 2000: 298–99). This may help explain the complexity of structure in chapter 1, which seems to skip from one form of disaster to penitence for sin and back again in verses 12–22.

Also embedded here in its depiction of a mournful populace is a cry for redress and an accusation that its punishment has gone too far. Certainly, the people cry out that they have violated the covenant and thus could be considered treaty breakers and are therefore subject to the curses that accompany such an agreement. Examples of the treaty formula, such as Deuteronomy 28:15–68 and the Sefire treaty (ancient inscription found in northern Syria), provide a systematic list of curses for disobedience (Hillers 1964: 58–60). It is in their explicit recitation of curses, however, that justice is traditionally found.

Lament for a Destroyed City

Lamentations 1:1–19—In detailing the plight of Jerusalem, the author presents a graphic picture of an empty city: "How lonely sits the city that once was full of people!" (v. 1). While the people of Judah have been taken into exile (v. 3), the once crowded "roads to Zion" are empty of pilgrims (v. 4). Now "daughter Zion" is left to cry over her departed princes and the mocking by her foes, who "have seen her nakedness," and there are "none to comfort her" (vv. 6–9).

Lament for Ur—In what became a standard liturgy of mourning and a means of reminding both the gods and the people of the previous disaster to the great Sumerian city of Ur, the priests recited this lamentation for a "desolate city" in whose midst "was uttered nothing but laments and dirges." They are told that "Ur was granted kingship, it was not granted an eternal reign" (Pritchard 1969: 617).

What seems to be the case in this extremity of destruction, however, is a form of punishment that exceeds these legal limits. In that case there is a cry for both mercy and for justice. Thus in Lamentations 1:10–12 the writer describes a personified Zion as a woman accused of harlotry and stripped of her clothing. This sort of punishment is acceptable according to the legal codes of the ancient Near East; it is referred to in Isaiah 47:3; Nahum 3:5; Jeremiah 13:22; and Ezekiel 16:37 and clearly represents the stripping of the temple of Jerusalem by the Babylonians in 2 Kings 25:8–17.

What is not acceptable to the penitent is the subsequent rape of the helpless woman, the metaphor for the "rape of Zion" and the violation of the temple precincts. It could be claimed that she had been justifiably shamed before her neighbors, but she/Zion does not deserve this physical violation of her person/temple (Dobbs-Allsopp and Linafelt 2001: 79). Her enemies have not only "stretched out their hands over all her precious things," but they have also invaded her "sanctuary" (Lam. 1:10). Having suffered this extra punishment, Zion now cries out, challenging all who can hear whether "there is any sorrow like my sorrow . . . which the LORD inflicted" (Lam. 1:12). In this way, the people may be making a case for the restoration of the temple once their term of punishment is complete (see Isa 40:1–5 for the eventual end of this penalty and a promise of restoration).

Once some time had passed and the memory of the day of destruction had become less vivid, the exilic and postexilic communities must have developed a slightly different lament form to express their reaction to their loss. While they would continue to express their sorrow, their emphasis was now on penitential prayer. This type of prayer expressed praise for their God, supplication in the face of their condition of separation from Zion, an abject confession of sin, and a recitation of the history of God's grace that had restored them in the past (Boda 2001: 186–87). For example, Leviticus 26:40–45 promises that "if they confess their iniquity and the iniquity of their ancestors," then they are assured by God that "I will remember my covenant . . . and I will remember my land." This public proclamation of their sins is a literary form that most likely came into the Israelite genre during the exilic period in Babylonia and continued to be used in the second temple (post–500 BCE) as part of the liturgy of worship.

Neo-Babylonian Judah

Despite the destruction of Jerusalem and subsequent exile of many of the people of Judah, it is unlikely that the land was left empty. The reality of the situation is that significant portions of Judah continued to be fairly well populated after the Babylonian conquest. The political and economic realities of Babylonia's power struggle with Egypt dictated that Judah, like the other sections of Syria-Palestine, must remain a populated and productive region. The empire needed to feed its armies, and it needed laborers to produce and transport luxury items such as olive oil and wine back to the urban centers in Babylonia (Barstad 2003: 10–13). The Babylonian general Nebuzaradan even commented on his deliberate decision to leave vinedressers and farmers to till the soil (2 Kings 25:12). Furthermore, Judah's role as a buffer state between the two superpowers remained a constant of Near Eastern politics, since Nebuchadnezzar and his successors were unable to conquer Egypt.

However, the destruction of Jerusalem along with its governmental apparatus had some significant ripple effects. This was certainly a major blow to those areas that depended upon the urban center for their livelihood. Most of the cities and towns in immediate proximity to Jerusalem, as well as its western and eastern border fortresses, which relied on trade and the protection of the military for their survival, could not continue to support their population; and we may assume that political concerns would have prevented the reconstruction of Jerusalem itself. Still, in Judah proper, archaeological surveys indicate that some of the smaller towns and villages continued to survive, at least as rebuilt, marginal population centers (E. Stern 2001a: 321–25).

Thus the image of a land completely emptied of its people (2 Chron. 36:20–21) and left waiting for their return must be set aside (Barstad 2003: 14). It must be conceded, however, that the land lacked indigenous leadership, and there is no evidence to date of a priestly community or of prophets operating in Judah during the exile. The biblical text leaves a gap for this period of time, and it resumes only once the exile comes to an end after 538 BCE (Oded 2003: 71). It would certainly be to the advantage of the exiles to focus on their own plight and their manner of coping with the disaster of the fall of Judah, the destruction of Jerusalem and the temple, and their own displacement. It would only be natural for them to continue to portray Judah as the "promised land," as an inducement for the eventual triumphant return of the exiles (see Isa. 40:1–11). In addition, they created a theodicy explaining the purpose of their exile as just punishment for their disobedience to the covenant, and this set the stage for the next step in the history of the nation. The next chapter deals with elements of the exilic experience as well as the construction of a postexilic existence in the Diaspora and in a restored Jerusalem community.

Cyrus Captures Babylon, and the Exiles Return Home

In this final chapter we come full circle, once again examining the qualities and attributes of an Eden-like place and the overwhelming desire to return to that place where God dwells. A large proportion of the people of Judah were taken into exile by Nebuchadnezzar after the destruction of Jerusalem in 587 BCE. The exile itself lasts until 538 BCE, when the Persian king Cyrus issues a decree that among other things allows captive peoples to return to their homelands and rebuild their cities and temples. The Cyrus Cylinder, although a piece of political propaganda, does provide a clear look at the Persian policy of accommodation with local cultural and religious beliefs. As Isaiah 40 proclaims, it is now possible for those who wish to return to Jerusalem to travel the path that will lead to the rebuilding of that sacred place.

It does not really matter whether Cyrus understands that it is Yahweh who has provided him with his victory and transformed him into a savior figure for the exiles. This captivity, like that in Egypt, ends with the people being purified by the experience of exile and sets the stage for the restoration of the covenant and of Jerusalem. What is remarkable about the language used by the postexilic prophets and the stories that they tell to induce the people to return to Judah/Jerusalem/Zion is its similarity to the tales of Eden in Genesis and elsewhere in the biblical text. Our task here is to analyze the events surrounding Cyrus's capture of Babylon in 540 BCE and the development of the postexilic Jewish community in the diasporic communities and in Yehud/Jerusalem.

Wilderness Experience: Exile and Hope

The story of God's just wrath is echoed throughout the biblical narrative in various forms of the "wilderness experience." Metaphorically, the wilderness is that region where chaos reigns, in which no person or people have a clear identity. It serves as a place of abandonment, struggle, and purification that can be escaped only through the intervention of God.

Genesis 3—The story of the expulsion from Eden is the first example of the wilderness story. For Adam and Eve, any place other than Eden was a wilderness. Even so, as permanent exiles from paradise, they were given the gifts of procreation, work, and personal relationship with which to console themselves and with which to create a world of their own.

Genesis 6:5–8—The flood story contains the same elements of divine anger/disappointment that are found in the Eden story. Noah, as the only righteous human, was given the opportunity to survive and rebuild his world, but only after spending forty days amid the teeming floodwaters and an additional period of waiting as the torrent receded (Gen. 7:11–24). In this way, the later audience for this story learned that even the righteous must (1) demonstrate their obedience by acting on God's command and (2) have the patience necessary to survive the ordeal of disaster and separation from normalcy.

Numbers 14:1–24—Despite the evidence of Yahweh's power found in the manipulation of Pharaoh during the plagues in Egypt, the crossing of the Red Sea, the granting of manna and quail, and the defeat of the Amalekites, the spies that Moses sent into the promised land gave a negative report, and the people "complained against Moses and Aaron" and even called for the election of a new leader and a return to Egypt (14:1–4). God was so angry that at first the decision was to destroy them all and "make of you [Moses] a nation greater and mightier than they" (14:12). Moses interceded for the people, arguing that the nations would see the destruction of the people as a failure on God's part to carry out the promise of a new land (14:13–16). The final decision was to forbid the unfaithful adults, who had seen God's saving acts, from entering the land, leaving them to die in the wilderness (14:20–24). In that way, the forty years of wilderness wandering culled the disobedient from the nation and prepared them under Joshua's leadership to conquer the land with God's help.

> **Jeremiah 29:10–11**—Despite the destruction of Jerusalem and many of the cities of Judah, the prophet assures the people that they have not been abandoned by their God. However, they must have patience and confidence in God's intention to once again set a term of exile in the wilderness during which the nation is to purify itself: "Only when Babylon's seventy years are completed will I visit you, and I will fulfill to you my promise and bring you back to this place . . . to give you a future with hope." This hope is then fulfilled according to the words of Second Isaiah (the putative author of Isa. 40–55): "Speak tenderly to Jerusalem, and cry to her that she has served her term, that her penalty is paid" (Isa. 40:2).

Historical Overview of Postexilic Events

From 587 to 540 BCE the Neo-Babylonian Empire, under the leadership of Nebuchadnezzar and his successor Nabonidus, controlled the fate of the exiled peoples and administered what remained of the people of Judah, their towns, and most of the territory of Syria-Palestine. While the Neo-Babylonians were unable to extend their control to Egypt, they still commanded most of what had been the former Assyrian Empire. It should also be noted that their allies, the Medes, as well as other re-emergent kingdoms on the Iranian plateau, functioned in this period as potential rivals to the rulers of Babylon. Under the leadership of Cyrus II, a coalition of peoples from Media, Elam, and Anshan (Persia) would eventually push aside the Neo-Babylonians and establish the largest of all the ancient Near Eastern empires, stretching from the Nile to the Aegean and east to the Indus Valley (Briant 2002: 21–23).

During their period of exile, we can assume that some of the people taken from their home countries by the Neo-Babylonians chose to assimilate into Mesopotamian society. This would have involved changing their names, abandoning or suppressing their cultural identity, and blending into the cosmopolitan mix of nations that inhabited Mesopotamia. Some may have taken Jeremiah's injunction to "build houses and live in them; plant gardens and eat what they produce" and "seek the welfare of the city where I have sent you into exile" (Jer. 29:6–7a) as a license to set aside former allegiances in favor of the winning side. However, those who read Jeremiah's letter to the exiles more carefully would have noted the prophet's instruction to "pray to the LORD on its [Babylon's] behalf, for in its welfare you will find your welfare" (29:7b). This injunction clearly states the proposition that Yahweh has not abandoned them permanently to the wilderness of exile and will continue to bless those who stand firm on their covenantal obligations. In fact, as Jeremiah states later in his letter, there is to be a set time limit to their exile after which they can expect that Yahweh will restore them to their homes and they will once again realize the benefits of calling upon God, who will hear them and respond favorably to their needs (29:12).

Echoes of the familiar wilderness story retold here in the narrative of the exile provide one more example of how the storyteller answers the question of which god is truly the most powerful. This narrative also reiterates the benefits of the covenant relationship in binding the people to Yahweh. Throughout their history the Israelites are repeatedly reminded that the God who is revealed in the story of the establishment of the covenant with Abraham and Moses is the same God who can and will safely guide the people through places of chaos and anarchy into the promised land. In this place of safety, chaos can never reign. However, the cycle of disobedience, which is also an essential element of this story, reminds the people that they are responsible for their actions each time they disobey the covenant. They should therefore not be surprised when they are once again cast into the wilderness to suffer yet another period of purification (Matthews 2000: 44).

What makes it possible for Second Isaiah to proclaim an end to the exiles' term of punishment is the capture of Babylon by the Persian king Cyrus II in 540 BCE. Cyrus's rise to power begins about 559 when he becomes king of Anshan (Persia) and initiates hostilities with the Median king Astyages. Unfortunately, the principal source for the conflict between the Persians and the Medes is the sixth-century Greek historian Herodotus. This chronicler often takes an uncritical view of his data, apparently accepting biased reports from both sides, and concentrates on telling a good story, like the long-drawn-out recitation of the "founder myth" involving Cyrus's escape from death as an infant, his upbringing by a shepherd, and his eventual rise to power (compare Moses' infancy story in Exod. 1:8–2:10). The Babylonian Chronicle contains a couple of references to Cyrus's conflict with Astyages, but again it is uncertain whether this document, prepared for Nabonidus's court in Babylon, provides an unbiased account. It does tell us that Astyages was betrayed by his own army commanders and turned over to Cyrus, and this then forms the basis for the unification of Median and Persian forces (Briant 2002: 31–32).

Also contributing to Cyrus's eventual success are the administrative policies and style of the Babylonian ruler Nabonidus. Much of what is known about Nabonidus comes from his royal archives and from the accounts told by his enemies (Sack 1992: 973–75). What these admittedly biased documents tell us is that he made some far-reaching changes in the religious establishment in Babylon, removing Marduk as the city's patron deity and replacing him with Sin, the patron god of

Harran (Beaulieu 1989: 212–19; Kuhrt 1983: 90). This also significantly diminished the power of the Marduk priesthood, creating a source of unrest that eventually led to the king's downfall. Making matters even worse, Nabonidus spent much of his time and efforts protecting the Arabian trade routes. He shifted his official residence for a ten-year period (553–543) to Tema in northern Arabia, and he delegated his powers in Babylon to his son Belshazzar (Millard 1985: 76–78; Beaulieu 1989: 155–60; 169–85).

Nabonidus's obsession with Arabia and his attempts to diminish the importance of the religious establishment in Babylon apparently created an opening for Cyrus. Once the Persian king had consolidated his control of the tribes of his own land and in Media, he began a series of military campaigns that added most of Anatolia to his territory. Having thereby "surrounded" Babylon (controlling lands to the east and north of Mesopotamia), Cyrus marched on Babylon in 540 BCE. His eventual victory and rebuilding of the Marduk temple in Babylon is reported in the Cyrus Cylinder, which served as part of his official propaganda campaign. It describes an easy victory facilitated by the god Marduk. Other ancient sources (Herodotus 1.188–91 and Xenophon, *Cyropaedia* 7.5.7–32, 58) suggest a much higher level of resistance by the Neo-Babylonians (Haerinck 1997: 26–27). Regardless of who is telling the story, all agree that Nabonidus was captured by the Persians, that the images of the gods he had held hostage in Babylon were returned to their cities, and that Babylonia became a Persian vassal state (Beaulieu 1989: 231–32).

That Cyrus is mentioned in both Greek and Babylonian sources is an indication of the impact he had on the ancient world. His influence and that of the emerging Persian Empire transformed not only the political landscape but also basic administrative policies, brought ease of trade and transportation under a "pax Persica," and fostered an acceptance of cultural pluralism in the midst of an overarching imperial hegemony. The various districts or satrapies of the Persian Empire would all duly pay their taxes, provide a basic level of obeisance, send their men to fight in the huge armies gathered by the Persian kings, and adopt Persian styles of architecture and city planning. However, once the Persian bureaucracy had placed them into understandable categories, they would also be allowed to maintain their own religious practices and, in many cases, be directed by governors appointed from their own ethnic group (Hoglund 1991: 62–64; Balentine 1996: 138–39). In this way, Persian hegemony could be interpreted as relatively benevolent, and this may help to explain the very favorable treatment that Cyrus receives in the biblical text.

Of course, the biblical account also heavily relies on the issuance of Cyrus's royal decree. Cyrus's document is a typical piece of political propaganda justifying his conquest of Babylon and asserting divine favor as the

Cyrus Cylinder and Isaiah

The similarities in language and focus between the Cyrus Cylinder (Hallo and Younger 2000: 314–16 [2.124]) and the pronouncements of Second Isaiah (Isa. 44:28–45:13) have long been noted by scholars (S. Smith 1944: 72). It is quite likely that the author of this portion of Isaiah was familiar with both the text of the Persian decree and the propagandistic style common to the Persian court (Blenkinsopp 2002: 249). Significantly, however, he chose to replace the role played by the Babylonian god Marduk with Yahweh (Fried 2002: 392). Below I will first quote a portion of the Cyrus Cylinder and then provide a comparative section of Isaiah's proclamation concerning Cyrus. I have noted significant words or phrases in bold type.

1. Justification for hostilities:
"An incompetent person was installed to exercise lordship over his country. . . . He put an end to the regular offerings. . . . By his own plan, he did away with the worship of Marduk, the **king of the gods**; he continually did evil against his (Marduk's) city. Daily, . . . he [imposed] the corvée upon its inhabitants unrelentingly, ruining them all."
"**I am the LORD, who made all things**, . . . who frustrates the omens of liars, . . . who confirms the word of his servant, and fulfills the prediction of his messengers, who says of Jerusalem, 'It shall be inhabited,' and of the cities of Judah, 'They shall be rebuilt, and I will raise up their ruins'" (Isa. 44:24–26).

2. Divine intervention:
"Upon (hearing) their cries, the lord of the gods became furiously angry [and he left] their borders; and the gods who lived among them forsook their dwellings, angry that he had brought (them) into Babylon. . . . Marduk . . . surveyed and looked throughout all the lands, **searching for a righteous king** whom he would support. He called out his name: Cyrus, king of Anshan; he **pronounced his name** to be king over all (the world)."
"Who has **roused a victor from the east**, summoned him to his service? He delivers up nations to him, and tramples kings under foot" (Isa. 41:2).
"I stirred up one from the north, and he has come, from the rising of the sun he was **summoned by name**" (Isa. 41:25).
"**Thus says the LORD to his anointed**, to Cyrus, whose right hand I have grasped to subdue nations before him and strip kings of their robes, to open doors before him—and the gates shall not be closed" (Isa. 45:1).
"**I call you by your name**, I surname you, though you do not know me" (Isa. 45:4b).

"I will fulfill my intention, **calling** a bird of prey from the east, the man for my purpose from a far country. I have spoken, and I will bring it to pass; I have planned, and I will do it" (Isa. 46:10–11).

3. Cyrus's actions:
"He (Cyrus) **shepherded** with justice and righteousness all the black-headed people, over whom he (Marduk) had given him victory. . . . Marduk . . . ordered him to march to his city Babylon . . . he **went at his side**. . . . He made him enter his city Babylon without fighting or battle; he saved Babylon from hardship. He delivered Nabonidus, the king who did not revere him, into his hands."
"[I am the LORD,] who says of Cyrus, 'He is my **shepherd**, and he shall carry out all my purpose'" (Isa. 44:28a).
"I will **go before you** and level the mountains, I will break in pieces the doors of bronze and cut through the bars of iron" (Isa. 45:2).

4. Results of the victory:
"All the people of Babylon, all the land of Sumer and Akkad, princes and governors, bowed to him and kissed his feet. They rejoiced at his kingship and their faces shone."
"When I [Cyrus] **entered Babylon in a peaceful manner**, I took up my lordly reign in the royal palace amidst rejoicing and happiness. . . . And I daily attended to his [Marduk's] worship. . . . I sought the welfare of the city of Babylon and all its sacred centers."
"I have aroused Cyrus in **righteousness**, and I will **make all his paths straight**; he shall build my city and set my exiles free, not for price or reward, says the LORD of hosts" (Isa. 45:13).

5. Fate of the exiles:
"I returned the (images) of the gods to the sacred centers . . . whose sanctuaries had been abandoned for a long time, and **I let them dwell in eternal abodes**. I gathered all their inhabitants and returned (to them) their dwellings."
"[I am the LORD,] who says of Jerusalem, 'It shall be rebuilt,' and of the temple, '**Your foundation shall be laid**'" (Isa. 44:28b).

basis for his success. It also emphasizes his role as restorer of the city of Babylon and of its temples. In this way, he models himself as a legitimate claimant to the rule of Babylon rather than as a foreign invader and usurper. Assyrian texts from the reign of Ashurbanipal (667–627 BCE) contain similar language and may in fact be the scribal foundation for the statements made by Cyrus (Kuhrt 1983: 92–93). The magnanimous terms of the decree generally focus on Babylon and its immediate vicinity. Subsequent reports, such as that found in the Babylonian Chronicle, mention only the return of the Babylonian gods to their temples (Grayson 1975: 110).

While the Persian king may also have been extending his aim of restoration to all the exiled peoples, this can only be inferred based on his statement that the images of all the gods held captive in Babylon were to be returned to their homelands and to their rebuilt temples. Such a policy would have garnered some favor from these exiled peoples, and it would also have provided an impetus on the part of the government to (1) rebuild previously underpopulated areas, restoring them to revenue-creating status, and (2) pacify potentially divisive or hostile nations by acknowledging their right to worship their own gods without hindrance as long as their political allegiance was clearly given to the Persian king. It also provided the justification for Isaiah's transference of the traditional language and themes associated with the Davidic ruler to Cyrus (see Pss. 2, 18, 20; Fried 2004: 180).

Retelling the Cyrus Story

The recitation of the events surrounding Cyrus's capture of Babylon and his decision to restore the temples of all captive gods was transformed in the message of Isaiah and in subsequent postexilic accounts into a general celebration of Yahweh's omnipotence and mercy. For the prophet, the story was removed from the mundane realm of political rivalry and military clashes. It took on the familiar ring of the contest-between-gods theme that runs throughout the Old Testament. While the Neo-Babylonians had been used by God to punish the people of Judah, there was a definite time limit to this punishment, and there was a promise that the offending conqueror would in turn face divine wrath (Jer. 25:8–14). Ultimately, the Deity would once again step in to save and restore the now purified people of God. This had been a certainty in the message of Jeremiah (Jer. 29:10–14), and it is simply a matter of having patience and trust that Yahweh would keep the promise made through these messengers (Isa. 44:24–26).

Although Cyrus "did not know" Yahweh, one might expect, according to this voice of Isaiah, that the great conqueror would eventually join those "from the rising of the sun and from the west" in acknowledging "that there is no one besides me [Yahweh]" (Isa. 45:6; Blenkinsopp 2002: 249). This does not imply conversion to the faith of the Israelite covenant. However, it does provide recognition, as Cyrus does in his own document, of divine intervention in his success. The idea that a foreign ruler's eyes would be opened to the truth of Yahweh's majesty is also found in the statements of praise made by the amazed Nebuchadnezzar in Daniel 4:34–35: "I blessed the Most High, and praised and honored the one who lives forever. . . . There is no one who can stay his hand or say to him, 'What are you doing?' "

Subsequently, the references to Cyrus as the instrument of God's restoration of the people of the covenant became standard fare in the books of Chronicles and in Ezra. Their retelling of the story from their own theological perspective, with only casual resemblance to standard bureaucratic style or to Cyrus's actual text, is an indication of the way a story can grow and be transformed to fit the needs of a particular group (Grabbe 1998: 128). For example, the biblical account, written in Hebrew rather than the more standard diplomatic language of Aramaic, reckons the capture of Babylon and the issuance of Cyrus's decree as in "the first year of Cyrus." However, that king had ruled Persia for over a decade prior to 538 (H. Williamson 1985: 8–9). Of course, what mattered to the exiles was the opportunity that Cyrus's action afforded them, and thus it was indeed "year one" for them.

For our purposes in trying to understand the storytelling process, the very repetition of the phrase, "In the first year of King Cyrus of Persia," in postexilic literature provides yet another example of how God employs other nations and their rulers to carry out the divine plan (compare Isa. 10:5; Jer. 21:4–7; Ezek. 30:24–26). This repeated phrase in Ezra and in Chronicles indicates to the audience that Yahweh has won another contest with the gods of the nations. Just as they have so often been reminded that Yahweh had "brought you out of Egypt" (Exod. 20:2; Ps. 81:10; Amos 2:10), they are assured in this formula statement that the end of the exile has been engineered by their God as well.

Completing the portrayal of Cyrus's intent are additional references in Ezra indicating the provision of money to hire workers and purchase the supplies needed to rebuild the temple in Jerusalem (Ezra 3:7). Furthermore, the king commands the restoration of the sacred vessels so that they can be carried back with the returning exiles and their cultic use may be resumed (Ezra 1:7–11; 5:14–15; 6:5). Of particular interest to the later political and social situation in Jerusalem is the account of how the Persian-appointed governor, Zerubbabel, rebuffs "the adversaries of Judah and Benjamin" from taking part in rebuilding "a house of our God" (Ezra 4:3). It is made quite clear that their authority to rebuild the temple and to deny these people, who had not experienced the purification of the exile, the privilege of assisting in its construction comes directly from the Persian king. In this way the account in Ezra functions as a means of authenticating and strengthening the "returned" community's claim to the land against that of the "people of the land" (compare Ezra 3:3; 9:1–2; Neh. 10:31–32), who had not gone into exile and were therefore "considered to be religiously compromised" (Blenkinsopp 2003: 101).

Portrayal of Cyrus in Postexilic Accounts

Unlike most other foreign rulers, Cyrus is universally portrayed in a favorable light in the biblical narrative. Much of the material is centered on his decree and is quite repetitive. The principal difference from the Isaiah account is the addition of details regarding the reconstruction of the Jerusalem temple and the restoration of the sacred vessels. This suggests a standardization of language by the Chronicler and the priestly editors of postexilic literature when refering to the salvific role of Cyrus as part of God's plan for restoration of the people (Japhet 1993: 1076–77).

Ezra 1:1–3—"In the first year of King Cyrus of Persia, in order that the word of the LORD by the mouth of Jeremiah might be accomplished, the LORD stirred up the spirit of King Cyrus of Persia so that he sent a herald throughout all his kingdom, and also in a written edict declared: 'Thus says King Cyrus of Persia: The LORD, the God of heaven, has given me all the kingdoms of the earth, and he has charged me to build him a house at Jerusalem in Judah. Any of those among you who are of his people . . . are now permitted to go up to Jerusalem in Judah, and rebuild the house of the LORD, the God of Israel—he is the God who is in Jerusalem.'"

2 Chronicles 36:22–23—"In the first year of King Cyrus of Persia, in fulfillment of the word spoken by Jeremiah [Jer. 25:12], the LORD stirred up the spirit of King Cyrus of Persia so that he sent a herald throughout all his kingdom and also declared in a written edict: 'Thus says King Cyrus of Persia: The LORD, the God of heaven, has given me all the kingdoms of the earth, and he has charged me to build him a house at Jerusalem, which is in Judah. Whoever is among you of all his people, may the LORD his God be with him! Let him go up.' "

Ezra 4:3—"But Zerubbabel, Jeshua, and the rest of the heads of families in Israel said to them [the 'adversaries of Judah and Benjamin'—4:1], 'You shall have no part with us in building a house to our God; but we alone will build to the LORD, the God of Israel, as King Cyrus of Persia has commanded us.'"

Creating the New Eden in Jerusalem

Once Persian policy created the opportunity for them to leave, a portion of the exiles did choose to return to Jerusalem and to Judah. Signaling this new era, they and their descendants told the story of their return and the reconstruction of Jerusalem as an effort to re-create an ideal place, identified once again with the claim that it is "the place where God dwells"

(Joel 3:21; Zech. 8:3). The story begins with Isaiah's cry: "In the wilderness prepare the way of the LORD, make straight in the desert a highway for our God" (Isa. 40:3). In this way, the prophet calls on creation to acknowledge its Lord and Master. The prison doors of exile are to be opened, and those who had been thrust out of God's presence will once again experience the "glory of the LORD" and proclaim without fear or doubt from the heights of Zion: "Here is your God!" (Isa. 40:9). In this way, the people are to be restored to an earthly Eden, and the age-old term of punishment can indeed be said to have been served; the "penalty is paid" (Isa. 40:2).

Of course it will take more than the return of the exiles to create a new Eden. They must rebuild their homes, bring the land back into cultivation, restore the walls and the dignity of the city of Jerusalem, and most important of all rebuild the temple of Yahweh and restore the sacrificial cult. These tasks, however, will prove to be more difficult than the prophets' words suggest. While Isaiah may call for the mountains to be "made low" and the leveling of all "uneven ground" (Isa. 40:4), the reality of their task must have struck the returnees quickly. The funds provided by the Persian government were expended within the first few years, and the foundation of the temple, laid in the second year of the return amid great celebration (Ezra 3:8–13), remained a testament to a good beginning, while arguments arose between the returned exiles and the "people of the land" over its construction (Ezra 4:1–4).

They were finally able to rebuild their temple, with the further assistance of the Persian king Darius, in 515 BCE. This must have led to great rejoicing and could be seen as the basis for the prophet Haggai's promise that once it was completed, God's Spirit would again abide with them and the prosperity associated with the covenant would be restored to the land (Hag. 2:5–9). Full circle is achieved when God declares the intention to return to Zion (Zech. 6:3). The wrath that had come upon the nation and had resulted in God's decision to abandon the temple (Ezek. 10:4–19), the city of Jerusalem (Jer. 21:5–6), and the land of Judah is now at an end (see the ray of hope in Jer. 4:27).

In contrast to the message of the preexilic and exilic prophets (Jer. 23:5–6; Ezek. 34:23–24), however, there is no mention of a restored monarchy in the postexilic era. This is most likely a reflection of the political realities of the Persian period as well as a sign of the dominance of the priestly community.

Ultimately, the story of the return contains the usual episodes of tense argument between various factions, disagreements over the role that should be played by the Persian-appointed governors and the high priest, and the shape that worship will take in the restored province of Yehud. The new world of the restored Jerusalem community will, over a period of two centuries or more, result in the development of a na-

Eden Theme: From Exile to Restoration

Prior to the exile the prophets spoke of the land of Israel as if it was indeed Eden-like. Although this favored portion of creation would be stripped of all life and life-giving properties by a wrathful God, once its period of punishment was past a general restoration would occur, bringing both the people and its resources back as it once again assumed the character of a garden like that of Eden.

> **Joel 2:3**—"Fire devours in front of them, and behind them a flame burns. Before them the land is like the garden of Eden, but after them a desolate wilderness." Joel describes how the land had been "like the garden of Eden." Then it had been devastated by a horde under God's direction as punishment for the nation's violations of the covenant.

This literary usage of the Eden image by Joel is also taken up in the message of the prophets Isaiah and Ezekiel, who had predicted the renewal of Israel's relationship with God and the restoration of the promised land once both had been cleansed from their iniquities (Barton 2001: 73). No better end to their sufferings could be imagined.

> **Isaiah 51:3**—"For the LORD will comfort Zion; he will comfort all her waste places, and will make her wilderness like Eden, her desert like the garden of the LORD." Zion, which had been left in ruins by the army of Nebuchadnezzar and the neglect of decades, would experience a general renaissance.
>
> **Ezekiel 36:35**—"They will say, 'This land that was desolate has become like the garden of Eden; and the waste and desolate and ruined towns are now inhabited and fortified.'" What matters is not so much the return of the people, but the "physical transformation of the environment" from a wasteland into a paradise. This in turn provides the people with all they need, including security (Block 1998: 363).
>
> **Joel 3:18**—"In that day the mountains shall drip sweet wine, and the hills shall flow with milk, and all the stream beds of Judah shall flow with water; a fountain shall come forth from the house of the LORD." Just as the Eden of Genesis 2:8–14 contained all that was necessary for life and was well watered, this image of the restored nation describes an idyllic place. It also points to the temple as the source for life-giving water in much the same way as it is described in Ezekiel 47:1–12 and Zechariah 14:8 (Barton 2001: 109; Barker 1991: 69).

tional identity tied to temple worship and social custom. For instance, the commemoration of the destruction of the first temple, described in Zechariah 7–8, is most likely the result of a compromise between civil and religious authorities and is designed to provide the restoration community with an opportunity to express collective mourning and to elicit collective memories of the events that had led to the fall of Jerusalem in 587 BCE (Hoffman 2003: 205).

Reshaping the Returned Community

A century after the first group of exiles returned to Jerusalem and the temple had been rebuilt, a brewing crisis arose over the future shape of the community and its understanding of itself. This can be seen in the confrontation between Ezra and the members of the Yehud community who had engaged in mixed marriages with the "people of the land" (Ezra 9:1–4). Ezra's role in this drama, which reflects the postexilic priestly attitude as well as Persian government policy, appears to be based on his concern that the Yehud community was in danger of losing its Jewish identity and thus, once again, being on the verge of expulsion from their restored land.

The confrontational manner in which the story of Ezra's dealing with this crisis is told speaks to a real sense of anxiety over the physical and social survival of the people (Eskenazi 1988: 190–91). Since Ezra's view is portrayed as the dominant one, we may assume that a majority of the community wished to demonstrate their willingness to be purified of "foreign" influences. A constancy of ritual practice and adherence to the rule of the law would thus replace the potential dangers of social change and assimilation that were manifested, in part, by the mixed marriages and the concern over the inability to speak Hebrew among the younger generation (Neh. 13:23–24), yet another "ingredient of national identity" (Blenkinsopp 1988: 363). This attempt at social engineering was also manifested in the desire to define "proper" marriage partners. Those matches that had previously been deemed acceptable, due to a lack of females among the returnees, the desire to obtain land or other property, or some other social or economic factor, would, under this new social order, be forbidden (Eskenazi and Judd 1994: 274–77).

Furthermore, the reforms of Ezra and Nehemiah, as representatives of the Persian government, would necessarily reflect the official policies of the empire (Hoglund 1992: 223). If it was Persian strategy (1) to use Yehud as a military buffer against Egyptian or Edomite expansion (signaled by the rebuilding of Jerusalem's walls and its revived status as an urban center) and (2) to reinforce ethnic identity among those peoples who had been resettled or had been returned to former homelands, then royal governors, judges, and magistrates would have been required to issue proclamations and procedures to get this done (Neh. 13:1–3, 23–30; Ezra 9:1–5). What is interesting here is that both the enhanced status of Jerusalem and the policy of endogamy, which may serve the purposes of empire, also serve the desires of exclusivist voices among the Jewish community. Ezra and

---

Restoration of Jerusalem's Role as God's Dwelling Place

The steps necessary to the complete restoration of Jerusalem as the religious focal point of the Jewish people include the rebuilding of the temple, the reemergence of the cultic community, and the return of Yahweh to the place where his name dwells.

Ezekiel 43:1–9—The return of God's glory to the holy precincts of the temple is the crowning step in Ezekiel's description of his restoration vision. The temple is certified as "the place of my throne and the place for the soles of my feet, where I will reside among the people of Israel forever" (v. 7).

Zechariah 8:3–5—Zechariah describes the benefits that will accompany God's return to Zion:

1. "Jerusalem shall be called the faithful city," a sentiment also found in Isaiah 1:26, where Zion becomes the "faithful city" based on God's decision to purify and to restore it (Childs 2001: 21). This contrasts with the negative view of Jerusalem in Micah 1:5, which associates the city in the eighth century with gross idolatry.
2. "The mountain of the LORD of hosts shall be called the holy mountain." This clause indicates the restoration of the sacred nature of Zion with God once again in residence. Joel 3:17 also posits how the divine presence in Zion/Jerusalem in the postexilic temple will allow the city to resume its role as God's "holy mountain" (Barton 2001: 107). As Zechariah puts it, in his vision of a restored paradise, the old may securely "sit in the streets of Jerusalem. . . . And the streets of the city shall be full of boys and girls playing." Perfection is achieved through the resumption of God's presence.

However, when the society of Jerusalem after the rebuilding of the temple did not prove to be perfect, Zechariah's message (Zech. 8:20–23) refocused on a future time when perfection might indeed be achieved through the return of all of the exiles (Tollington 1993: 28).

Nehemiah, adherents of what has been called the "Yahweh-alone party" (M. Smith 1971: 127–28), would be able to use the backing of the empire to enforce their reforms as a way to "purify" Palestinian Judaism. Their intent, therefore, was to restore it to the model of Jewish identity that their group advocated.

There was also an ideological aspect to the marriage policies of Ezra and Nehemiah. It was their intention to create an identifiable people who adhered to a particular set of cultural and religious values. They found that the best way to do this was through a policy of exclusion, which in turn required a genealogical foundation to prove who was actually a member of that community. This explains in part the extensive genealogical lists found in Ezra and Nehemiah that chronicle the lineage of the returned households and provide the basis for both membership in the covenant community and status within the priestly ranks (Ezra 2:1–63; 8:1–20; Neh. 7:5–69; 12:1–26).

Civil administrators and their priestly allies thus required members of the community to adhere to and publicly advocate the proscribed policy of purification and cultural identity as the only true means of gaining God's support and as the manifestation of their acceptance of the covenant. The policies of a theology of separation were reinforced by the legal injunctions found in the Holiness Code, Leviticus 17–26, which provided the foundation for the strict rules of ritual purity and priestly authority. In acknowledging their obedience to each of God's laws, the people were to repeat the litany "I am the LORD your God" (Lev. 19:10–35). They were to recognize the necessity to obey God's injunction, "Consecrate yourselves therefore, and be holy; for I am the LORD your God" (Lev. 20:7), and they were to accept their special blessings and responsibilities based on God's decision to "separate you from the peoples" (Lev. 20:24; compare Exod. 19:4–6).

That the authorities were not entirely successful in universalizing this social doctrine can be seen in the book of Ruth. Although the author(s) of Ruth has set the story in the settlement period, "in the days when the judges ruled" (1:1), it would not be lost on the audience that the story concludes with a genealogy clearly pointing to a mixed origin for King David (4:13–22). What better argument could the critics of Ezra and Nehemiah make than one that clearly demonstrates the value rather than the impurity of mixed marriage (Bush 1996: 18–30; Korpel 2001: 224–27)? Thus the argument could be made that the emphasis on exogamy in the story of Ruth the Moabite represents a postexilic attempt to counterbalance the insistence in Ezra and Nehemiah on endogamy. The inclusion of the genealogy of David and its link to an exogamous marriage would also strengthen the case among those who venerated

---

Universalism Theme

The universalism theme demonstrates the power of Yahweh over all other deities. It is a type of instruction, in story form, for the people of the covenant that contains a tale in which a non-Israelite fervently recognizes Yahweh's power or accepts the Israelite God as his or her own God.

Joshua 2:9–11—The Jericho prostitute Rahab recites to Joshua's spies the saving acts of Yahweh in aiding the Israelites to cross the Red Sea and to defeat the Amorite kings Sihon and Og. Then she states, "The LORD your God is indeed God in heaven above and on earth below."

Ruth 1:15–17—Naomi urges Ruth to go "back to her gods," but Ruth insists that she will remain with her mother-in-law and pledges that "your God [will be] my God."

2 Kings 5:15—After following the instruction of the prophet Elisha and being cured of his leprosy, the Syrian general Naaman proclaims: "Now I know that there is no God in all the earth except in Israel."

Daniel 2:47—After Daniel successfully interprets the king's dream, Nebuchadnezzar proclaims, "Truly your god is God of gods and Lord of kings and a revealer of mysteries." The Babylonian king makes a similar statement in Daniel 4:34–37 after he is restored from a period of insanity, proclaiming his praise of "the King of heaven, for all his works are truth, and all his ways are justice."

---

the memory of David as Israel's ideal king (see Sasson 1989: 178–87 for a summary of various views).

To better understand how the story of Ruth could be of value to segments of the postexilic community, we need to give particular attention to its emphasis on membership in the community. Just as Ezra and Nehemiah were trying to define who had the right to participate in Jewish ritual in the temple and who could be identified as a member of the covenant community, the story of Ruth revolves around similar issues of social and legal acceptance.

At a basic social level, the personal sense of identity in the culture of ancient Israel was defined for each individual by his or her membership in a household, a clan, and a tribe, and by age and gender (Matthews 2004b: 218–22). Recognition of membership within a specific group was further defined by the location of the person's home village or town, the geographical region within Israelite territory, and the geopolitical relations with the kinship group's neighbors as well as other tribes and nearby states. As a rule, it would be unnecessary for a person in this ancient society to think about his or her identity beyond these factors. However, the book of Ruth centers on the dilemma of social identity. Having left her homeland of Moab and her parents' household, Ruth had to struggle to be accepted by her adopted community of Bethlehem so that she could resume a normal life there.

The statement of faith that she expresses (Ruth 1:16–17) fits well into the universalism theme often found in the stories of the Old Testament (Matthews 2000: 63–89). As a non-Israelite she binds herself to the religion of Israel, and once she has been fully accepted into that community, through her association with her mother-in-law Naomi and then with her husband Boaz, her search for identity ends. The idyllic conclusion to her story is the fulfillment of all her hopes for the future, and the "prize" for Israel is the origin story for their ideal king, David (Bovell 2003: 182–83). In microcosm, then, Ruth's search can be compared to that of the community of exiles, who must reaffirm their devotion to Yahweh through the purifying experience of the exile so that they may return to their proper place and be confirmed once again as the people of the covenant with all of its benefits.

The voice of Isaiah found in chapter 56 would have appreciated Ruth's social dilemma. The empathy that this prophetic voice has for those who are being excluded from full temple worship or from the covenant community certainly speaks to Ruth's need to fit in and be accepted. Isaiah's more inclusive message expresses the belief that one "who keeps the sabbath . . . [those] who choose the things that please me and hold fast my covenant" are not to be cut off, shunned, or denied access to the temple (vv. 2–5). Isaiah takes a step back in the tradition of the people to the principles upon which the Mosaic covenant had been established, opening the potential community up to foreigners and proselytes (Childs 2001: 457–58). In his view, the return to the land, to God's "holy mountain" (56:7a), is not just for a few, but for all those "outcasts" gathered there by God. If their faith approaches that of Ruth, then their sacrifices "will be accepted on my altar" (56:7b).

Conclusion

In the end, the Persian administration would have had the final say on the maintenance of order and on the smooth running of the province of Yehud. It is quite possible that imperial policy, which may not have taken into account local and regional opinion, may also have helped to reshape legal activity and social maintenance to meet its own, larger needs. The empire's concerns were primarily over defensive postures within disputed regions and maintenance of protocol and recognition of the rights of posted garrisons in conquered territories. It is not surprising then that the Persian bureaucracy developed the general sense that people who can be fitted into identifiable groups and patterns are easier to control. The reforms imposed by Nehemiah and Ezra suggest both imperial meddling and cultural incursion by the advocates of diasporic Judaism and its more rigid concept of law and ethnic identity. However, the fact that minority voices, such as the story of Ruth and portions of the postexilic prophets, do appear in the text is a testament to the diversity of how Israel told its story.

Of course, the story does not end here. The apocalyptic visions of Daniel 7–12 and of Zechariah 9–14 attest to the continued reuse of biblical traditions and themes to fit new historical and social situations. These late prophetic voices offer a sense of hope to the people as new masters (the Greeks and the Romans) take physical and political control of their lives. They point to a future day when, through God's intervention and powers of deliverance (Dan. 12:1–3), the earth at last will take on Eden-like qualities. On that day the climate will be perfect, the people will live in the perpetual light of God, life-giving waters will flow out of Jerusalem, and God will assume the position of "king over all the earth" (Zech. 14:6–9).

Glossary

annunciation: the announcement or declaration by a representative of God (e.g., angel, priest, prophet) of the coming birth of a child.

apocalyptic: a type of literature dealing with "end things," which is characterized by word or number symbols, monstrous visions, and predictions of final battles.

apology: a literary defense of a character (e.g., the Apology of David, the stories in 1 Samuel defending David's claim to the throne).

apostasy: departure from the right worship of God.

apotropaic: designed to ward off evil or danger, usually describing a ritual act (e.g., painting the doorposts with blood prior to the Passover in Egypt—Exod. 12:7).

ark of the covenant: the gold-covered box created to house the Ten Commandments. It was carried by the Levites and was kept in the holy of holies of the tabernacle during the wilderness period.

assimilation: the process of transforming an outsider into a member of a group.

call narrative: the story about a person's call to a divinely ordained office, such as a judge or a prophet (see Isa. 6).

canon: those books designated by a faith community as Holy Scripture and as the standard for faith and practice.

canonical: items such as clothing, ritual practices, or books of Scripture that conform to a general rule of orthodoxy.

Chronicler: unknown author of the books of Chronicles during the fifth century BCE. He drew material, such as genealogies, from Genesis and apparently had access to the text of the books of Samuel and Kings, although the Chronicler's use of these sources is selective in an attempt to promote a pro-Davidic agenda.

contest between gods: a recurrent theme designed to demonstrate Yahweh's supremacy over the gods of other nations (e.g., plague sequence in Exod. 5–12).

covenant: a contractual agreement between Yahweh and the chosen people that promises land and children in exchange for exclusive worship and obedience.

Covenant Code: one of the seven bodies of Israelite law (Exod. 20:18–23:33) and considered to be the oldest; it contains both casuistic and apodictic forms of legal pronouncement.

covenant-renewal ceremony: a ritual used several times by Israelite leaders to reinforce the importance of the covenant with Yahweh and to mark a major turning point in the history of the nation.

cultic site: place where religious activity takes place (e.g., temple).

Decalogue: the Ten Commandments (Exod. 20:1–17; Deut. 5:6–21).

deuterocanonical books: the collection of books, also known as the Old Testament Apocrypha (e.g., 1 and 2 Maccabees, Judith, and Baruch), written between 300 BCE and 100 CE that are contained in the Septuagint and the Vulgate (Latin Bible) and are accepted as authoritative by Roman Catholics and Eastern Orthodox but not by Protestants and Jews.

Deuteronomic Code: a late-seventh-century BCE law code (Deut. 12–26) that updates some of the legal stipulations found in the earlier Covenant Code and may be associated with Josiah's reform movement.

Deuteronomistic Historian: the name given to the sixth-century author(s) or editor(s) of the long and complex history found in Deuteronomy through 2 Kings, called the Deuteronomistic History. It is characterized by a strict moralism and a view of Israelite history in which the people continually fail to obey the covenant and therefore deserve Yahweh's punishment.

Diaspora: the scattering of the people of Israel and Judah throughout the countries and regions of the Near East following the destruction of Samaria (721 BCE) and Jerusalem (587 BCE).

diasporic Judaism: the life and practice of Jews outside Palestine. The major impetus for the development of the Diaspora was the Babylonian exile. Diaspora Judaism found continued vitality among Jews who remained in the lands of the exile or who emigrated from Palestine in the centuries following the exile.

disqualification story: a story designed to eliminate a person or a family from succession to the throne of Israel or from inheriting the covenantal promise.

divine assembly: the divine company that serves Yahweh in the form of messengers and that is portrayed surrounding the enthroned Yahweh (e.g., Job 1:6).

Divine Warrior: Yahweh depicted in the role of a combatant in warfare in defense of the people of Israel.

egalitarian ideal: as expressed by the prophets, this ideal of society considered every head of household within the covenant community equal under the law. However, this did not discount the reality of social divisions based on wealth, gender, and political status.

enacted prophecy: a prophecy that includes an action by the prophet designed to attract attention and reinforce the message (see Ezek. 4–5).

endogamy: the practice and policy of marrying only within one's own identifiable group.

etiology: a story designed to explain the origin of an event, the background of a place name, or the basis for a tradition.

everlasting covenant: a pledge made by God to David in which Yahweh promises that there will always be a king of the line of David ruling in Jerusalem (2 Sam. 7:7–17).

exogamy: the practice and policy of marrying only outside one's own identifiable group.

framework story: a narrative that has an outline structure that can be applied whenever a similar set of events occur or that can be used as the basis for a drama.

genealogy: the listing of the familial histories of several generations of a people, clan, or profession (e.g., priests).

Hebrew canon: the set of thirty-nine books (grouped differently and counted as twenty-four in the Hebrew Bible) commonly accepted by Jews and Protestants as Holy Scripture. It does not include the deuterocanonical books.

hegemony: a political situation in which a powerful nation or empire exercises extensive influence over the policies and actions of neighboring states.

henotheism: belief in the existence of many gods conjoined with the choice to worship only one of them.

herem: an element of "holy war" in Israelite warfare that requires the complete destruction of all persons, animals, and property as a dedicatory sacrifice to Yahweh.

ḥesed: "everlasting love," a covenantal term that is used as the basis
for Yahweh's willingness to make a covenant with the people of
Israel and Judah.

high place: *bamah* in Hebrew; a hilltop that provides the setting for a
local shrine.

Holiness Code: a portion (Lev. 17–26) of the Priestly source (strand
of Old Testament tradition focusing on sacrifice and ritual),
probably dating to the fifth century BCE, that reiterates the
command to "be holy" and is concerned with matters of ritual
purity.

holy of holies: the most holy portion of the tabernacle, and later the
Jerusalem temple, that housed the ark of the covenant. Only the
high priest was allowed to enter this sacred precinct.

inclusio: a literary device in which the same element occurs at the
beginning and at the end of a literary unit (e.g., ABCA pattern).

infrastructure: the public works projects that aid communication,
travel, and economic activity (e.g., roads, bridges, irrigation
canals, and dams).

Jeroboam's sin: the actions taken by King Jeroboam I to establish a
separate identity for the northern kingdom. They were used by
the biblical writers as the hallmark of the "evil king."

Jewish identity movement: theology of the postexilic era
characterized by emphasis on Sabbath worship, use of Hebrew
in liturgy, development of a canon of scriptures, ritual purity
and dietary laws, and endogamous marriage practice.

liturgy: the outline of the body of material recited or sung and the
stages of a worship service.

motif: a repeated story element in a narrative.

murmuring motif: a recurrent theme in the wilderness period
consisting of complaints by the Israelites about their needs for
food and water or rebellion against Moses' leadership and the
resulting punishment by God. The murmuring motif is paired
with a culling process designed to eliminate the unfaithful.

myth: a story that centers on the origin of events or things (see
etiology) and usually involves the activities of gods.

oracle: a prophetic speech.

prophetic immunity: protection given to a prophet when he or she
speaks in God's name that prevents people from killing the
messenger because of a negative message.

reflection story: a type of story in which the audience is given the
opportunity to reflect on the implications of what would be to
them an unusual, even frightening tale.

remnant: the portion of the community who, according to the prophets, will survive God's wrath and rebuild the nation.

ritual purification: the steps taken to transform persons or objects into a "clean" or "pure" religious state. Impurity can be caused by contact with the dead or the diseased or through sexual activity. Some individuals, like the high priest, must maintain an even higher level of ritual purity in order to carry out sacred duties.

Sabbath: the celebration of Yahweh as the creator God and the commemoration of the creation event by ceasing work one day each week.

Sea Peoples: groups of invaders who, about 1200 BCE, attacked many of the population centers along the eastern Mediterranean coast, weakening both the Egyptians and the Hittites and destroying the Syrian port of Ugarit. Some, later known as the Philistines, settled along the southern coastal plain of Canaan.

Second Temple period: the stage in Jewish history following the construction of the second temple in Jerusalem (515 BCE) until the destruction of Herod's temple in Jerusalem in 70 CE by the Romans.

Septuagint: the Greek translation of the Hebrew Bible by the Jews of Alexandria, Egypt, in the fourth through second centuries BCE; it contains the Old Testament Apocrypha (deuterocanonical books) and is abbreviated LXX (the roman numeral for seventy, the number of scholars originally thought to have done the translating).

seventy elders: that group of men selected to help administer the Israelites and who represented them at major events.

Sheol: the "pit," or abode of the dead. Apparently, both the righteous and the wicked go there after death. There is no indication in the Hebrew tradition of punishment or reward and little indication of anything that happens in Sheol. Older translations of the Bible often translated *Sheol* as "hell," but that is incorrect.

Shephelah: the low hills in western Canaan separating the coastal plain from the central hill country to the east.

sons of the prophets: apprentice prophets, such as those who served Elijah and Elisha as a support group and as messengers.

stele: an inscribed monument, usually carved on stone, or a pillar erected to commemorate a military victory or other important event.

theodicy: an explanation for God's actions, most often found in the words of the prophets, intended to exonerate God from the charge of being unjust or evil.

theophany: the appearance by God to a human being (e.g., the "burning bush" in Exod. 3:2).

trickster: a character who constantly struggles to outwit other characters and generally ends up being tricked.

universalism: a theme in biblical narrative that attempts to demonstrate that Yahweh is a universal god rather than a deity localized to Israel alone.

utopia: an idyllic place, unassociated with the regular world, that contains absolute peace and harmony.

wife-sister motif: a theme in the ancestral narratives that appears three times and in which the patriarch portrays his wife as his sister in order to deceive a local ruler.

Wisdom literature: a type of literature that concentrates on how one should live and the basic values and common sense of a culture.

x + 1 formula: a literary or ritual formula in which 1 is added to a number of special or sacred significance (esp. prime numbers like 3 or 7 or politically or religiously significant numbers like 10 or 12) in order to signal either continuous behavior (cf. Amos 1:3) or the completion of a waiting period.

Yahweh: one of the Hebrew names for the Israelite God in the Bible, which is sometimes anglicized as *Jehovah*. This name is associated with the J, or Yahwist, source (strand of Old Testament tradition referring to God as Yahweh). In English translations of the Bible, *Yahweh* is usually translated as "Lord."

Works Cited

Alexander, T. D. 1994. "Abraham Reassessed Theologically: The Abraham Narrative and the New Testament Understanding of Justification by Faith." In *He Swore an Oath: Biblical Themes from Genesis 12–50*, edited by R. S. Hess, G. J. Wenham, and P. E. Satterthwaite, 7–28. 2nd ed. Carlisle, Eng.: Paternoster; Grand Rapids: Baker.

———. 1995. *From Paradise to the Promised Land*. London: Paternoster.

Alonso-Schökel, L. 1976. "Sapiential and Covenant Themes in Genesis 2–3." In *Studies in Ancient Israelite Wisdom*, edited by J. L. Crenshaw, 472–79. New York: Ktav.

Amit, Y. 1990. "Biblical Utopianism." *Union Seminary Quarterly Review* 44/1–2:11–17.

Andersen, F. I., and D. N. Freedman. 1989. *Amos*. Anchor Bible. Garden City, NY: Doubleday.

Anderson, A. A. 1989. *2 Samuel*. Word Biblical Commentary. Dallas: Word.

Ash, P. S. 1995. "Solomon's? District? List." *Journal for the Study of the Old Testament* 67:67–86.

———. 1998. "Jeroboam I and the Deuteronomistic Historian's Ideology of the Founder." *Catholic Biblical Quarterly* 60:16–24.

Ashley, T. R. 1993. *The Book of Numbers*. New International Commentary on the Old Testament. Grand Rapids: Eerdmans.

Balentine, S. E. 1996. "The Politics of Religion in the Persian Period." In *After the Exile: Essays in Honour of Rex Mason*, edited by J. Barton and D. J. Reimer, 129–46. Macon, GA: Mercer University Press.

Barker, M. 1991. *The Gate of Heaven: The History and Symbolism of the Temple in Jerusalem*. London: SPCK.

Barr, J. 1992. *The Garden of Eden and the Hope of Immortality*. Minneapolis: Fortress.

Barrick, W. B. 1996. "On the Meaning of בֵּית־הַבָּמוֹת and בָּתֵּי־הַבָּמוֹת and the Composition of the Kings History." *Journal of Biblical Literature* 115:621–42.

Barstad, H. M. 2003. "After the 'Myth of the Empty Land': Major Challenges in the Study of Neo-Babylonian Judah." In *Judah and the Judeans in the Neo-Babylonian Period*, edited by O. Lipschits and J. Blenkinsopp, 3–20. Winona Lake, IN: Eisenbrauns.

Barton, J. 2001. *Joel and Obadiah*. Louisville: Westminster/John Knox.

Batto, B. 1984. "Red Sea or Reed Sea: How the Mistake Was Made and What *Yam Sûp* Really Means." *Biblical Archaeology Review* 10/4:57–63.

Beaulieu, P.-A. 1989. *The Reign of Nabonidus, King of Babylon, 556–539 B.C.* New Haven: Yale University Press.

Becking, B. 1992. *The Fall of Samaria: An Historical and Archaeological Study*. Leiden: Brill.

———. 2000. "From Exodus to Exile: 2 Kings 17,7–20 in the Context of Its Co-text." In *Studies in Historical Geography and Biblical Historiography*, edited by G. Galil and M. Weinfeld, 215–31. Leiden: Brill.

Birch, B. C. 1997. *Hosea, Joel, and Amos*. Old Testament Library. Louisville: Westminster/John Knox.

Bleibtreu, E. 1991. "Grisly Assyrian Record of Torture and Death." *Biblical Archaeology Review* 17/1:53–61, 75.

Blenkinsopp, J. 1988. *Ezra–Nehemiah: A Commentary*. Old Testament Library. Philadelphia: Westminster.

———. 2000. *Isaiah 1–39*. Anchor Bible 19. New York: Doubleday.

———. 2002. *Isaiah 40–55*. Anchor Bible 19a. New York: Doubleday.

———. 2003. "Bethel in the Neo-Babylonian Period." In *Judah and the Judeans in the Neo-Babylonian Period*, edited by O. Lipschits and J. Blenkinsopp, 93–108. Winona Lake, IN: Eisenbrauns.

Block, D. I. 1998. *The Book of Ezekiel, Chapters 25–48*. New International Commentary on the Old Testament. Grand Rapids: Eerdmans.

Boda, M. J. 2001. "From Complaint to Contrition: Peering through the Liturgical Window of Jer 12,1–15." *Zeitschrift für die alttestamentliche Wissenschaft* 113:186–97.

Boehm, O. 2004. "Child Sacrifice, Ethical Responsibility and the Existence of the People of Israel." *Vetus Testamentum* 44:145–56.

Boer, R. 1996. *Jameson and Jeroboam*. Atlanta: Scholars Press.

Boshoff, W. 2000. "Jeroboam Ben Nebat in the Deuteronomistic History." In *Past, Present, Future: The Deuteronomistic History and the Prophets*, edited by J. C. de Moor and H. F. Van Rooy, 19–35. Leiden: Brill.

Bosman, H. 1988. "Adultery, Prophetic Tradition and the Decalogue." In *"Wünschet Jerusalem Frieden": Collected Communications to the XIIth Congress of the International Organization for the Study of the Old Testament, Jerusalem 1986*, edited by M. Augustin and K.-D. Schunck, 21–30. Frankfurt am Main: Lang.

Bovell, C. 2003. "Symmetry, Ruth and Canon." *Journal for the Study of the Old Testament* 28:175–91.

Brett, M. G. 2000. *Genesis: Procreation and the Politics of Identity*. London: Routledge.

Brettler, M. 1989. "Ideology, History and Theology in 2 Kings xvii 7–23." *Vetus Testamentum* 39:268–82.

Briant, P. 2002. *From Cyrus to Alexander: A History of the Persian Empire*. Winona Lake, IN: Eisenbrauns.

Brinkman, J. A. 1984. *Prelude to Empire: Babylonian Society and Politics, 747–626 B.C.* Philadelphia: Occasional Publications of the Babylonian Fund, University Museum.

Broshi, M. 1978. "Estimating the Population of Ancient Jerusalem." *Biblical Archaeology Review* 4/2:10–15.

Brown, W. P. 1990. "The So-Called Refrain in Isaiah 5:25–30 and 9:7–10:4." *Catholic Biblical Quarterly* 52:432–43.

Bush, F. 1996. *Ruth, Esther*. Word Biblical Commentary. Dallas: Word.

Cahill, J. M. 2003. "Jerusalem at the Time of the United Monarchy: The Archaeological Evidence." In *Jerusalem in Bible and Archaeology: The First Temple Period*, edited by A. G. Vaughn and A. E. Killebrew, 13–80. Society of Biblical Literature Symposium Series 18. Leiden: Brill.

Callender, D. E., Jr. 2000. "The Primal Human in Ezekiel and the Image of God." In *The Book of Ezekiel: Theological and Anthropological Perspectives*, edited by M. S. Odell and J. T. Strong, 175–93. Atlanta: Society of Biblical Literature.

Carey, J., ed. 1999. *The Faber Book of Utopias*. London: Faber and Faber.

Carlson, R. A. 1993. "David and the Ark in 2 Samuel 6." In *History and Traditions of Early Israel*, edited by André Lemaire and Benedikt Otzen, 17–23. Leiden: Brill.

Carroll, R. P. 1986. *Jeremiah*. Old Testament Library. Philadelphia: Westminster.

Childs, B. S. 1974. *The Book of Exodus*. Old Testament Library. Philadelphia: Westminster.

———. 2001. *Isaiah*. Old Testament Library. Louisville: Westminster/John Knox.

Chirichigno, G. C. 1987. "The Narrative Structure of Ex. 19–24." *Biblica* 68:457–79.

Clancy, F. 1999. "Shishak/Shosheng's Travels." *Journal for the Study of the Old Testament* 86:3–23.

Clements, R. E. 1980. *Isaiah and the Deliverance of Jerusalem*. Journal for the Study of the Old Testament: Supplement Series 13. Sheffield: JSOT Press.

Cogan, M. 2001. *1 Kings*. Anchor Bible 10. New York: Doubleday.

Cogan, M., and H. Tadmor. 1988. *II Kings*. Anchor Bible 11. Garden City, NY: Doubleday.

Cohen, M. E. 1988. *The Canonical Lamentations of Ancient Mesopotamia*. Potomac, MD: Capital Decisions Limited.

Cohn, R. L. 1985. "Literary Technique in the Jeroboam Narrative." *Zeitschrift für die alttestamentliche Wissenschaft* 97:23–35.

Cook, S. L. 1995. *Prophecy and Apocalypticism: The Postexilic Social Setting*. Minneapolis: Fortress.

———. 1999. "Creation Archetypes and Mythogems in Ezekiel: Significance and Theological Ramifications." *Society of Biblical Literature Seminar Papers*, 123–46. Atlanta: Society of Biblical Literature.

Cornelius, I. 1988. "Paradise Motifs in the 'Eschatology' of the Minor Prophets and the Iconography of the Ancient Near East." *Journal of Northwest Semitic Languages* 14:41–83.

Cross, F. M. 1973. *Canaanite Myth and Hebrew Epic: Essays in the History of the Religion of Israel*. Cambridge, MA: Harvard University Press.

Dalley, S. 1984. *Mari and Karana: Two Old Babylonian Cities*. London: Longman.

———. 1985. "Foreign Chariotry and Cavalry in the Armies of Tiglath-Pileser III and Sargon II." *Iraq* 47:31–48.

Davies, E. W. 1995. *Numbers*. Grand Rapids: Eerdmans.

Day, J. 1990. *Psalms*. Sheffield: Sheffield Academic Press.

Dever, W. G. 2003. *Who Were the Early Israelites and Where Did They Come From?* Grand Rapids: Eerdmans.

De Vries, S. 1985. *1 Kings*. Word Biblical Commentary. Waco: Word.

Dillard, R. B. 1987. *2 Chronicles*. Word Biblical Commentary. Waco: Word.

Dobbs-Allsopp, F. W., and T. Linafelt. 2001. "The Rape of Zion in Thr 1,10." *Zeitschrift für die alttestamentliche Wissenschaft* 113:77–81.

Donner, H. 1977. "Separate States of Israel and Judah." In *Israelite and Judaean History*, edited by J. Hayes and J. M. Miller, 381–434. Philadelphia: Westminster.

Dorsey, D. A. 1991. *The Roads and Highways of Ancient Israel*. Baltimore: Johns Hopkins University Press.

Douglas, M. 1992. "No Free Gifts: Introduction to Mauss's Essay on *The Gift*." In *Risk and Blame: Essays in Cultural Theory*, by M. Douglas, 155–66. London: Routledge.

Dozeman, T. B. 1981. "The Way of the Man of God from Judah: True and False Prophecy in the Pre-Deuteronomic Legend of 1 Kings 13." *Catholic Biblical Quarterly* 44:379–93.

Edelman, D. V. 1995. "Solomon's Adversaries Hadad, Rezon and Jeroboam: A Trio of 'Bad Guy' Characters Illustrating the Theology of Immediate Retribution." In *The Pitcher Is Broken: Memorial Essays for Gösta W. Ahlström*, edited by S. W. Halloway and L. K. Handy, 166–91, Journal for the Study of the Old Testament: Supplement Series 190. Sheffield: Sheffield Academic Press.

Eilberg-Schwartz, H. 1990. *The Savage in Judaism*. Bloomington: University of Indiana Press.

Eliade, M. 1975. *Myths, Dreams and Mysteries: The Encounter between Contemporary Faiths and Archaic Realities*. New York: Harper & Row.

Emerton, J. A. 1990. "The Site of Salem, the City of Melchidezedek (Genesis XIV 18)." In *Studies in the Pentateuch*, edited by J. A. Emerton, 45–71. Supplements to Vetus Testamentum 41. Leiden: Brill.

Eskenazi, T. C. 1988. *In an Age of Prose: A Literary Approach to Ezra–Nehemiah*. Atlanta: Scholars Press.

Eskenazi, T. C., and E. P. Judd. 1994. "Marriage to a Stranger in Ezra 9–10." In *Second Temple Studies*, vol. 2, *Temple Community in the Persian Period*, edited by T. C. Eskenaszi and K. H. Richards, 266–85. Journal for the Study of the Old Testament: Supplement Series 175. Atlanta: Scholars Press.

Evans, C. D. 1983. "Naram-Sin and Jeroboam: The Archetypal *Unheilsherrscher* in Mesopotamian and Biblical Historiography." In *More Essays on the Comparative Method*, edited by W. Hallo et al., 97–125. Scripture in Context 2. Winona Lake, IN: Eisenbrauns.

Finkelstein, I. 1994. "The Archaeology of the Days of Manasseh." In *Scripture and Other Artifacts*, edited by M. Coogan et al., 169–87. Louisville: Westminster/John Knox.

———. 2003. "The Rise of Jerusalem and Judah: The Missing Link." In *Jerusalem in Bible and Archaeology: The First Temple Period*, edited by A. G. Vaughn and A. E. Killebrew, 81–101. Leiden: Brill.

Fleishman, J. 2001. "On the Significance of a Name Change and Circumcision in Genesis 17." *Journal of the Ancient Near Eastern Society of Columbia University* 28:19–32.

Fleming, D. E. 1999. "A Break in the Line: Reconsidering the Bible's Diverse Festival Calendars." *Revue biblique* 106:161–74.

Fortier, M. L., and R. F. Fortier. 1992. *The Utopian Thought of St. Thomas More and Its Development in Literature*. Lewiston, NY: Mellen.

Fox, M. V. 1974. "The Sign of the Covenant." *Revue biblique* 81:557–96.

Fretheim, T. E. 1991. *Exodus*. Interpretation Bible Commentary. Louisville: Westminster/John Knox.

Fried, L. S. 2002. "Cyrus the Messiah? The Historical Background to Isaiah 45:1." *Harvard Theological Review* 95:373–93.

———. 2004. *The Priest and the Great King: Temple-Palace Relations in the Persian Empire*. Winona Lake, IN: Eisenbrauns.

Frisch, A. 1994. "Jerusalem and Its Parallels: Five Cities Paired with Jerusalem in the Bible." *Abr-Nahrain* 32:80–95.

———. 2000. "Jeroboam and the Division of the Kingdom: Mapping Contrasting Biblical Accounts." *Journal of the Ancient Near Eastern Society of Columbia University* 27:15–29.

Frolov, S., and V. Orel. 1999. "David in Jerusalem." *Zeitschrift für die alttestamentliche Wissenschaft* 111:609–15.

Galambush, J. 1999. "Castles in the Air: Creation as Property in Ezekiel." *Society of Biblical Literature Seminar Papers*, 147–72. Atlanta: Society of Biblical Literature.

Galil, G. 1995. "The Last Years of the Kingdom of Israel and the Fall of Samaria." *Catholic Biblical Quarterly* 57:52–65.

Gammie, J. G. 1989. *Holiness in Israel*. Overtures to Biblical Theology. Minneapolis: Fortress.

Gitin, S. 1998. "Philistia in Transition: The Tenth Century BCE and Beyond."

In *Mediterranean Peoples in Transition: Thirteenth to Early Tenth Centuries BCE*, edited by S. Gitin et al., 162–83. Jerusalem: Israel Exploration Society.

Goldberg, H. E. 1996. "Cambridge in the Land of Canaan: Descent, Alliance, Circumcision, and Instruction in the Bible." *Journal of the Ancient Near Eastern Society of Columbia University* 24:9–34.

Gosling, F. A. 1999. "Were the Ephraimites to Blame?" *Vetus Testamentum* 49:505–13.

Goulder, M. D. 1996. *The Psalms of Asaph and the Pentateuch*. Journal for the Study of the Old Testament: Supplement Series 233. Sheffield: Sheffield Academic Press.

Grabbe, L. L. 1998. *Ezra–Nehemiah*. New York: Routledge.

Grayson, A. K. 1975. *Assyrian and Babylonian Chronicles*. Locust Valley, NJ: Augustin.

Gross, W. 1978. "Lying Prophet and Disobedient Man of God in 1 Kings 13: Role Analysis as an Instrument of Theological Interpretation of an Old Testament Narrative Text." *Semeia* 15:97–135.

Habel, N. 1965. "The Form and Significance of the Call Narrative." *Zeitschrift für die alttestamentliche Wissenschaft* 77:297–323.

Hackett, J. A. 1984. *The Balaam Text from Deir ʿAllā*. Cambridge, MA: Harvard University Press.

Haerinck, E. 1997. "Babylonia under Achaemenid Rule." In *Mesopotamia and Iran in the Persian Period: Conquest and Imperialism, 539–331 BC*, edited by J. Curtis, 26–34. London: British Museum.

Hallo, W. W., and K. L. Younger, eds. 2000. *The Context of Scripture*. Vol. 2, *Monumental Inscriptions from the Biblical World*. Leiden: Brill.

Halpern, B. 2001. *David's Secret Demons: Messiah, Murderer, Traitor, King*. Grand Rapids: Eerdmans.

Hamilton, V. P. 1990. *The Book of Genesis, Chapters 1–17*. New International Commentary on the Old Testament. Grand Rapids: Eerdmans.

Hanson, P. D. 1975. *The Dawn of Apocalyptic*. Minneapolis: Fortress.

Harran, M. 1997. "The *Bĕrît* 'Covenant': Its Nature and Ceremonial Background." In *Tehillah le-Moshe*, edited by M. Cogan et al., 203–19. Winona Lake, IN: Eisenbrauns.

Hasel, G. F. 1981. "The Meaning of the Animal Rite in Genesis 15." *Journal for the Study of the Old Testament* 19:61–78.

Hauser, A. J. 1987. "Two Songs of Victory: Exodus 15 and Judges 5." In *Directions in Biblical Hebrew Poetry*, edited by E. R. Follis, 265–84. Journal for the Study of the Old Testament: Supplement Series 40. Sheffield: JSOT Press.

Hayes, J. H. 1963. "The Tradition of Zion's Inviolability." *Journal of Biblical Literature* 82:419–26.

Hayes, J. H., and J. K. Kuan. 1991. "The Final Years of Samaria (730–720 BC)." *Biblica* 72:153–81.

Helyer, L. R. 1983. "The Separation of Abram and Lot: Its Significance in the Patriarchal Narratives." *Journal for the Study of the Old Testament* 26:77–88.

Hess, R. S. 1994. "The Slaughter of the Animals in Genesis 15: Genesis 15:8–21 and Its Ancient Near Eastern Context." In *He Swore an Oath: Biblical Themes from Genesis 12–50*, edited by R. S. Hess, G. J. Wenham, and P. E. Satterthwaite, 55–65. 2nd ed. Carlisle, Eng.: Paternoster; Grand Rapids: Baker.

Hillers, D. 1964. *Treaty-Curses and the Old Testament Prophets*. Rome: Pontifical Biblical Institute.

———. 1972. *Lamentations*. Anchor Bible. Garden City, NY: Doubleday.

Hobbs, T. R. 2001. "Hospitality in the First Testament and the 'Teleological Fallacy.'" *Journal for the Study of the Old Testament* 95:3–30.

Hoffman, Y. 2003. "The Fasts in the Book of Zechariah and the Fashioning of National Remembrance." In *Judah and the Judeans in the Neo-Babylonian Period*, edited by O. Lipschits and J. Blenkinsopp, 169–218. Winona Lake, IN: Eisenbrauns.

Hoffmann, H.-D. 1980. *Reform und Reformen*. Abhandlungen zur Theologie des Alten und Neuen Testaments 66. Zürich: Theologischer Verlag.

Hoglund, K. G. 1991. "The Achaemenid Context." In *Second Temple Studies*, vol. 1, *Persian Period*, edited by P. R. Davies, 54–72. Sheffield: Sheffield Academic Press.

———. 1992. *Achaemenid Imperial Administration in Syria-Palestine and the Missions of Ezra and Nehemiah*. Society of Biblical Literature Dissertation Series 125. Atlanta: Scholars Press.

Holder, J. 1988. "The Presuppositions, Accusations, and Threats of 1 Kings 14:1–18." *Journal of Biblical Literature* 107:27–38.

Hopkins, D. C. 1997. "The Weight of Bronze Could Not Be Calculated: Solomon and Economic Reconstruction." In *The Age of Solomon*, edited by L. K. Handy, 300–311. Leiden: Brill.

Hoppe, L. J. 2000. *The Holy City: Jerusalem in the Theology of the Old Testament*. Collegeville, MN: Liturgical Press.

Hurowitz, V. 1994. "Inside Solomon's Temple." *Bible Review* 10/2:24–37, 50.

Janzen, W. 1994. *Old Testament Ethics: A Paradigmatic Approach*. Louisville: Westminster/John Knox.

Japhet, S. 1993. *I & II Chronicles*. Old Testament Library. Louisville: Westminster/John Knox.

Jeremias, J. 1995. *Amos*. Old Testament Library. Louisville: Westminster/John Knox.

Johnstone, W. 1998. *Chronicles and Exodus: An Analogy and Its Application*. Journal for the Study of the Old Testament: Supplement Series 275. Sheffield: Sheffield Academic Press.

Junker, H. 1953. "Die Entstehungszeit des Ps 78 und das Deuteronomium." *Biblica* 34:487–500.

Keys, G. 1996. *The Wages of Sin: A Reappraisal of the "Succession Narrative."* Journal for the Study of the Old Testament: Supplement Series 221. Sheffield: Sheffield Academic Press.

Kitchen, K. A. 1986. *The Third Intermediate Period in Egypt (1100–650 B.C.)*. 2nd ed. Warminster: Aris & Phillips.

Kletter, R. 1999. "Pots and Polities: Material Remains of Late Iron Age Judah in Relation to Its Political Borders." *Bulletin of the American Schools of Oriental Research* 314:19–54.

Knauf, E. A. 1997. "*Le roi est mort, vive le roi!* A Biblical Argument for the Historicity of Solomon." In *The Age of Solomon*, edited by L. K. Handy, 81–95. Leiden: Brill.

Knight, D. A. 1995. "Political Rights and Powers in Monarchic Israel." *Semeia* 66:93–117.

Knoppers, G. N. 1990. "Rehoboam in Chronicles: Villain or Victim?" *Journal of Biblical Literature* 109:423–40.

———. 1995. "Aaron's Calf and Jeroboam's Calves." In *Fortunate the Eyes That See: Essays in Honor of David Noel Freedman in Celebration of His Seventieth Birthday*, edited by A. B. Beck et al., 92–104. Grand Rapids: Eerdmans.

———. 2000. "Is There a Future for the Deuteronomistic History?" In *The Future of the Deuteronomistic History*, edited by T. Romer, 119–34. Leuven: Peeters.

Korpel, M. C. A. 2001. *The Structure of the Book of Ruth*. Assen: van Gorcum.

Kraus, H.-J. 1988. *Psalms 1–59*. Translated by Hilton C. Oswald. Continental Commentary. Minneapolis: Augsburg.

———. 1989. *Psalms 60–150*. Translated by Hilton C. Oswald. Continental Commentary. Minneapolis: Augsburg/Fortress.

Kuhrt, A. 1983. "The Cyrus Cylinder and Achaemenid Imperial Policy." *Journal for the Study of the Old Testament* 25:83–97.

Lasine, S. 1992. "Reading Jeroboam's Intentions: Intertextuality, Rhetoric, and History in 1 Kings 12." In *Reading between*

Texts: Intertextuality and the Hebrew Bible, edited by D. N. Fewell, 133–52. Louisville: Westminster/John Knox.

Leene, H. 2000. "Ezekiel and Jeremiah: Promises of Inner Renewal in Diachronic Perspective." In *Past, Present, Future: The Deuteronomistic History and the Prophets*, edited by J. C. de Moor and H. F. Van Rooy, 150–75. Leiden: Brill.

Levenson, J. D. 1985. *Sinai and Zion: An Entry into the Jewish Bible*. San Francisco: Harper & Row.

———. 1993. *The Death and Resurrection of the Beloved Son*. New Haven: Yale University Press.

Levinson, B. M. 2003. "You Must Not Add Anything to What I Command You: Paradoxes of Canon and Authorship in Ancient Israel." *Numen* 50:1–51.

Lincoln, B. 1994. *Authority: Construction and Corrosion*. Chicago: University of Chicago Press.

Linville, J. 1997. "Rethinking the 'Exilic' Book of Kings." *Journal for the Study of the Old Testament* 75:21–42.

Lohfink, N. 1994. *Theology of the Pentateuch: Themes of the Priestly Narrative and Deuteronomy*. Edinburgh: Clark.

Lundbom, J. R. 1998. "Parataxis, Rhetorical Structure, and the Dialogue over Sodom in Genesis 18." In *The World of Genesis: Persons, Places, Perspectives*, edited by P. R. Davies and D. J. A. Clines, 136–45. Journal for the Study of the Old Testament: Supplement Series 257. Sheffield: Sheffield Academic Press.

Machinist, P. 1983. "Assyria and Its Image in the First Isaiah." *Journal of the American Oriental Society* 103:719–37.

———. 1995. "The Transfer of Kingship: A Divine Turning." In *Fortunate the Eyes That See: Essays in Honor of David Noel Freedman in Celebration of His Seventieth Birthday*, edited by A. B. Beck et al., 105–20. Grand Rapids: Eerdmans.

MacIntosh, A. A. 1997. *Hosea*. Edinburgh: Clark.

Malina, B. J. 1986. "The Received View: What It Cannot Do: III John and Hospitality." *Semeia* 35:171–86.

Malul, M. 1990. "Adoption of Foundlings in the Bible and Mesopotamian Documents: A Study of Some Legal Metaphors in Ezekiel 16.1–7." *Journal for the Study of the Old Testament* 46:97–126.

Margalith, O. 2000. "The Riddle of Genesis 14 and Melchizedek." *Zeitschrift für die alttestamentliche Wissenschaft* 112:501–8.

Master, D. M. 2001. "State Formation Theory and the Kingdom of Ancient Israel." *Journal of Near Eastern Studies* 60:117–31.

Matthews, V. H. 1981. "Pastoralists and Patriarchs." *Biblical Archaeologist* 44:215–18.

———. 1991a. "Hospitality and Hostility in Judges 4." *Biblical Theology Bulletin* 21:13–21.

———. 1991b. "The King's Call to Justice." *Biblische Zeitschrift* 35:204–16.

———. 1992. "Hospitality and Hostility in Genesis 19 and Judges 19." *Biblical Theology Bulletin* 22:3–11.

———. 1994. "The Anthropology of Slavery in the Covenant Code." In *Theory and Method in Biblical and Cuneiform Law: On Revision, Interpolation, and Development*, edited by B. Levinson, 117–33. Journal for the Study of the Old Testament: Supplement Series 181. Sheffield: JSOT Press.

———. 1999. "The Unwanted Gift: Implications of Obligatory Gift Giving in Ancient Israel." *Semeia* 87:91–104.

———. 2000. *Old Testament Themes*. St. Louis: Chalice.

———. 2002. *A Brief History of Ancient Israel*. Louisville: Westminster/John Knox.

———. 2004a. "David and the Ark." *The Bible Today* 42/3:143–47.

———. 2004b. *Judges and Ruth*. Cambridge: Cambridge University Press.

Matthews, V. H., and D. C. Benjamin. 1997. *Old Testament Parallels: Laws and Sto-*

ries from the Ancient Near East. 2nd ed. Mahwah, NJ: Paulist Press.

Mays, J. L. 1976. *Micah.* Old Testament Library. Philadelphia: Westminster.

McCarter, P. K. 1984. *II Samuel.* Anchor Bible 9. Garden City, NY: Doubleday.

McClung, W. A. 1983. *The Architecture of Paradise: Survivals of Eden and Jerusalem.* Berkeley: University of California Press.

McConville, J. G. 2002. *Deuteronomy.* Downers Grove, IL: InterVarsity.

McDonough, S. M. 1999. "'And David Was Old, Advanced in Years': 2 Samuel XXIV 18–25, 1 Kings I 1, and Genesis XXIII–XXIV." *Vetus Testamentum* 49:128–31.

McKenzie, S. L. 2000. "The Divided Kingdom in Deuteronomistic History and in Scholarship on It." In *The Future of the Deuteronomistic History,* edited by T. Romer, 135–45. Leuven: Peeters.

Millard, A. R. 1985. "Daniel and Belshazzar in History." *Biblical Archaeology Review* 11/3:73–78.

Miller, J. M., and J. H. Hayes. 1986. *A History of Ancient Israel and Judah.* Philadelphia: Westminster.

Miller, P. D., and J. J. M. Roberts. 1977. *The Hand of the Lord: A Reassessment of the "Ark Narrative" of 1 Samuel.* Baltimore: Johns Hopkins University Press.

Moberly, R. W. L. 1990. "Abraham's Righteousness (Gen 15:6)." In *Studies in the Pentateuch,* edited by J. A. Emerton, 103–30. Leiden: Brill.

Monson, J. M. 1999. "The Temple of Solomon: Heart of Jerusalem." In *Zion, City of Our God,* edited by R. S. Hess and G. J. Wenham, 1–22. Grand Rapids: Eerdmans.

Mullen, E. T., Jr. 1987. "The Sins of Jeroboam: A Redactional Assessment." *Catholic Biblical Quarterly* 49:212–32.

Murphy, R. E. 1996. *The Tree of Life: An Exploration of Biblical Wisdom Literature.* 2nd ed. Grand Rapids: Eerdmans.

Na'aman, N. 1991. "The Kingdom of Judah under Josiah." *Tel Aviv* 18:3–71.

———. 1993. "Population Changes in Palestine Following Assyrian Deportations." *Tel Aviv* 20:104–24.

Nakhai, B. A. 1994. "What's a Bamah? How Sacred Space Functioned in Ancient Israel." *Biblical Archaeology Review* 20/3:18–29, 77–78.

Nelson, R. D. 2002. *Deuteronomy.* Old Testament Library. Louisville: Westminster/ John Knox.

Noble, P. R. 1997. "Amos' Absolute 'No.'" *Vetus Testamentum* 47:329–40.

Noort, E. 1995. " 'Land' in the Deuteronomistic Tradition—Genesis 15: The Historical and Theological Necessity of a Diachronic Approach." In *Synchronic or Diachronic? A Debate on Method in Old Testament Exegesis,* edited by J. C. de Moor, 129–44. Leiden: Brill.

Ockinga, B. G. 1988. "The Inviolability of Zion—a Pre-Israelite Tradition?" *Biblische Notizen* 44:54–60.

Oded, B. 1979. *Mass Deportation and Deportees in the Neo-Assyrian Empire.* Wiesbaden: Reichert.

———. 2000. "The Settlements of the Israelite and the Judean Exiles in Mesopotamia in the 8th–6th Centuries BCE." In *Studies in Historical Geography and Biblical Historiography,* edited by G. Galil and M. Weinfeld, 91–103. Leiden: Brill.

———. 2003. "Where Is the 'Myth of the Empty Land' to Be Found? History versus Myth." In *Judah and the Judeans in the Neo-Babylonian Period,* edited by O. Lipschits and J. Blenkinsopp, 55–74. Winona Lake, IN: Eisenbrauns.

Ollenburger, B. C. 1987. *Zion: The City of the Great King.* Journal for the Study of the Old Testament: Supplement Series 41. Sheffield: JSOT Press.

Ottosson, M. 1988. "Eden and the Land of Promise." In *Congress Volume: Jerusalem, 1986,* edited by J. A. Emerton, 177–88. Vetus Testamentum Supplement 40. Leiden: Brill.

Parker, S. B. 1996. "Appeals for Military Intervention: Stories from Zinjirli and the Bible." *Biblical Archaeologist* 59:213–24.

Patton, C. L. 1995. "Psalm 132: A Methodological Inquiry." *Catholic Biblical Quarterly* 57:643–54.

Pritchard, J. B., ed. 1969. *Ancient Near Eastern Texts Relating to the Old Testament*. 3rd ed. Princeton: Princeton University Press.

Propp, W. H. 1990. "Eden Sketches." In *The Hebrew Bible and Its Interpreters*, edited by W. H. Propp, B. Halpern, and D. N. Freedman, 189–203. Winona Lake, IN: Eisenbrauns.

Prouser, O. H. 1996. "Suited to the Throne: The Symbolic Use of Clothing in the David and Saul Narratives." *Journal for the Study of the Old Testament* 71:27–37.

Rad, G. Von. 1961. *Genesis*. Translated by John H. Marks. Old Testament Library. Philadelphia: Westminster.

Redford, D. B. 1967. "Literary Motif of the Exposed Child: Ex 2:1–10." *Numen* 14:209–28.

Rendsburg, G. A. 1992. "Notes on Genesis XV." *Vetus Testamentum* 42:266–72.

Renz, T. 1999. "The Use of the Zion Tradition in the Book of Ezekiel." In *Zion, City of Our God*, edited by R. S. Hess and G. J. Wenham, 77–103. Grand Rapids: Eerdmans.

Roberts, J. J. M. 1973. "The Davidic Origin of the Zion Tradition." *Journal of Biblical Literature* 92:329–44.

———. 2002. "The Enthronement of Yhwh and David: The Abiding Theological Significance of the Kingship Language of the Psalms." *Catholic Biblical Quarterly* 64:675–86.

Röllig, W. 1999. "El-Creator-of-the-Earth." In *Dictionary of Deities and Demons in the Bible*, edited by K. van der Toorn et al., 280–81. 2nd ed. Leiden: Brill.

Sack, R. H. 1992. "Nabonidus." In *Anchor Bible Dictionary*, edited by D. N. Freedman, 4:973–76. 6 vols. New York: Doubleday.

Salters, R. B. 2000. "Structure and Implication in Lamentations 1." *Scandinavian Journal of the Old Testament* 14:293–300.

Sarna, N. M. 1989. *Genesis = Be-reshit: The Traditional Hebrew Text with the New JPS Translation*. JPS Torah Commentary: Philadelphia: Jewish Publication Society.

Sasson, J. M. 1966. "Circumcision in the Ancient Near East." *Journal of Biblical Literature* 85:473–76.

———. 1989. *Ruth*. 2nd ed. Sheffield: JSOT Press.

———. 2000. " 'The Mother of All . . .' Etiologies." In *"A Wise and Discerning Mind": Essays in Honor of Burke O. Long*, edited by S. M. Olyan and R. C. Culley, 205–20. Providence: Brown Judaic Studies.

Sawyer, J. F. A. 1992. "The Image of God, the Wisdom of Serpents and the Knowledge of Good and Evil." In *A Walk in the Garden: Biblical, Iconographical and Literary Images of Eden*, edited by P. Morris and D. F. Sawyer, 64–73. Journal for the Study of the Old Testament: Supplement Series 136. Sheffield: JSOT Press.

Schaefer, K. 2001. *Psalms*. Collegeville, MN: Liturgical Press.

Schenker, A. 2000. "Jeroboam and the Division of the Kingdom in the Ancient Septuagint: LXX 3 Kingdoms 12.24a–z, MT 1 Kings 11–12; 14 and the Deuteronomistic History." In *Israel Constructs Its History: Deuteronomistic Historiography in Recent Research*, edited by A. de Pury et al., 214–57. Journal for the Study of the Old Testament: Supplement Series 306. Sheffield: Sheffield Academic Press.

Schmitt, J. J. 1995. "Samaria in the Books of the Eighth-Century Prophets." In *The Pitcher Is Broken: Memorial Essays for Gösta W. Ahlström*, edited by S. W. Holloway and L. K. Handy, 355–67. Journal for the Study of the Old Testament: Supplement Series 190. Sheffield: Sheffield Academic Press.

Schniedewind, W. M. 1993. "History and Interpretation: The Religion of Ahab and Manasseh in the Book of Kings." *Catholic Biblical Quarterly* 55:649–61.

———. 1999. *Society and the Promise to David: The Reception History of 2 Samuel 7:1–17.* New York: Oxford University Press.

Shanks, H. 1999. "Everything You Ever Knew about Jerusalem Is Wrong (Well, Almost)." *Biblical Archaeology Review* 26/6:20–29.

Shaw, C. S. 1997. "The Sins of Rehoboam: The Purpose of 3 Kingdoms 12.24A–Z." *Journal for the Study of the Old Testament* 73:55–64.

Sherry, J. F., Jr. 1983. "Gift Giving in Anthropological Perspective." *Journal of Consumer Research* 10:157–68.

Simkins, R. A. 1994. *Creator and Creation.* Peabody, MA: Hendrickson.

Smith, M. 1971. *Palestinian Parties and Politics That Shaped the Old Testament.* New York: Columbia University Press.

Smith, M. S. 1990. *The Early History of God.* San Francisco: Harper & Row.

———. 2001. *The Origins of Biblical Monotheism: Israel's Polytheistic Background and the Ugaritic Texts.* New York: Oxford University Press.

Smith, R. L. 1984. *Micah–Malachi.* Word Biblical Commentary. Waco: Word.

Smith, S. 1944. *Isaiah, Chapters XL–LV: Literary Criticism and History.* London: Oxford.

Speiser, E. A. 1964. *Genesis.* Anchor Bible 1. Garden City, NY: Doubleday.

Stern, E. 2001a. *Archaeology of the Land of the Bible: The Assyrian, Babylonian, and Persian Periods (732–332 B.C.E.).* New York: Doubleday.

———. 2001b. "Pagan Yahwism: The Folk Religion of Ancient Israel." *Biblical Archaeology Review* 27/3:20–29.

Stern, P. 1995. "The Eighth Century Dating of Psalm 78 Re-argued." *Hebrew Union College Annual* 66:41–65.

Stordalen, T. 1992. "Man, Soil, Garden: Basic Plot in Genesis 2–3 Reconsidered." *Journal for the Study of the Old Testament* 53:3–26.

Stratton, B. J. 1995. *Out of Eden: Reading, Rhetoric, and Ideology in Genesis 2–3.* Journal for the Study of the Old Testament: Supplement Series 208. Sheffield: Sheffield Academic Press.

Stuart, D. 1987. *Hosea–Jonah.* Word Biblical Commentary. Waco: Word.

Stuhlmueller, C. 1990. "Psalm 46 and the Prophecy of Isaiah Evolving into a Prophetic, Messianic Role." In *The Psalms and Other Studies on the Old Testament,* edited by J. C. Knight and L. A. Sinclair, 18–27. Nashotah, WI: Nashotah House Seminary.

Tadmor, H. 1982. "Traditional Institutions and the Monarchy: Social and Political Tensions in the Time of David and Solomon." In *Studies in the Period of David and Solomon and Other Essays: Papers Read at the International Symposium for Biblical Studies, Tokyo, 5–7 December, 1979,* edited by T. Ishida, 239–57. Winona Lake, IN: Eisenbrauns.

Thompson, J. A. 1980. *The Book of Jeremiah.* New International Commentary on the Old Testament. Grand Rapids: Eerdmans.

Thureau-Dangin, F. 1907. *Die sumerischen und akkadischen Königsinschriften.* Leipzig: Hinrichs.

Toews, W. I. 1993. *Monarchy and Religious Institution in Israel under Jeroboam I.* Society of Biblical Literature Monograph Series 47. Atlanta: Scholars Press.

Tollington, J. E. 1993. *Tradition and Innovation in Haggai and Zechariah 1–8.* Journal for the Study of the Old Testament: Supplement Series 150. Sheffield: Sheffield Academic Press.

Tomes, R. 1993. "The Reason for the Syro-Ephraimite War." *Journal for the Study of the Old Testament* 59:55–71.

Toorn, K. van der. 1994. "David and the Ark." *Journal of Biblical Literature* 113:209–31.

Tuell, S. 2000. "The Rivers of Paradise: Ezekiel 47:1–12 and Genesis 2:10–14." In *God Who Creates: Essays in Honor of W. Sibley Towner*, edited by W. P. Brown and S. D. McBride Jr., 171–89. Grand Rapids: Eerdmans.

Turner, L. A. 1990. *Announcements of Plot in Genesis*. Journal for the Study of the Old Testament: Supplement Series 96. Sheffield: Sheffield Academic Press.

Ussishkin, D. 1990. "Notes on Megiddo, Gezer, Ashdod, and Tel Batash in the Tenth to Ninth Centuries B.C." *Bulletin of the American Schools of Oriental Research* 277/278:71–91.

———. 1997. "Lachish." In *Oxford Encyclopedia of Archaeology in the Near East*, edited by E. M. Meyers, 3:317–23. New York: Oxford University Press.

Van Seters, J. 1992. *Prologue to History: The Yahwist as Historian in Genesis*. Louisville: Westminster/John Knox.

Van Winkle, D. W. 1995. "1 Kings XII 25–XIII 34: Jeroboam's Cultic Innovations and the Man of God from Judah." *Vetus Testamentum* 46:101–14.

Viviano, P. A. 1987. "2 Kings 17: A Rhetorical and Form-Critical Analysis." *Catholic Biblical Quarterly* 49:548–59.

Walsh, J. T. 1989. "The Contexts of 1 Kings XIII." *Vetus Testamentum* 39:355–70.

Weinfeld, M. 1983. "Zion and Jerusalem as Religious and Political Capital: Ideology and Utopia." In *The Poet and the Historian*, edited by R. E. Friedman, 75–115. Harvard Semitic Studies 26. Chico, CA: Scholars Press.

Weinstein, J. M. 1998. "Egyptian Relations with the Eastern Mediterranean World at the End of the Second Millennium BCE." In *Mediterranean Peoples in Transition: Thirteenth to Early Tenth Centuries BCE*, edited by S. Gitin et al., 188–96. Jerusalem: Israel Exploration Society.

Weiser, A. 1962. *The Psalms*. Old Testament Library. Philadelphia: Westminster.

Wells, J. B. 2000. *God's Holy People: A Theme in Biblical Theology*. Journal for the Study of the Old Testament: Supplement Series 305. Sheffield: Sheffield Academic Press.

Wenham, G. J. 1987. *Genesis 1–15*. Word Biblical Commentary. Waco: Word.

Whitelam, K. W. 1986. "The Symbols of Power: Aspects of Royal Propaganda in the United Monarchy." *Biblical Archaeologist* 49:166–73.

———. 2001. "Constructing Jerusalem." In *"A Land Flowing with Milk and Honey": Visions of Israel from Biblical to Modern Times*, edited by L. J. Greenspoon and R. A. Simkins, 105–26. Omaha: Creighton University Press.

Whitney, J. T. 1979. "'Bamoth' in the Old Testament." *Tyndale Bulletin* 30:125–47.

Widengren, G. 1984. "Yahweh's Gathering of the Dispersed." In *In the Shelter of Elyon*, edited by W. B. Barrick and J. R. Spencer, 227–45. Journal for the Study of the Old Testament: Supplement Series 31. Sheffield: JSOT Press.

Williamson, H. G. M. 1985. *Ezra, Nehemiah*. Word Biblical Commentary. Waco: Word.

Williamson, P. R. 2000. *Abraham, Israel and the Nations: The Patriarchal Promise and Its Covenantal Development in Genesis*. Journal for the Study of the Old Testament: Supplement Series 315. Sheffield: Sheffield Academic Press.

Willis, J. T. 1997. "Isaiah 2:2–5 and the Psalms of Zion." In *Writing and Reading the Scroll of Isaiah: Studies in Interpretive Tradition*, edited by C. C. Broyles and C. A. Evans, 1:295–316. Vetus Testamentum Supplement 70.1. Leiden: Brill.

Willis, T. M. 1991. "The Text of I Kings 11:43–12:3." *Catholic Biblical Quarterly* 53:37–44.

Wilson, R. R. 1983. "Israel's Judicial System in the Preexilic Period." *Jewish Quarterly Review* 74:229–48.

Wolff, H. W. 1974. *Hosea*. Translated by Gary Stansell. Hermeneia. Philadelphia: Fortress.

Wyatt, N. 1990. "David's Census and the Tripartite Theory." *Vetus Testamentum* 40:352–60.

Younger, K. L. 1998. "The Deportations of the Israelites." *Journal of Biblical Literature* 117:201–27.

———. 1999. "The Fall of Samaria in Light of Recent Research." *Catholic Biblical Quarterly* 61:461–82.

Zadok, R. 1988. *The Pre-Hellenistic Israelite Anthroponymy and Prosopography.* Leiden: Brill.

Zakovitch, Y. 1985. "Reflection Story—Another Dimension of the Evaluation of Characters in Biblical Narrative." *Tarbiz* 54:165–76.

Zevit, Z. 1990. "Three Ways to Look at the Ten Plagues." *Bible Review* 6/3:16–23, 42–43.

———. 2001. *The Religions of Ancient Israel: A Synthesis of Parallactic Approaches.* New York: Continuum.

Index of Scripture and Other Ancient Writings

Index of Subjects